MERCHANTS AND MERCHANDISE

MERCHANTS AND MERCHANDISE

THE EXPANSION OF TRADE
IN EUROPE 1500-1630

J.N. BALL

ST. MARTIN'S PRESS   NEW YORK

HF
493
B34
1977b.

Printed in Great Britain
by Redwood Burn Ltd, Trowbridge and Esher

CONTENTS

PREFACE

The present work is an attempt to bring together the results of the research of others and to make it accessible to the student in a manageable compass. The period covered is crucial in the evolution of European society, its most dramatic originality as seen by many being the opening of direct contact with the New World and the Orient. Whilst not denying the impact of this expansion, this account seeks to lay its main emphasis on trade within western Europe and to consider trades with the outside world for the effect they had on the pattern of commerce within the limits of Europe itself.

To deal adequately even with the major themes has imposed many choices. Most important, it was decided that it was best to select rigorously, but, it is hoped, not too arbitrarily, some cities, some merchant families, and some commodities for detailed analysis, where existing monographs seemed to offer the opportunity of treatment in some depth, rather than to aim at a fully comprehensive treatment.

Limitations imposed both by the chance of surviving original sources and the research that has been done on them to the present time has also meant that it did not seem practicable to pose a standard set of questions to be answered. Only in some places has a discussion of the rate of merchant profit, for example, been possible. Statistical series offering the opportunity of studying long-term fluctuations of trade are rare for the sixteenth century, and their reliability has rightly been questioned. Without going at length into the debate about the value of such early economic statistics, the writer is nevertheless not so pessimistic as those who deny the utility of all attempts to quantify early modern social and economic phenomena. All reservations made, economic history without quantities lacks its vital third dimension.

The temptation to engage in the design of a complete 'macroeconomic' picture has, however, been resisted. Of so broad a canvas, we do not know enough even roughly to delineate the area occupied by trade in the whole economy, though we may conclude with some confidence that it was a growing part of that whole. For some recent brilliant attempts to approach the sixteenth-century economy as a whole the reader may turn to such books as Frédéric Mauro's *Le xvie siècle européen—aspects économiques* and the global synthesis of Immanuel Wallerstein's *The Modern World System*.

My thanks are due to Prof. J.S. Bromley for his encouragement, his criticism of a draft version and especially for the time he spent applying his great editorial experience to indicate faults of style as well as content. I am also grateful to Prof. W. Minchinton, who also read the manuscript and offered many suggestions. Mr A.C. Duke was kind in the loan of books and articles, especially on the Netherlands, to which he had drawn my attention. It nevertheless goes almost without saying that I retain the responsibility for the remaining faults and shortcomings of this book.

Southampton,
December, 1976

1 INTRODUCTION

The years around 1500 are still regarded as a convenient and satisfactory point at which to draw a line between the later middle ages and the early modern period of European history, despite a recent well-justified tendency to emphasise the essential unity of a period extending from the fifteenth century to the seventeenth or eighteenth. This emphasis on continuity is certainly preferable in the social and economic sectors to an over-dramatisation of the revolutionary character of the early sixteenth century, yet it is by no means improper to call attention once again to the importance of short-term factors affecting economic development. The sixteenth century dawned to new political situations in many parts of western Europe, which accelerated existing tendencies towards economic expansion. In 1490, America was still undiscovered, but by 1503 the Castilian monarchy, freshly established in its domestic authority, and recently triumphant over the last survivals of the Moorish occupation of the Iberian peninsula, had already set up the organisation which was to control the expanding trade with the Indies. In 1490, the Portuguese explorations of the west coast of Africa had only just passed the Cape of Good Hope, but by 1499 the first cargoes of pepper and spices reached Lisbon directly from India. Precisely in 1500 Pedro Alvares Cabral made the first landfall on the coast of Brazil. Though it is not the intention of this book to deal in detail with the trade between Europe and the rest of the world for its own sake, the impact upon the pattern of trade within Europe made by these events is one of its major themes, and there is no doubt that the influence of the new routes to the Orient and of the opening of mainland America was felt very quickly, even if their maximum effects were not exerted until the century was well advanced.

Politically, the most important single factor was the growth of the Spanish empire, not only in America but also in Europe. From 1519 the House of Habsburg ruled Spain, the Holy Roman Empire and the Netherlands, and was on the point of consolidating its control over almost the whole of Italy. There is no doubt that however imperfect the political unity of the empire of Charles V, it was a potent force for greater economic and financial integration. Its political strength stemmed in large degree from the concentration within its borders of most of the economically advanced centres of western Europe, and was

11

further increased as the supply of gold and silver from Mexico and Peru
was channelled into the European economy through Spain.

At the same time the pressure of the Ottoman Turks was increasingly
being felt at the eastern extremities of Europe. From the capture of
Constantinople in 1453 to the incorporation in the Ottoman empire of
Syria and Egypt by 1516, and that of the major part of Hungary in
1526, the economic interests of the major Italian city-states, with the
important exception of Venice, were increasingly diverted towards the
west.

These events were superimposed on factors which were perhaps
more fundamental, but operated more slowly. Historians are in general
agreement that the European economy underwent a prolonged period of
stagnation during the late fourteenth and early fifteenth centuries, but
that it was beginning to show significant signs of revival from about
1450 onwards. Fundamental to this change of climate was the beginning
of a general increase in population which was to continue in most areas
throughout the sixteenth century, and in some, well into the seventeenth.
The first major outbreak of bubonic plague in the middle of the fourteenth century may well have reduced the population of Europe by 25
per cent on average, and by much more in the worst-hit areas. It was
followed for a century or more by further outbreaks affecting more or
less wide areas of the continent, which restrained the natural tendency
of the population to increase again, often severely affecting areas which
had been relatively lightly hit by the first wave. The evidence for the
decline of the population of the major cities of western Europe is matched by that for the rural areas, both in Mediterranean and in northern
Europe. The abandonment of peasant holdings, even of whole villages,
produced social tensions as landlords fought to impose more severe
tenurial conditions on the survivors to protect their own income, whilst
land also went out of cultivation following the drop in the demand of
the larger towns for food. The incomes of both the surviving peasantry
and the workers in the towns often rose in real terms as prices fell more
steeply than wages.

In many parts of Europe political conditions deteriorated in the
fifteenth century. The Hundred Years War between France and England
harmed both monarchies and disrupted town and countryside in France,
leading to a political disintegration which threatened to become social.
In Castile the internal conflict reached a climax in civil war in the 1460s,
while in Catalonia tensions between landlord and tenant combined with
political considerations to produce a crisis which was not effectively
settled until 1486. It is not easy to explain why these trends were

reversed, in some areas from about 1450 and almost everywhere from 1500 onwards. Political reconstruction in France, England and Spain, and even the abnormal period of peace in Italy following the treaty of Lodi of 1454, may well have been of greater importance than the lessening incidence of plague. Improved nutritional standards had undoubtedly followed the increased supply and cheapness of basic foodstuffs in the preceding period of reduced demand, but it is striking that the new trend towards a general increase of the population was able to maintain itself over a long period, in the face of what are widely recognised as worsening conditions, as the pressure on available land resources led to the recultivation of less productive soils and food prices began to rise faster than the incomes of the poor.

The evidence for the increase of population during the course of the sixteenth century may not be satisfactory by modern standards of demographic measurement, but the lack of suitable census material can be made good in general terms by the use of the indirect evidence of prices and wages. In estimating the rate of population growth allowance has to be made for the increasing efficiency of governments in enumerating their populations, balanced by the increasing inducement to evade censuses, the object of which was largely fiscal. In the last analysis, however, the evidence drawn from a wide variety of sources and places points conclusively to a rising population trend throughout the greater part of the century in most areas, continuing in some into the early decades of the seventeenth century. Contemporary observers confirm the impression derived from statistical sources. In 1483, a chronicler of Erfurt wrote that 'within these twenty years, there has not been any real pestilence, and seldom is there seen a couple but they have eight, nine or ten children.'[1] Nearly a century later, the comments of towns and villages in New Castile which returned the *Relaciones Topográficas* ordered by Philip II were almost unanimous in looking back on the preceding years as a period of growth in population.[2] Pressure on land was seen everywhere in the recultivation of waste lands, the decreasing size of peasant holdings, the migration of population to the towns, and the increase of landless 'vagabonds'. In France, steady progress during the first half of the sixteenth century was seriously interrupted by the Wars of Religion after 1560. In Italy the recovery of the late fifteenth century received an early setback during the wars between France and Spain which were largely fought on her territory, but seems to have been resumed after about 1530. Despite serious outbreaks of plague in the 1570s the population of the city-states of north Italy was greater in 1600 than it had been in 1500.

It is equally certain that the rate of growth in the towns and cities was more rapid than in the countryside. If sixteenth-century Europe remained overwhelmingly rural, and if the mass of smaller towns was still intimately related to agriculture, the larger towns and cities came to rely on a wider area for their food supply. Even in Italy, where the urban economies were undergoing considerable stresses, the cities expanded. Milan grew by as much as 40 per cent between 1540 and 1590, and it was paralleled by many of the smaller cities of the north, such as Verona, Como, Bergamo, Brescia and Pavia, the last of which may even have doubled in size. Venice and Naples remained among the largest cities of Europe. Venice expanded from just over 100,000 persons in 1509 to 130,000 in 1540, and to over 160,000 before its population was reduced to 120,000 by the plagues of the 1570s. In Spain, whilst the towns of the Mediterranean littoral, especially Barcelona, failed to expand greatly, those of Castile, both on the coast and in the interior, saw a growth which in some cases exceeded that of anything in Italy. Between 1530 and the 1590s Seville grew from 50,000 to over 100,000 inhabitants, making it more than twice the size of any other Castilian city, including Madrid, which despite a rapid expansion from 14,000 to 37,000 after it became the fixed capital of Spain during the reign of Philip II, was to see its most outstanding growth only in the first half of the seventeenth century. The picture was the same in Old Castile as in Andalucía. Burgos nearly doubled in size, and even towns such as Zamora and Soria, away from the main currents of national commerce, expanded significantly. Only in the far north-west was there a decline in the sixteenth century, as population migrated southwards towards the centres of the greatest economic expansion. [3]

The demographic history of France is relatively poorly documented for this period, as is that of England, but urban expansion, though checked in some areas by the Wars of Religion, was evident on both the Mediterranean and Atlantic coasts, especially in Marseilles and Bordeaux, whilst inland centres such as Lyons and Tours as well as Paris experienced considerable growth. In the Netherlands, the late fifteenth century was not a propitious time for a growth of population, but Antwerp was an outstanding exception. From the 1490s, however, recovery was general, and growth continued until about 1570, when Antwerp had about 100,000 inhabitants. The revolt against Spanish rule was to hit the Netherlands severely, especially in the southern provinces, both in the towns and the countryside, but the greater security of the rebellious northern provinces and extensive migration from the south enabled them to maintain the expansion of their population into the seventeenth century. The population of Leiden rose from 12,000 in 1581 to 44,000 in 1622, by which time Amsterdam had reached the size of Antwerp at its greatest.[4]

In the long run, the expansion of agricultural production was to fail to keep pace with the expansion of population, except in the most favoured regions. In some areas the raising of sheep for wool production expanded more rapidly than arable farming, and it was fortunate, especially for southern Europe and the Mediterranean, that the great reservoirs of grain production in eastern Europe became available to meet a growing deficiency in the west and south. Only in the more fertile and technically advanced areas, as in England, parts of France and the Netherlands, was it possible to increase overall production by the planting of vegetables and grass crops in alternate years in place of allowing the land to lie fallow between crops of grain, or substantially to increase yields by maintaining a better balance between animal farming and arable to increase the supply of animal fertilisers. In most of the poorer low-yielding areas the traditional fallow, sometimes for two years out of three or even more, prevented an expansion of the grain crop except by the extension of the area of cultivation into lands which were even less productive. In the east, however, the extent of land available for such expansion provided an escape from the cycle of declining productivity, and stimulated the great expansion of demesne-farming by the landlords of the Vistula basin, on the basis of wage labour and of increasing labour services from the peasantry in place of money rents. The dependence of western and southern Europe on these areas was to become more regular in the second half of the sixteenth century, when climatic conditions in the Mediterranean increased the number of years of below-average yields. Consequently grain became an even more important commodity in long-distance trade.

Reliable figures for the trend of industrial production are even more difficult to obtain from sixteenth-century records than those for the movement of population. For the most part, historians have been forced to rely on arguments based on the relative movement of prices in order to conclude that in general industrial production more successfully kept pace with growing demand than did that of agriculture. Nevertheless there are useful indicators in some areas for the production of cloth, by far the most important manufactured article in the early modern economy, and for the production of important ancillary raw materials such as alum, in which a virtual monopoly position was enjoyed by a small number of centres of production. Such evidence enables us to conclude that, with a considerable fluctuation between regions of specialist cloth production, there was a sustained growth in volume sufficient to meet the increased demand of the classes of society which formed the market for goods of high quality. It remains much more doubtful whether there was much extension of the mass market of the rural and urban poor; indeed there is good evidence to the contrary.

The relative growth in the money supply was a feature of the sixteenth-century economy which has received considerable attention from historians, and whatever differences of emphasis are placed upon it as a causal factor, there is no doubt that there was a pronounced reversal of the trend of price levels, beginning in the late fifteenth century, and continuing throughout the sixteenth century. Stable or falling price levels were replaced by the steady upward movement which is often a sign of economic expansion. There is evidence however that the incomes of the wage-earners in the towns failed in the long run to keep pace with the rise in prices, especially of agricultural produce, and therefore that they suffered a decline in living standards compared with the relatively favourable period of the late middle ages. Their demand for manufactured goods must have fallen as a higher proportion of their incomes was spent on food, and also on taxes, as in most countries the pressure of rising state expenditure fell upon them. Although the peasantry may have prospered from rising agricultural prices, they too suffered from the burdens of increased taxation and debt. The conditions were thus not created for the expansion of a mass consumer market, but rather for a market of those classes, especially merchants and professional men, who benefited most from the rise in prices. Whatever reservations we may have about such a theory, it remains broadly accepted, and it cannot be emphasised too much that, with the exception of foodstuffs, sixteenth-century international trade was largely confined to articles whose market was socially narrow, but expanding the more rapidly as the growing profits were dissipated in conspicuous consumption by classes which were themselves expanding in size.

At the turn of the fifteenth and sixteenth centuries Europe was on the brink of a change in the pattern of its trade which was to throw the Atlantic seaboard into increasing prominence at the expense of the Mediterranean, but it is a major theme of this book that the process was a slow one, occupying the whole of the sixteenth century, that early signs were to be detected from the mid-fifteenth century, and that the factors involved were a complex mixture of the commercial, the financial and the political. In this slowly changing balance, the new source of supply of the precious metals in the New World was an important element, since the major currents of trade were to be attracted towards the points at which the supply of currency entered and circulated through the European economy.

The westward swing of the centre of commercial gravity was no sudden consequence of the chance discovery of America, but was prepared by a series of factors, some of which had begun to exercise their effect far back in the middle ages. The oldest was the Christian *Reconquista* in the Iberian peninsula. By the mid-thirteenth century the Atlantic coast had been entirely cleared of Moorish occupation. First the coast of Portugal and then, after the battle of Las Navas de Tolosa in 1212 had paved the way for Christian entry into the basin of the Guadalquivir, the whole of the coast as far east as the Straits of Gibralter was re-occupied. Though the frontier between Castile and the Moorish kingdom of Granada remained relatively stable for another two-and-a-half centuries, navigation through the Straits became much safer for Christian vessels. The way was opened for the Genoese, the Venetians and the Florentines to develop the sea route to Flanders and England which soon led to the decline of the fairs of Champagne as the principal meeting point of north and south. From the late thirteenth century the Italians established their trading colonies in Bruges, and dominated the exports of English wool and metals such as lead and tin, which they obtained in exchange for spices, silks and alum obtained in the Levant.

With the fifteenth century, the relationship of Genoa and Venice with the Levant began to change. Even earlier the beginnings of a retreat were discernible, as the collapse of the Mongol empire cut off the Genoese from their direct contacts with China, where silks had been bought in the thirteenth century. The end of the fourteenth century had seen serious disturbances of Italian trade in the Levant itself. Though these were of a temporary nature, they were harbingers of worse to come. The establishment of the power of the Ottoman Turks, first in Asia Minor and then in the Balkans, posed a long-term threat to communications between the Mediterranean and the Black Sea, in the face of which Venice and Genoa failed to pursue a consistent policy. Whilst they sought to maintain the failing strength of the Byzantine empire, at the same time they treated with the Turks. Interruptions in the sailings of the annual galleys between Venice and her bases in the Black Sea at Trebizond and Tana became more and more frequent, with serious consequences for the supply of grain.[5] The development of an overland route to the Black Sea through Moldavia proved an only partly satisfactory alternative, and the fall of Constantinople in 1453 spelt further difficulties for the Venetians and the Genoese. The latter struggled to maintain their colonies in the Crimea, but were forced finally to withdraw from Caffa in 1475. The effects of Turkish expansion were felt very widely in western Europe. Not only was the food supply of Genoa and Venice affected, but a sharp crisis occurred in the supply of alum for the cloth industry, fortunately solved by the discovery of important deposits at Tolfa in the Papal States.

The Genoese reacted more effectively to shift the balance of their trade to the west than did the Venetians, whose position at the head of the Adriatic was less favourable for such a radical change. The Genoese attempted to gain control of the new trade in alum from the Papal States, and pursued a vigorous policy to extend their grip on the trade of the western basin of the Mediterranean. In this they were assisted by the decline of the Catalans, hit both by the Turkish expansion in the Levant and by domestic troubles. The Genoese sought the gold of the Sudan and the coral of Tunisia in the ports of north Africa, obtained alternative supplies of silk in Granada and Valencia, and of sugar in Sicily and the newly colonised Portuguese islands of the Atlantic. They had been established in strength in Seville from the early days of its occupation by Castile, using it not so much as a stepping-stone on the voyages to England and Flanders as a centre for trade with the Canaries. Not being committed to the cause of the *Reconquista,* they were able at the same time to maintain their relations with the Moorish kingdom of Granada, establishing a consulate at Málaga which supervised their important trade with north-west Africa. In one of its aspects, the enterprise of the Genoese-born Christopher Columbus was an attempt to realise the old Genoese dream of re-establishing direct commercial contact with the Far East, whilst welding it to the Castilian tradition of messianic conquest.

As the Genoese were shifting the emphasis of their trade to the western Mediterranean and the Atlantic, penetrating the Iberian peninsula more and more deeply with their capitalist expertise, the Castilians themselves were establishing stronger links with northern Europe. One aspect of the Hundred Years War had been the normal alliance of Castile with France against England and Burgundy, yet the commercial links between Castile and the Netherlands were becoming closer as Spanish wool began to replace English as the prime raw material of the Flanders cloth industry. Castilian merchants in Bruges had obtained privileges as extensive as those of the Hanseatic League as early as 1348. By 1486, 30 per cent of the vessels entering the Zwin canal were Castilian, accounting for over half of the recorded tonnage. Castilian influence in Brittany was also increasing from the late fourteenth century, much of the trade of St Malo, Morlaix and Nantes being carried in Castilian vessels. They also appeared in growing numbers in Bordeaux and La Rochelle, as well as in Normandy. As early as 1347, Nantes had seventeen resident Castilian merchants and ten ship-masters. At least one French authority considers that during the later years of the Hundred Years War, the French had largely abandoned productive functions to foreigners, with the consequence that later in the century Louis XI found himself without any economic basis for his policy of antagonism towards the reviving political powers of Castile and Aragon. After the French expulsion of the Jews in 1420, even some banking functions in France were performed by Castilians. At the same time, John II of Castile was prepared to exploit the opportunities of the war to inflict a crushing defeat on a combined English and Hanseatic fleet off La Rochelle, and negotiating from strength, he was able to extract truces from the English without being forced to make commercial concessions to the Hanseatics. From the 1420s, the Castilians virtually drove the Hanseatic merchant fleets from the Bay of Biscay. In 1428 Philip the Good agreed to convert the community of Castilian merchants in Bruges into a full gild, with the right to elect its own consuls from 1441. It remained dominated by the interests of Burgos, the principal centre for the wool trade, and disappointed Biscayan ship-owners were forced to find their compensation in the Mediterranean, where the contraction of Catalan trade and shipping, combined with the Genoese reliance on foreign ships for the expanding charter-work of their west Mediterranean traffic, opened the way to the vessels of Spain's northern ports.[6]

The Castilian offensive against the powerful Hanseatic League was an early sign of the beginnings of the decline of the commercial force which had dominated the maritime trade of northern Europe in the preceding centuries. Though Hanseatic ships continued to sail as far south as Portugal in search of salt, the fifteenth century saw the progressive liberation of the Atlantic coast of Europe from their direct presence. The French of Bordeaux and La Rochelle were exporting more of their salt, wine, wheat and woad in their own ships, or those of the Bretons, Basques and English. The Bretons had expanded the scale and range of their maritime trade considerably during the latter part of the fifteenth century, benefiting from the restoration of more peaceful conditions. They were to be found shipping the wines of Bordeaux and the salt of La Rochelle and Brouage to parts of northern France and to the Netherlands. To the south, they penetrated as far as Madeira in search of sugar.[7] The Normans too, especially those of Rouen, were expanding their activities. In 1477-8 no less than 606 ships are recorded entering or leaving Rouen, exporting wheat to England, Brittany and Spain, and importing salt, iron, wine and Breton canvas. Already the orbit of Rouen's trade stretched from Antwerp to Seville, into the Mediterranean as far as the Levant, and in the Atlantic to the Canaries, Madeira and the Azores.[8]

Relationships between the area bordering the North Sea and the Baltic region were also undergoing changes which were fundamentally to alter the trading pattern. The Hanseatic League had already passed the peak of its influence as the provider of the major link between the eastern Baltic, including Russia, and the north-west seaboard of Europe. Industrial change in the west was an important factor in this. The cloth manufactures of Flanders suffered severely from the political conditions of the fifteenth century, while the increasing competition of English cloth, rapidly replacing wool as England's principal export, took English merchants and ships into the Baltic. A mood of nationalist fervour brought about the temporary withdrawal in 1447 of the privileges of the Steelyard, the Hanseatic headquarters in London, followed by war between England and the Hanse in the 1470s. The Hanseatic policy of negotiating commercial privileges at a time when most western states had lacked satisfactory native sources of taxable wealth deriving from trade was increasingly seen as an intolerable affront to national pride. Though the English offensive was sporadic, and bore full fruit only at the end of the sixteenth century, the Hanseatics were coming under attack in other parts of western Europe throughout the fifteenth century, and did themselves further harm by reacting too sharply to what were initially no more than minor threats to their position. The arrival within their area of powerful Italian firms, manifestly superior in commercial technique and financial strength, caused both envy and unjustified anxiety. In 1397 the Prussian members of the League petitioned the Grand Master of the Teutonic Knights to forbid the entry of 'Lombards', and in 1412 the general assembly at Lüneburg prohibited the Italians from trading in the League's Baltic preserve.

The Dutch certainly presented the most real threat to the Hanseatic supremacy inside the Baltic. The identity of interest which had joined Amsterdam and Brill with the Hanseatics against Denmark and Norway in the fourteenth century was soon replaced by a growing rivalry which posed a far greater threat than the limited English penetration of the Baltic. The Dutch offensive was essentially based on a combination of a rapidly expanding cloth industry and a powerful merchant fleet evolved from a highly developed fishing industry. Dutch cloth, sold directly in the Baltic markets, dealt a severe blow to the linchpin of the Hanseatic system at Bruges, itself threatened by the decline of the Flanders cloth industry. Dutch herrings, cheaper and more plentiful than those of Skania, if not of such high quality, competed successfully in German markets, and ensured the development of a shipping more broadly based on the large number of small towns and villages of Holland and Zeeland. The demand for salt was also leading the Dutch to obtain it themselves from the west coast of France.[9] The Dutch were welcomed, both in Germany and the east Baltic, despite the official attitude of the Hanseatic League, and especially so in Scandinavia. The Wendish towns of the League, led by Lübeck, saw themselves increasingly bypassed, as was Hamburg at the western end of the overland route from Lübeck across the Jutland peninsula. The League made the mistake of a too aggressive defence of its interests, which was to reveal its own lack of unity.

Pressure on the Hanseatic League also came from another direction with the rise of the south German towns in the fifteenth century. Though the growth of the maritime route between Italy and north-west Europe had gravely affected the economic life of eastern France and western Germany, it had by no means been extinguished. With the political disturbances in France in the fifteenth century, it was natural that the most important points of contact within the heart of the continent should move southwards to Geneva and Lyons. Most of France was an increasingly passive market, and despite the existence of some centres of vitality such as the Papal court at Avignon, the royal court, and areas such as Guyenne, under English influence until 1453, foreign merchant colonies played the major role in long-distance trade. The contrast with the towns of southern Germany was very strong. Their position on the complex network of overland routes linking the Netherlands with Italy was strengthened by their proximity to the mineral resources of Bohemia and Hungary, which experienced a remarkable revival and a technical revolution in the late fifteenth century. Control of the exports of copper, tin, zinc and silver helped to create enormous concentrations of capital in the hands of the merchants of Augsburg and Nuremberg. The linen and fustian manufacturers of Swabia, especially around Lake Constance, were close to areas of flax cultivation and enjoyed easy access to supplies of Levantine cotton via Italy. The *Grosse Ravensburger Gesellschaft* (the Great Company of Ravensburg) made the small town the headquarters of the largest commercial partnership of fifteenth-century Europe, controlling thirteen agencies and factories in Germany, Switzerland, Italy, Spain, France and the Netherlands, and trading in silk and saffron as well as linen goods. The south Germans had been long established at Venice in the *Fondaco dei Tedeschi,* where they were able to obtain their supplies of raw cotton in exchange for the silver of the Austrian, Bohemian and Hungarian mines, vital to Venice's trade with the Levant. In Genoa, the Germans were important in the trade in mercury as well as other metals and Spanish wool. Near Gandía in Valencia they operated a sugar plantation.[10]

To the north and east the merchants of central and southern Germany penetrated into the area previously dominated by the Hanseatic League. Their intrusion was even less easily opposed than that of the English and Dutch either by trade boycott or war, since the new arrivals were equally subjects of the Holy Roman Emperor, and came to represent at least as serious a threat as the competition of the Dutch. Nuremberg merchants had begun to extend their operations northwards to Frankfurt from the fourteenth century, and by its end had established a foothold in Lübeck at the heart of the western sector of the Hanseatic League, producing the hysterical complaint that one Nuremberger sold as much in one day as the Lübeckers in a year.[11] Not only did they supply Lübeck with spices, metals and Italian luxury goods, but also with cloth from Cologne and Flanders, posing a direct threat to the Hanseatic trade at Bruges. Measures taken against them remained largely ineffective, and were frequently circumvented by the marriage of Nuremberg merchants to women of Lübeck, which opened to them the privileges of citizenship and even membership of the most exclusive commercial fraternities.

Though Lübeck was one of the strongest citadels of Hanseatic trade, it was not the only one to be breached. At Leipzig and Breslau, and at Cracow, Poznan and Lwow in Poland, south German merchants found a positive welcome, and were soon competing effectively with the Prussian towns of the League, eventually penetrating to the Baltic itself. Equally menacing to the interests of the Hanseatic towns was the south Germans' establishment of a trade route from west to east, linking Frankfurt with Nuremberg, Leipzig and Poznan, which enabled them to tap the produce of the Polish interior as it descended the rivers. By the end of the fifteenth century even the valuable fur trade had come within the south German orbit. The gravitational pull of the new route was sufficient to lead Breslau to quit the Hanseatic League in 1474, and to encourage some of the landowners of Mecklenburg and Livonia to route some of their exports of grain and timber to the south-west in return for Flemish and Italian luxuries.

The south German encroachment on the territories of the Hanseatic

League was only one aspect of an evolution which was to place them in a dominant position in European commerce and finance during the first half of the sixteenth century. Their establishment in strength in the Netherlands, especially at Antwerp, was another. Half a century before the first arrivals of spices in the Netherlands via the new Portuguese route around the Cape of Good Hope, the south Germans were already carrying spices by the overland route from Venice to Antwerp. Though they never entirely replaced the sea route through the Straits of Gibraltar, the growth of the spice trade of the south Germans combined with the transfer of some of the maritime traffic to create an important factor in the rise of Antwerp to its pre-eminence in northern Europe, which coincided remarkably with that of the great merchant and finance houses of Nuremberg and Augsburg. Brabant cloth also found its way from Antwerp to Italy and beyond through their hands. The devaluation of the money of account in the Netherlands in 1465 not only stimulated industry but also led to an over-valuation of silver which exercised a magnetic attraction to the south Germans, who also found greater quantities of English cloth available in the Netherlands following the English devaluation of 1464.[12]

In the matter of commercial organisation and business techniques the contrast between the north Italian cities and their distant merchant colonies and the rest of western Europe was perhaps at its strongest in the late fifteenth century. By then, the greater Italian cities had evolved business methods to a point which neither saw nor needed much further change until the emergence of the modern industrial economy. Although it is untrue to say that all merchants were sedentary by the end of the middle ages (indeed some of the greatest travelled most), the development amongst the larger firms of a fixed headquarters from which the dependent 'factories' were controlled by a senior partner had already a long history behind it. The forms of business partnership were extremely varied. Many partnerships were of quite short duration, especially in southern Europe, where they might be limited to a single trading voyage, or dissolved after a few years, even if they were immediately reformed on almost exactly the same terms. The most primitive form of partnership in southern Europe was the *compagnia,* the fundamental characteristic of which was the communal living and feeding of the partners. The *commenda,* also very common in late medieval Italy, was a form in which the merchant who travelled with the goods of the firm was supplied with capital by a partner who remained at home, the former providing little but his time and commercial experience. In such cases, the partner who provided the capital usually took the major share of the profits, and bore most of the monetary risks. The *societas* was a partnership in which two or more persons contributed the capital and controlled the business, sharing the profits or losses in proportion to the capital they contributed.

Some of the largest companies of medieval Italy greatly transcended the average in both size and duration. The Bardi of Florence lasted for seventy years, the partnership being renewed every six or seven years. The company's solid basis within the family was normally the best guarantee of its survival through successive generations, with a variable number of subordinate partners forbidden to engage in commercial activities outside the company. Beyond the principal partners, such firms frequently accepted deposits of capital by outsiders, which led them to develop quasi-banking functions, and very often eventually to the lending of money on a large scale to governments, with all the risks usually attendant upon a policy of 'lending long' and 'borrowing short'.

All companies in the later middle ages, whether great or small, were characterised by a lack of specialisation in their trading activities, a feature which lasted with very few exceptions throughout the sixteenth and seventeenth centuries, with retail sales, the financing and organisation of transport by land and sea, banking and monetary exchange functions carried on side by side in the same organisation. The largest firms were, however, distinguished by their use of dependent agencies in the major commercial centres of Europe. During the fifteenth century, the Italian firms were becoming increasingly 'capitalist' in character, with larger numbers of salaried employees and commission agents in various centres, a larger number of partners, and a more and more complex pattern of interlocking relationships between companies, with a parent body approaching close to the modern 'holding company'. By then, even the *commenda* partnerships were tending to last for longer periods.

These developments were being imitated elsewhere, and in some areas of southern Germany, to some extent surpassed. The *Grosser Ravensburger Handelsgesellschaft* was fundamentally an association of three families from Ravensburg, Constance and Buchorn, but its lesser partners came from a much wider region throughout Swabia as far away as Ulm. It existed for no less than 150 years, from 1380 to 1530, during which time over 300 persons from 120 separate families were involved in it, without detracting from the permanent domination of the three principal families, who at the end of the fifteenth century owned about 430,000 florins of its total capital of 590,000.[13]

In Genoa, the process of evolution towards a more impersonal form of company organisation had gone even further. In the fifteenth century companies were often founded for more specialised purposes, such as the transport of salt, alum or mercury, though still investing some of their capital in subsidiary activities. In such firms the domination of a single individual or family had disappeared both in the title of the company and in practice. The capital was normally divided into 24 shares or carats, which were in practice further subdivided, often in a complex manner, the shares or parts of them being saleable without notice or further formalities, offering easy access to capital seeking investment. The company was able to take the risks of specialisation precisely because those who invested in it were also investing in other enterprises.[14] In this way too, individuals found themselves able to modify their investment policy more or less at will as market conditions varied. Thus the evolution towards the joint-stock companies of northern Europe in the seventeenth century had already been sketched out in the special conditions of fifteenth-century Italy.

The evolution of company organisation in Italy had led very early to the development of banking functions allied to commercial enterprise. The first step was probably the simplification of private contracts by reliance on either verbal agreement or simple documents such as recognizances of debt and letters of payment, avoiding the need for recourse to registration before a notary. Though the number of commercial contracts to be found in the increasing quantity of business records which have survived shows a relative increase, it must be recognised that they form only a very small fraction of the contracts which must have been drawn up, and it is unwise to conclude that their use expanded at the rate at which they multiply in our sources. Nevertheless as banking developed, the transfer of funds from one merchant to another was increasingly effected in the ledgers of the bank by simple verbal instructions, except where distance made the use of a written order essential. The development of mercantile credit was considerably eased by this method of transfer, and for long-distance transactions the letter of exchange was in full use in southern Europe and in the major centres of the north-west by the beginning of the fifteenth century. By that time also, public banking, supported by the state, had emerged in some centres in Italy and eastern Spain. In Genoa the *Casa di San Giorgio* had developed by 1411 from a body which had originated for the purpose of funding the debt of the Commune into a stable banking institution, and was paralleled in Barcelona and Valencia by municipally controlled banks or *Taulas.*

Great emphasis has been placed by some historians on the importance amongst the techniques of later medieval capitalism of changes in the science of book-keeping. There can be no doubt about the facts. Both the theory and the practice of 'double-entry' book-keeping were well-established among Italian business firms before the beginning of the fifteenth century. Its basic principle was that all transactions should be recorded twice, as a credit to one account and a debit to another, and should be expressed in the same monetary unit. In its fully developed form it involved the keeping of separate accounts for each customer and for each factory or dependency of the enterprise, with the debit and credit entries arranged on alternate pages of the ledgers, or later often on opposite pages. By encouraging a more and more detailed breakdown of the activities of a company it made possible a much closer control over its affairs, and most important, facilitated the production of a regular balance-sheet of profits and losses, assets and liabilities.[15]

Whilst such a system of accounting lies at the heart of modern business methods, there is considerable room for doubt concerning the extent to which it was practised in even the economically most advanced areas of late medieval Europe, and whether the firms which used it were necessarily more efficient and successful than those which did not. A recent specialist in the history of accountancy has dismissed the 'metaphysical' view of double-entry book-keeping taken by historians such as Werner Sombart, who saw it as an essential part of the mystique of the evolving 'spirit of capitalism'. It seems clear, in the first place, that many of those merchants who practised double-entry book-keeping did not strike a regular balance, and that very often there is no indication in the ledgers which survive that profits were regularly transferred to a capital account. Very much later, some large joint-stock companies seem to have been able to survive without using the double-entry technique at all. The Dutch East India Company did not use it in the seventeenth century, and the Sun Fire Insurance Office of London only adopted it in full form in 1890, whilst the Capital and Counties Bank was not employing it at the time of its merger with Lloyds Bank in 1918. The same writer concludes that the system did not 'by itself determine the range of data to be included in a particular setting, nor impose a particular pattern of internal ordering and re-ordering of data', that 'systematic accounting of past business results has a decidedly limited part to play in business decision-making', and that 'the double-entry system is not essential for the provision of information about past results or costs in different lines of activity'. He refers specifically to the example of the English farmer Robert Loder, who, despite a most primitive form of account-book, had a 'Remembrance' book kept from

1610 to 1620 containing the most sophisticated calculations in the form of exercises on the hypothetical profits which would result from various courses of action and included the charging of depreciation.[16]

There can be no doubt, however, that the use of double-entry accounting methods spread rapidly in late medieval Italy. The formation of partnerships certainly increased the need for clearer book-keeping methods, and was responsible for the taking of periodic inventories, whilst the use of employees as factors and agents increased it further. Perhaps the earliest surviving evidence of an accounting system which made use of double-entry methods is that of a Sienese partnership trading at the fairs of Champagne in the late thirteenth century. By the end of that century Sienese bankers were using two account books, the *libro dell' entrate e dell'uscita,* and the *libro dei creditori e dei debitori.* The Florentine house of the Peruzzi, which went bankrupt in 1343, kept its registers in two parts for credit and debit, though the evolution of its book-keeping was only completed when the debit and credit entries for each customer were written on opposite pages of the same book. This last development was probably introduced first of all in Venice, as the late-fourteenth-century Florentine accounts kept in this way were described as being *alla Veneziana,* though no Venetian examples have survived. The practice of the inventory has been shown by recent research to have been current in fifteenth-century Florence at least, partly because the Florentine taxation system compelled merchants to present a statement of their wealth.

As far as Europe outside Italy and the Italian mercantile communities abroad is concerned, the organisation of the individual merchant enterprise reveals a strong contrast. Even where the Italians had penetrated in northern Europe it remains doubtful how far their methods had been imitated by local merchants. The very supremacy of the Italians in the fields of banking and international exchange prevented Netherlanders and English from successful competition based on emulation. It is certain that there was little osmosis of business methods from the Italians in Bruges to their Hanseatic trading companions. Hanseatic organisation generally remained loyal to a relatively small-scale individual enterprise, with relatively simple techniques, and even the largest merchants of north-east Europe and of France were less accustomed to the handling of accounts or even business correspondence than Italians of more modest rank. The typical Hanseatic grouping was the small partnership in a variety of forms. Neither the *Sendeve,* a partnership in which a servant bought and sold goods on the orders of a principal who took the financial risks, nor the *Wederlegginge,* a partnership of equals but limited to a single venture, similar to the Italian *commenda,* was as typical of Hanseatic organisation as the *Gegenseitige Ferngesellschaft.* Effectively, this was a partnership between merchants in different places, who agreed to act as mutual agents for each other. Though it was relatively well suited to the simple geographical pattern of Hanseatic trade along an east-west axis, it had serious weaknesses. The partnership lacked common capital or organisation, and its existence was normally not revealed to outsiders. The lack of properly co-ordinated book-keeping led to many disputes between partners, in which neither had authority to arbitrate.

As late as the early sixteenth century, a merchant of Reval and another of Rostock had a partnership in which no mutual settlement was made between 1507 and 1523. These deficiencies were matched by a rigid conservatism in book-keeping techniques. Double-entry was not to be found before the sixteenth century, and inefficient book-keeping may well have been the cause of the failure of some of the wealthiest Hanseatic merchants, such as Heinrich Veckinchusen of Lübeck in the early fifteenth century.[17] There were few banking centres or organised money markets east of the Rhine, and the deep suspicion of credit trans-actions remained characteristic of many Hanseatics, even after the open-ing of a bank in Lübeck in 1410, significantly by Italians from Perugia. After the death of its principal partner in 1449 the bank went into liquidation, and later in the century it was left to south Germans to open other banking houses. Under the influence of the less-developed east, where trade by barter was still common, the Hanse even began officially to place barriers in the way of the further extension of credit as the basis of its trade. In 1401 the Diet of the League at Lübeck for-bade sales or purchases on credit in Flanders except between members. In 1462 the London Steelyard demanded an end to credit deals, especially for the purchase of cloth. Such measures may well have enjoyed a paradoxical short-term success, but were symptomatic of the measures taken by the Hanseatics in the fifteenth century to crush their western competitors.

In many ways other than the purely geographical, the sixteenth century was to see a slow process of adoption of business techniques which had been the prerogative of the Italians, but also of the independent evolution of solutions which were sometimes similar products of similar economic circumstances, sometimes radically new techniques which owed little to the Italian examples.

Notes

1. K.F. Helleiner, 'The Population of Europe from the Black Death to the Eve of the vital Revolution', *Cambridge Economic History of Europe,* IV, Ch. 1. See also, R. Mols, 'Population in Europe 1500-1700', *The Fontana Economic History of Europe—the sixteenth and seventeenth centuries,* Ch. 1.

2. N. Salomon, *La campagne de la Nouvelle Castille à la fin du xvie siècle, passim.*

3. R. Carande, *Carlos Quinto y sus banqueros,* I, p. 60.

4. Helleiner, loc. cit., p. 37.

5. M.N. Pélékidis, 'Venise et la Mer Noire du xie au xve siècle, *Venezia e il Levante fino al secolo XV,* pp. 541-82, at pp. 573-4.

6. J. Heers, *Gênes au xve siècle,* pp. 282-3.

7. H. Touchard, *Le commerce maritime breton à la fin du moyen âge, passim.*

8. M. Mollat, *Le commerce maritime normand à la fin du moyen âge,* pp. 126-32.

9. J. Heers, *L'Occident au xive et xve siècles—aspects économiques et sociaux,* p. 176.

10. Ibid., pp. 178-80.

11. P. Dollinger, *The German Hansa,* pp. 243-4.

12. H. van der Wee, *The growth of the Antwerp market,* II, pp. 80-3.

13. Heers, *L'Occident,* p. 195.

14. Heers, *Gênes,* pp. 204-6.

15. R. de Roover, 'Les origines du comptabilité à partie double', *Annales d'histoire économique et sociale,* 1937, pp. 270-1.

16. B.S. Yamey, 'Accounting and the rise of capitalism', *Studi in onore di Amintore Fanfani,* VI, pp. 835-57.

17. Dollinger, op. cit., p. 256.

TRADE INSTITUTIONS AND STATE POLICY

The sixteenth-century merchant, as his predecessor and successors, carried on his business in an environment bounded by existing forms of commercial organisation and the legislation of the state and municipal authorities. The extent to which this framework altered fundamentally during the century varied enormously from place to place. The advanced economies of Italy and the Netherlands retained the lead they had established in the later middle ages, but the century saw the slow adoption of their methods in other places. It is the purpose of this chapter to discuss the structure of organisations controlling trade, and the impact of state policy on them, leaving the organisation of the individual firm for separate treatment.

(1) The Fair

Though it had already been transcended in the most highly developed areas, the fair remained in most regions a seasonal focus for trade. Small local fairs provided, three or four times a year, a point of contact between the public and the pedlar or small retailer, and between the small market town and the world of long-distance trade. The greater fairs were relatively few in number. Those of Champagne had declined long before, with the growth of maritime trade between the Mediterranean and the Netherlands and England, and were replaced in the fifteenth century by those of Lyons and Geneva, better placed as intermediaries between Italy and south Germany. The greater fairs were also evolving into centres for international financial transactions, and this aspect of their life will be dealt with in the following chapter. Even in sixteenth-century Antwerp, however, the fairs still formed a series of peaks in the levels of commercial activity. The English Merchant Adventurers continued to concentrate their exports of cloth in fleets which sailed in time for the fairs, and the convent of the *Béguines* at Brussels always bought its spices at the St Bavo fair in Antwerp.[1] It is estimated that in Lyons the level of activity during the fairs was three or four times as great as the normal rate.[2] Late in the seventeenth century the French author Jacques Savary wrote that

> most of the wholesale merchants who deal with merchants in other
> towns usually bring their goods to the principal fairs, because the

merchants of all the other towns of the kingdom are to be found
there on the days established for the bringing of goods and moneys,
of which there is an excess in their own area, to bring to others
where they are lacking and require.[3]

The small local fairs were more numerous than the great international
ones, and in that sense much more typical of sixteenth-century Europe.
According to the *Relaciones Topográficas* ordered to be made by the
government of Philip II in the 1570s, New Castile had more than twenty
fair towns apart from those in the large cities. It was reported that at
Tendilla the St Matthew fair lasted for thirty days, and was dominated
by the sale of cloth manufactured in Segovia, Cuenca and other Spanish
centres, as well as of foreign woollens and silks. It was attended by merchants from Madrid, Toledo, Medina del Campo, and allegedly by
more Portuguese than any other Castilian fair.[4] Thus a fair based on a
town of a mere three thousand inhabitants could attract a national
clientele. The initiative of the local landlord was undoubtedly an
important factor in its existence, and it was said to bring him a quarter
of a million *maravedís* in *alcabala* (sales tax) at three per cent. Far to
the east, on the Polish-Moldavian frontier, the fairs of Sniatyn, Sipeniti
and Lintesti were centres for the exchange of Moldavian cattle for
Polish textiles and farm implements on a barter basis, whilst those of
Lanciano attracted trade in the south Adriatic to an extent which at
times gave Venice cause for concern.

The privilege of holding a fair was much sought after. In the early
sixteenth century Valladolid fought hard but unsuccessfully for the
transfer of the fair of Medina de Rioseco, and amongst the greater, the
example of Lyons well illustrates the mingling of political and economic
factors in such a struggle. During the last years of the Hundred Years
War, the French Crown wished to encourage the development of a commercial and financial centre, and the citizens of Lyons made out a case
for themselves based on their proximity to the frontier with Savoy and
the routes to Italy and Switzerland. By the beginning of the reign of
Louis XI Lyons was holding a fair four times a year for a period of a
fortnight, during which trade was carried out free of taxes, foreign
money was allowed free circulation, and special machinery was set up
for the rapid settlement of commercial disputes. Lyons was launched
on the rapid commercial expansion which soon had a bad effect on the
prosperity of the fairs of Geneva, previously the supreme centre of
Alpine Europe. The royal support on which Lyons' privileges depended
proved fickle. In 1484, the young Charles VIII was persuaded by pres-

sure from merchants of the Languedoc, jealous of Lyons' capture of
their spice trade, that the fairs of Lyons were the cause of a drainage
of money from the kingdom, and they were consequently suppressed.
Only persistent lobbying by the merchants of Lyons, combined with the
rivalry between other cities for the honour, secured their re-establishmen
after an interval of four years, but until 1494 only bi-annually. From
that date, however, their continuing prosperity was assured.[5]

The privileges of the Lyons fairs followed typical lines. Fundamental
to all was the royal guarantee of safe conduct for the foreign merchant
and his goods, even if France should be at war with his own country,
and respect for the confidentiality of business papers. Foreign merchants
were also exempted from the *droit d'aubaine,* so that in the event of
their death whilst in Lyons, their property could be returned to their
heirs. Exemption from taxation was restricted to those foreign merchants who did not settle with their families or own property in the city.
The Lyons fairs were thus in an excellent position to exploit the revival
of trade between Italy and the Netherlands by the overland route which
followed the restoration of more peaceful conditions. The Medici had
transferred their banking branch from Geneva to Lyons as early as 1464,
and the fairs of the former entered a period of decline, the departure of
the Italian banking community being only partially compensated by an
increase in the number of German merchants, trading especially in
metals. Geneva's survival as an international as opposed to a regional
centre was henceforward dependent on her position on the road betweer
Lyons and south Germany.[6]

(2) Merchant Colonies Abroad

Antwerp grew into the most important commercial centre of northern
Europe on the basis of colonies of foreign merchants, encouraged to
settle there by the grant of privileges which helped to turn it from a
town of fairs into one of permanent residence. As these colonies became
more vital to the prosperity of the city, so their jealous protection of
their privileges intensified. Antwerp perhaps became too dependent on
its foreign colonies, even though recent writers consider that the role
of the natives should not be underestimated. In such a situation, the
interplay of political rivalries could be very dangerous. In the opinion
of the historian of the southern merchant colonies—Italians, Spaniards
and Portuguese—the toleration of religious differences shown by the city
authorities and by the Emperor Charles V rebounded when the 'dangerous fanaticisms' they had welcomed exploded against the less tolerant
policy of Philip II. A strongly organised 'nation' of merchants was able

to hold the threat of withdrawal over the head of the city government, and in 1567 the English Company of Merchant Adventurers carried the threat into practice. Though they found in the short run it was impossible to find a completely satisfactory alternative centre for their cloth export trade, in the longer run Antwerp was to lose its place as the staple for the distribution of English cloth in European markets, and with it one of the keystones of the commercial system which it had established in the first half of the century.

Though Antwerp may be an extreme case, it was not untypical either of the sixteenth century or earlier times. Merchant colonies residing abroad had evolved their organisation during the later middle ages. The 'nation' functioned as a charitable body, with a strong religious element, as well as a commercial group, and was usually governed by a consul and other officers. The merchants of Lucca living in medieval Bruges elected their consul by ballot for an annual term. He acted as their representative with the town authorities, and was also the representative of his native city. He exercised judicial authority over his members, within limits set by the overruling power of the Count of Flanders, and the laws of the town. Membership of the 'university' was compulsory, and it was made practically impossible for a merchant to carry on trade if he refused to join. The autonomy of the colony from both local and home control varied enormously. At the beginning of the sixteenth century the Florentine consul in Bruges was appointed in Florence by the Captain of the Guelph party and the Consul of the Sea.[7]

The Consulate of the Sea was an even older institution in Mediterranean cities, having existed in Pisa since the thirteenth century. That of Barcelona provided a code which was widely imitated around the Mediterranean, and formed the basis of modern maritime law. The Consulates of the Sea controlled the organisation of the port and shipping, and enjoyed the jurisdiction over commercial cases, offering more rapid procedures than the ordinary courts of law. They came to be imitated even in inland towns, for example in Burgos after the union of Castile and Aragon, when Catalan institutions greatly influenced the archaic Castilian organisation of industry and trade. In 1494 Burgos was granted a *Consulado* for the administration of the 'university' of merchants, with autonomous jurisdiction over commercial cases. It was soon imitated by its rival Bilbao, and the sense of regional independence remained strong enough for the two cities to lead separate 'nations' in Bruges. The relative slowness of France to adopt the home consulate system is striking. One was set up in Toulouse in 1549, followed by Rouen in 1556 and Paris in 1563. From this date forward, however, there was a remarkable spread of the fashion, despite the troubled times, and no less than forty-nine more were established in the next few years.[8]

The merchant operating abroad was thus used both to privileges allowed by the local administration, and to discipline imposed by his own community.

(3) The 'Regulated' Company

Whereas in most of Europe the individual merchant operated freely within this framework, the English and to a lesser extent the north Germans adopted forms of organisation which at least theoretically restricted the individual's activity at home and abroad. The English Regulated Company was perhaps unique. The Society of Merchant Venturers exporting cloth to the Netherlands was by the sixteenth century the most important, but was based on the same principles as the Merchants of the Staple who had exported raw English wool to Calais from the high middle ages. The merchant who wished to engage in the trade was compelled to join the company. After 1564 the Merchant Adventurers were able to rely on a royal charter which allowed them to control admission to the trade and regulated its conduct. It chartered shipping for the seasonal voyages, and established quotas for its members' shipments of cloth. Its official concern for the exclusion of outsiders or 'interlopers', combined with its attempt to achieve a fair share of the market amongst its members, had been typical of the medieval gilds from which it had evolved. Yet its 'monopoly' was not that of an entirely closed group. Admission was in principle open on payment of a relatively nominal entry fine. Its insistence on its value to English trade became more strident as it was increasingly challenged by interlopers who refused to join it, and as in the second half of the sixteenth century the volume of English cloth exports ceased to expand. Around the turn of the century its secretary, John Wheeler, defended it in a widely circulated tract. His argument was that the company guaranteed an 'orderly trade', the quality of the goods and commercial experience. The interests of existing members were guaranteed by the rules restricting the 'stint' of new entrants to four hundred cloths a year for their first three years of membership, rising to the maximum of one thousand after fifteen years. The concern for fair shares, perhaps stronger during the contraction of exports following the boom of the 1540s and early 1550s, nevertheless remained almost entirely theoretical, since there is evidence that many members exceeded the maximum 'stint' by a considerable amount. Sir Thomas Gresham, for example, is recorded as having exported 4,500 cloths in a single shipment. The exclusion of those engaged in London's retail trade helped to ensure that the members were of relatively high social status, mostly substantial men of the great Livery Companies, especially the Mercers; many younger sons of the landed gentry also sought their fortunes in the trade.

The affairs of the Merchant Adventurers were controlled by a Governor and a Court of 24 Assistants, based usually in the Netherlands. They were thus also the governing body of the English 'nation' in Antwerp, with power of imprisonment of members, and exercising jurisdiction not only over trade questions but over morals, and even enjoying the power to fine non-members for 'interloping'. This powerful corporation boasted in 1575 that 'the experience of the past sixty years hath shown that to whatsoever place the English keep their marts, thither all other nations follow to traffic.'[9] Although this was a ludicrously over-simplified explanation of the rise of Antwerp, their withdrawals, beginning in 1567, certainly helped to intensify the economic crisis there.

The English trade to the Baltic was similarly organised through the Eastland Company. Far into the seventeenth century it retained its monopoly, and its regulations, codified only in 1618, were exceptionally rigid. Any ship's captain who wished to load goods for a member of the company had to enter a bond promising to pay the dues levied by the Crown of Denmark on passage through the Sound and by the Baltic states where the goods were consigned, not to carry the goods of non-members, and to unload only at the staple port of Elbing in Prussia. Merchants could only load their goods for shipment after seeing a certificate that the captain had promised to fulfil the conditions. Members were forbidden to employ foreigners as factors at Elbing, and limitations were placed on the duration of credit terms. The company frequently justified its monopoly on the usual ground that unity gave strength, and that an individual merchant unprotected by the company would be forced to sell at a lower price than members could obtain. From the English government's point of view the company also helped to stimulate the growth of home shipping by its insistence on the charter of English vessels.[10] Thus not only was the balance of trade improved but England's naval potential was increased. Whether or not the company's arguments were sound, they were certainly acceptable to the government. In fact the quantities of cloth it exported, according to the evidence of the Sound Toll Registers, reached their peak by 1620, and thereafter fluctuated at lower levels, essentially no doubt as a consequence of the disturbed conditions during the Thirty Years War and of the varying success of Dutch competition.

From the early years of the seventeenth century, the Regulated Companies were coming under increasing attack, sharing the unpopularity of other forms of monopoly in internal industry and trade. The criticism was particularly strong in Parliament, where it formed part of the wider attack on the Crown launched by the Common Lawyers, who were beginning to develop doctrines favouring the principle of free trade.[11] The close relations which existed between the Crown and the great chartered companies were normally good enough to enable them to withstand such attacks, and they succeeded in surviving the Civil War and Commonwealth with their privileges virtually intact. From the time of Elizabeth I they had provided the Crown with valuable financial support, in a country where financial organisation long continued in a state of relative backwardness. This interdependence increased during the long political struggles of the seventeenth century, and was not permanently affected by such episodes as the notorious Cockayne project of 1615 which temporarily substituted a rival monopoly group for that of the Merchant Adventurers in English cloth exports.[12] In other areas of trade, however, the new pressure for liberty of individual enterprise, particularly strong in the provincial ports, which saw in the position of the great companies the principal guarantee of the domination of London in overseas trade, was more effective. The revival of trade with Spain after the conclusion of peace in 1604 at first saw the restoration of the position of the Spanish Company, but after 1605 its monopoly was taken away and the trade 'opened'. It is not easy to say whether this had a favourable effect on Anglo-Spanish trade, as contemporary comments vary, but complaints were made against the small-scale traders whose lack of experience and limited power in Spanish markets allegedly turned the terms of trade against England at a time when great opportunities theoretically existed.[13] Certainly the trade did not fulfil expectations, though a sceptical diplomat wrote that 'howsoever they complain there, I have gathered from out of some of themselves that their gains are great here: but your Lordships and my poor self are only made partakers of their Oes, not of their Alleluias.'[14] The controversy around the question of the role of monopoly companies and the level of trade remained unresolved among contemporaries, and modern historians are hardly nearer to agreement.

(4) The Hanseatic League

If the English chartered companies revealed the close contact of the state and commercial organisation, the Hanseatic League was the principal example of a trading community which existed to make up for the lack of a unified state power.[15] Its hey-day was ended by the sixteenth

century, which saw its decline and disintegration under the pressures
of increasing competition and political troubles in Germany. In origin it
had been a broad league to defend the common interests of merchants
over a wide area of north Germany, Poland and Prussia, which by the
late fourteenth century had been converted into a league of the principal
towns. Its extent was variable: entry to it was easy, and withdrawal
hardly more difficult, so that it cannot be said that its membership was
in any way static. In many cases it remained nominal, so that although
as many as seventy towns might be members simultaneously, its affairs
were in practice dominated by a few of the most important. Nevertheless, the use of Hanseatic trading privileges was restricted to merchants
who resided in member towns or in their 'factories' or 'counters' elsewhere, and in the fifteenth century was further restricted to those who
were natives of the member towns. Its ultimate governing body, the
General Assembly, gathered together representatives of all member
towns, but met relatively infrequently, and the city of Lübeck acted as
the permanent leader of the organisation. The great distances and expense
involved in travel to General Assemblies were mitigated by the division
of the League first into 'thirds' and later into 'quarters', which met more
frequently, but the regional assemblies were the most active, since they
represented areas of greater geographical cohesion and identity of commercial interests. Though it was essentially a League of towns, one territorial prince was a member—the Grand Master of the Teutonic Knights
of Prussia, whose close control over the towns developed within the
Order's territory made him their natural representative, although only
the merchants of the six principal towns enjoyed the practical benefits
of membership. The Order gave the Hanseatic League some prestige, and
was a useful support in political conflicts in eastern Europe, but its own
ambitions sometimes meant that the League was dragged into difficulties
in its relations with foreign states.

The League lacked much on the formal plane which inhibited its
dealings with the states in which its members traded. It never achieved
a recognised legal personality, lacking a seal, but in practice the dominant role of its leading member-towns was an adequate substitute. Its
trading counters succeeded in establishing themselves as legal entities
where the League in general failed, and exercised effective discipline
over the merchants of the member-towns. Four of its counters emerged
as by far the most important, those of Novgorod, Bergen, London and
Bruges, providing a network which linked Muscovy with the rich commercial centres of the North Sea, and thence with southern Europe. All
merchants of member-towns who passed through any of the trading posts

were expected to register their presence, to submit to the local statutes
of the counter, and to reside in the houses within its boundaries. The
government of the counter's affairs lay in the hands of annually elected
Aldermen, and each counter had a treasury, replenished from a small
tax on goods. Towards the end of the middle ages the autonomy of the
counters became more restricted, and the nomination of the most important officers at Novgorod fell under the control of Visby and Lübeck.
That of London (the Steelyard) was unique in having two Aldermen,
one a German, the other English. Though the latter was sometimes of
German origin, he was always a citizen of London, elected by the merchants of the Steelyard but installed by the King, and was often the Lord
Mayor. His function was to mediate between the Hanseatic merchants
and the English, at the same time as he was their representative. The
counter of Bruges was by far the most important of the four principal
centres. Its individuality consisted in the lack of a specially designated
commercial and residential quarter, so that its members were more
physically integrated with the local community than elsewhere. Its
assembly of 1457, just before the beginning of its decline, numbered
over six hundred participants, whilst the diplomatic relations of its Aldermen extended not only throughout the territories of the Dukes of Burgundy, but also to France and even Castile and Aragon. From the Hanseatic point of view it was also especially valuable in that it provided a
point of contact with the advanced business methods of the Italians,
and with their reserves of capital and credit.

Apart from its major counters the trade of the League was carried
on through a large number of lesser 'factories', judicially indistinguish-
able from them, and with a similar organisation. Some of them came to
rival the counters in size, especially those of Pskov and Copenhagen.
Like the counters, they tended to lose their autonomy in the fifteenth
century, and fell under the control of a single Hanseatic city or, in the
west, more often one of the great counters. Sometimes there were conflicts of jurisdiction between the counters, as that between London and
Bergen over the factory at Boston, eventually settled by an unsatisfactory condominium in 1474.

The loose formal structure of the Hanseatic League contrasted with
its commercial power. During a crisis the gap was often filled by the
establishment of more specific leagues of a financial and military character between individual Hanseatic towns. During the fifteenth century
these became more frequently necessary as political conditions in the
Holy Roman Empire brought the towns more and more into conflict
with the rising power of the territorial princes. In 1418, Lübeck, recently

formally recognised as the head of the League, proposed a permanent alliance of forty or more member-towns, on the basis of collective security. This project proved too ambitious and more was achieved by smaller leagues on a regional basis. In matters of politics as well as commerce, the Hanse acted more effectively by means of *ad hoc* methods than by formal acts of the whole body. Its commercial power enabled it to exert considerable political pressure on back-sliding members or on outside powers. Its methods of reconciling internal divisions were well tried, ranging from the mediation of neighbouring towns to the use of the General Assembly as a final arbiter, all recourse to outside authorities, even the Emperor, being expressly forbidden by Instructions dating from 1381. From time to time a town might be expelled or temporarily excluded from the benefits of membership. Occasionally even the largest suffered this punishment, for example Bremen in 1427 and Cologne in 1471, but military action against a member-town was never contemplated.

In its dealings with outside powers the League employed able diplomats, to supplement the skills and experience of the Aldermen of the counters, and they did not hesitate to use as diplomatic weapons the threat of removal of a counter, or the temporary suspension of trade. This pressure was used quite frequently, against Poland, England, Flanders and France, sometimes simultaneously. As others found, the embargo was a two-edged weapon, which could rebound on its users if imposed too frequently, and it severely tested Hanseatic unity. Whilst the League was reluctant to use the ultimate sanction of war, it was compelled to resort to it more often in the fifteenth and sixteenth centuries, and it proved increasingly counter-productive. The interruptions to the commerce it was meant to protect, and the heavy expenditure, which had to be financed by taxes on the trade, reduced the number of members prepared to contribute to a few of the largest or most interested. The threat to the independence of the towns represented by the German princes equally failed to promote united action by the League, but they were saved by the equally deep rivalries between the princes themselves.

Whilst the League provided an element of common organisation of trade for the merchants of its members, the towns themselves were left to regulate their own merchant communities at home. These were normally gathered into a merchant gild, but also into fraternities according to their geographical area of specialisation—for example, the *England-fahrer* or the *Bergenfahrer*. It does not seem however that membership of these groupings was compulsory, and they were therefore quite different from the English Regulated Companies.

By the beginning of the sixteenth century the Hanseatic League was entering a critical period. The changing structure of European trade was unfavourable to its interests, and its unpopularity made it a target for the rising economic nationalism and growing commercial self-confidence of the Dutch and the English. These forces gradually broke such unity as the League had displayed: some cities turned away to orbit the newly prosperous commercial centres of south Germany, others were able to profit from their proximity to the North Sea to establish links with the expanding trade of the Iberian peninsula, whilst the least fortunate gradually saw their prosperity undermined. The towns suffered less than the merchant exporters and ship-owners, as the exchange of goods between the Baltic and the west and south of Europe expanded rather than contracted, but fell into the hands of western merchants. The temporary closure of the Novgorod counter from 1494 to 1514 dealt a blow to the League's trade with Muscovy from which it never recovered, and the Livonian member-towns revealed a typical regard for their local interests when they applied a prohibition on foreign merchants trading there to the western members of the League, against which Lübeck vainly protested. In Norway and the Netherlands, the weakening of the Hanseatic position was more gradual, but the counter of Bruges, already affected in the late fifteenth century, declined with the town, and negotiations with Antwerp never resulted in the full renewal of privileges which had existed there at earlier times.

Whilst the League was more successful in maintaining its position in England after the restoration of relations following the wars of 1472-6, the English were never reconciled to the refusal of the League to restore their reciprocal privileges in Prussia, but bided their time, until in the reign of Elizabeth their merchants were able to take the offensive. By the end of the century they had succeeded not only in penetrating German and Polish markets with English cloth sold directly and in revealing the increasing inner disunity of the League by negotiating privileges for themselves in Hamburg and Elbing, but also in 1598 finally bringing to an end the privileges of the Steelyard in London. The renewed commercial prosperity of some Hanseatic cities at the end of the sixteenth century resulted from the pursuit of an independent policy which spelt the end of the League as anything more than the shadowy unity which the Holy Roman Empire had itself become.

(5) The Joint-Stock Companies

The late sixteenth and early seventeenth centuries also saw the appearance in international commerce of a new kind of trading company, based on the joint-stock principle. The principle had made its appearance in state banks such as that of S. Giorgio at Genoa before the end of the middle ages, and was used for a few industrial enterprises of exceptional risk and high capital requirements. The most famous examples in international trade were the English and Dutch East India Companies, founded at the turn of the sixteenth and seventeenth centuries, but are not to be discussed in detail here, since they were established for trade outside Europe. They were in fact preceded by nearly half a century by the English Muscovy Company, and by twenty years by the Levant Company.

The Muscovy Company was founded in 1553, following the return of an expedition to Russia by the Archangel route in 1553.[16] Though the original motive of the expedition may have been the discovery of a north-east passage to China and the spice islands, the encouraging reception it received from the Tsar caused the abandonment of the more ambitious objective in favour of trade with Russia. The royal charter of 1555 gave the company a monopoly of the commerce with Russia and the right to trade anywhere in areas not frequented by English merchants before 1553. The risks of the enterprise of 1553 had been revealed by the return of only one of the three vessels which had left England, and the idea of the joint stock was to spread the risk more widely than existing forms of partnership permitted, especially as the individual business firm in England was of relatively small size compared with some of those on the continent. No less than 201 persons, including two women, were named in the Muscovy Company's charter, including high office-holders who provided a link with the royal court and helped to emphasise the diplomatic and political purpose of the Company's foundation. Peers of the realm and landed gentry emphasised the closer links which were developing in England between the country and the City of London. The majority of members were nevertheless drawn from the London merchant community, at least fourteen being Merchant Staplers and another 26 Merchant Adventurers. Over twenty members also helped to promote voyages to Guinea in the 1550s, giving colour to the view that the Muscovy Company was formed by a group which was anxious to see a greater geographical diversity in English trade. The basic share in the Company was fixed at £25 for the first voyage of 1553, and existing shareholders were called on for more in 1555 and again in 1557. By then Sir William Cecil had subscribed £100. It is difficult to say whether this was an average holding, but there is evidence that the Company was not dominated by a few individuals. It is probable that the original intention was that when a dividend was eventually paid, it should have included the return of the capital, but this was not put into effect. The success of the enterprise was only moderate, and by 1566 no dividend had been paid. Further calls for additional capital were made in 1570 and 1572, but not all of the shareholders responded. The scale and range of the business had certainly expanded however, and by the 1570s stretched from Narva on the Baltic as far as Persia by the overland route through Russia. This development failed to expand, however, after the revival of English trade to the Middle East through the Mediterranean.

The Muscovy Company operated in Russia through a system of factors, who were apparently employees rather than shareholders, and some difficulties arose because they sometimes traded on their own account as well as that of the Company. It is certain that around 1586 the capital was wound up and a new Company formed, exhibiting a greater concentration of control among a dominant group of ten or twelve shareholders. By this time the custom of returning capital as well as profit every few years was well established, though some shareholders continued to re-invest for long periods. In the 1590s one man had over £3,000 invested out of a total of not much above £20,000. The Company increasingly resembled a Regulated Company, though it remained formally a joint-stock company until around 1620.

The Levant Company followed a similar course of evolution.[17] English trade with the Mediterranean seems to have languished during the third quarter of the sixteenth century, for reasons which remain partly obscure. That it should have revived and expanded to new levels during a period when relations with Spain deteriorated into war is paradoxical, but explicable. As trade with Spain and Portugal became more difficult, it was in fact natural that the English should seek to display the inability of their enemy to prevent the passage of ships through the straits of Gibralter. The Crown took a considerable interest in the origins of the Levant Company, the Queen having paid the expenses of a mission to Constantinople to negotiate privileges for trade in Turkey, while the Secretary of State, Walsingham, encouraged the enterprise, seeing in it the prospect of increasing naval reserves and of cutting out foreign intermediaries in the trade in spices and silks, and in the already important market for English cloth in the Mediterranean. As much as the Muscovy Company, the Levant Company was the focus of diplomatic relations between England and foreign governments, and the agent of the Company at Constantinople was effectively the English ambassador, though characteristically the Company was compelled to cover his costs. A decade after its foundation the Company was reconstructed by an amalgamation with the Venice Company, bringing two complementary trades into a single organisation. It is not clear from the new charter how the Company was organised, and there are unfortunately many obscurities, especially in its financial history. Certainly in the time between the expiry of the original charter in 1588 and the grant of a new one in 1592 there was considerable discussion concerning the joint-stock basis of the new Company. Equally, there is certain evidence that by 1595 members were carrying on trade on their own account, with their own factors in the Mediterranean, and in 1598 an extra levy was imposed by the Company on all traders to Turkey. As a joint-stock experiment, therefore, the Levant Company was short-lived. It is not easy to say why the decision to revert to a 'regulated' basis was taken, but probably it was a sign of increasing self-confidence among the merchants in their ability to raise sufficient capital for individual enterprise, even though the trade was risky—more from the activities of Barbary corsairs than official enemies—and the vessels employed needed to be heavily armed and crewed. The profits of the trade could be very great and in the early seventeenth century some 'Turkey merchants' were among the most wealthy men in the City of London.

These early examples of joint-stock companies demonstrate the extent to which they shared the characteristics of the older Regulated Companies. Only gradually did the principle of the permanency of the capital take hold, and the royal charters cease to place a time limit on the existence of the companies. The earliest, the Russia Company, was exceptional in this respect, and the charter to the English East India Company in 1600 ran for only fifteen years. The process of evolution towards a permanent capital was essential before a full market in their shares could develop. They remained closer in spirit to the traditional partnership than is often realised. The English East India Company levied a fee of admission from new members, although they had purchased their share, and the character of new members was controlled in much the same way as in the Regulated Companies, preference being given to apprentices, employees and agents, and provision made for lower entry fines for the sons of members. The English companies also appear to have been more conservative in practice than their legal position demanded. Nevertheless, the essential characteristic of the joint-stock companies and the corporate trading with capital raised from members should not be underestimated from a practical point of view. That they came into use mainly for non-European trade shows that within the limits of the period, the need for large concentrations of capital in commerce was restricted to these specialised areas, in most of which the companies were forced to carry on activities which went beyond the merely commercial, intruding into the diplomatic and military spheres. Yet in origin they owed more to the initiative of private individuals than the state, which simply permitted them to exercise functions on its behalf. The English and Dutch joint-stock companies of the seventeenth century had this in common in contrast to the later developments in France under Colbert, where the state took the initiative and forced government officials and municipalities to contribute capital.

(6) The State and Trade

The question of the relationship between the state and commerce goes to the root of the concept of 'mercantilism' often said to characterise the seventeenth and eighteenth centuries.[18] Current historical thinking has not entirely abandoned the use of the term, though the older view of the conscious use of state power to encourage trade in the ultimate interest of the state has been substantially modified. Reduced to such a basic formulation, it might be said that mercantilism has always existed, and that the contrast drawn between the sixteenth to eighteenth centuries and earlier and later times has been over-dramatised. Even when Adam Smith analysed mercantilism in order to destroy its theoretical basis and substitute that of free trade and the division of labour, he was forced to make important concessions to the realities of the state's power and of conflict between states.

The problem of making generalised statements about the extent of the change in the attitude and role of the state in commercial affairs during the course of the sixteenth century and the early seventeenth is exceedingly difficult. If, at one extreme, we deny that anything approaching a conscious and consistent policy which took the encouragement of trade as an end in itself can be detected, it would be rash to assert at the other that the state was solely concerned with its own financial interest in the narrowest, fiscal, sense. What later came to be called 'mercantilism' enjoyed such coherence as analysts could give it largely from their concentration on the writings of men who were practising merchants, or were intimately connected with them, but most attempts to prove that state policy was or became dominated by their ideas have been unsuccesful. Most of the writers who form the canon of mercantilist thought belonged to the late seventeenth and eighteenth centuries, though the controversies about bullion and trade balances began in the 1620s, and even earlier the Hakluyts had written of colonial expansion as a source of essential commodities and a remedy for unemployment at home. The sixteenth-century state largely took its decisions relating to 'economic' matters in a condition of innocence of what we regard as commonplaces of elementary economic theory. It was superficially aware of changes which affected its interests, and took measures to protect them as it saw them, without benefit of abstract theory. It was not necessary that a government should have a sophisticated understanding of the quantity theory of money in order to see that its revenues were losing in purchasing power as prices rose, even if it could not always restore the position without political difficulty. The state's principal business was defence and the conduct of war, and in most of the larger states the importance of foreign trade and the power of the merchant community were small in relation to that of the land-owning class. In these circumstances it is not surprising that the interests of commerce, which was never in itself a single interest, were normally overridden by considerations of a different order. This is not to say that the state could afford to ignore commercial interests entirely, and it is reasonable to assert that there was a tendency during the sixteenth century for governments to take more note of them as their importance to society increased. Such a statement does not take us far, and many distinctions must be drawn. It is easy, for example, to criticise the Spanish monarchy for allowing its relatively easy access to bullion to distract it from the long-term necessity of providing conditions in which Castilian industry and trade could flourish and remain competitive, but it must be remembered that no state at the time had the power sufficiently to control economic life, however 'absolute' was its power in theory.

Things were very different where the state and commercial interests were more closely identified. Venice went to war with the Turks when its commercial interests were attacked, but at other times was prepared to suffer unpopularity in Christian Europe for its steady refusal to join in the 'crusade'. More typically, governments, not for the first time, used the threat of embargoes on trade as a diplomatic weapon in time of peace, and as a means of economic warfare, and were frequently forced to realise that the weapon was two-edged. Spain was forced to permit the Dutch to trade in the Iberian peninsula in the 1580s and 1590s because of her dependence on Baltic grain, although she would have preferred to deny the Dutch access to the salt of Setúbal and Cadiz which was essential to Dutch fishing. The torn economy of the Netherlands was patched together by the issue of licences for trade between north and south. If commerce had to accommodate itself to war, it is equally true that in certain circumstances war had to accommodate itself to commerce.

There was a tendency during the sixteenth century for the state's conception of its interests to become closer to that of a society in which commerce played an increasingly important role. What the English were calling the 'Common Weal' was a concept which continued to broaden, and was gradually preparing the way for an age in which trade rivalry would emerge as a prime determinant of a nation's foreign relations. By the middle of the seventeenth century the rivalry of England and the Dutch led to a series of wars which centred on trade and imperial quest-ions, for there was little else in dispute, and much in common, between the two societies. It was in such a world as this that the ideas most usually associated with 'mercantilism' flourished, not the world of con-flicting ideologies which deeply influenced the course of sixteenth-century politics. Though trade rivalry played its part in the sixteenth century, it is at least as accurate to argue that the Portuguese blockade of the Red Sea was as much a part of the ideological struggle between Christendom and Islam as it was part of a commercial struggle with Venice for the monopoly of the European spice market. That it was both at the same time epitomises the age. That it was an enterprise directed by the Crown.is a sign of the remarkable modernity of outlook of a government which needed to take the initiative where private enter-prise lacked the resources.

To a large extent all states operated under the sign of a 'bullionism' which narrowly equated the wealth of the state with the quantity of coinage in the royal coffers or, rather more broadly, within the realm. Agreement on this principle did not prevent the existence of tensions between the short-term fiscal needs of the state and the views of theo-rists of 'proto-mercantilist' outlook almost invariably resolved in favour of the short-term interest of the government. Often the imposition of customs duties on exports preceded those on imports, and progress towards a customs policy deliberately designed to encourage the export of manufactured goods and the import of raw materials was slow and erratic. The state had to balance the views of those who favoured the urgent expansion of manufacturing industry for export with the inter-ests of the domestic consumer as well as its own revenues.

In both Spain and France the construction of a 'mercantilist' policy by the government was urged by memoranda and petitions for long before it was applied in any serious or coherent way. The recommendat-ions of the Castilian *arbitristas* of the seventeenth century had been anticipated a century earlier by writers whose memoranda had only limited contemporary effect, and remained unprinted. In the early years of the sixteenth century the Castilian Crown placed some restriction on the import of foreign cloth with the intention of encouraging the native industry in centres such as Segovia and Cuenca, but allowed exceptions by licence. At the same time, however, the manufacturing interests complained of inadequate supplies of raw wool of high quality, allegedly the result of the Crown's favouring the export of wool through Burgos. In 1514 the manufacturers obtained the revival of a law of 1462 reserving one-third of the wool bought for export for domestic users. The clash of interest between merchant-exporters and manufacturers was sharp, and in the end the power of Burgos merchants, and the reliance of the Crown on the revenues from wool exports, was to triumph. Within a few years the Regent Cardinal Cisneros was to receive two memoranda which adumbrated in a striking way the concept of a nationalist economic policy. Pedro de Burgos analysed the system of wool sales in detail to show that it was in practice almost impossible for those making purchases for domestic industry to obtain adequate supplies because the exporting interests of Burgos were able to exploit their close contacts with the sheep-owners of the *Mesta* to purchase wool at low prices before the shearing. He recommended that the export of the finest-quality wool should be prohibited, and drew attention to the underdevelopment of the Castilian economy resulting from its concentration on the export of raw materials and the consequent import of manufactures. 'I say that in the trade in cloth Castile ought to be Flanders. . . [so that] the *alcabalas* and income of their highnesses would grow to a much greater quantity than they are today.'[19]

Such wide-ranging proposals remained largely unheeded as the Crown came to rely increasingly on the supply of precious metals from the Indies to satisfy its needs. Not even the more sophisticated proposals of Luis Ortiz, probably put forward in the aftermath of the state bankruptcy of 1557, stirred the government into any consistent action. Whilst Ortiz remained fundamentally within the 'bullionist' tradition, he wished to cure the drain of the precious metals by a programme of industrial development designed to prepare the way for the prohibition of the import of manufactures. Ortiz was no doubt unrealistic in supposing that a four-year plan could convert Castile into an economic copy of the Netherlands, and admitted that a further period might have to elapse before prohibition could be implemented without starving the domestic market of essential imports, but at least he saw that too hasty and drastic curtailment of imports would be disastrous.[20]

The opportunities which existed in the reign of Philip II were not taken, and only when the supply of American treasure began to slacken, and the Castilian economy was in deep crisis, did the ideas of the more famous *arbitristas* produce some sporadic and unsuccesful attempts of

the government to encourage new industrial developments, which were
limited to areas most obviously relevant to Spain's ability to continue
to wage the European wars, the abandonment of which was the prime
requisite for a cure of economic ills.

Amongst the greater states of Europe, Spain was an extreme example
of underdevelopment, but her major rival, France, occupied a midway
position. During the period of reconstruction following the end of the
wars of religion, the government of Henry IV was urged by writers such
as Barthélemy de Laffemas to develop the native silk industry of Tours
and to prohibit the import of Italian silks, and even to expand the production of raw silk. Such a plan revealed the sharp clash of interests
between the established commercial interest of Lyons and the ideal of
national industrial self-sufficiency. Lyons, its prosperity already undermined during the wars, reacted violently to the premature prohibition
of the import of Italian silks, and to the threat to its own silk-weaving
industry implied by the favouring of Tours and the attempt to bring its
organisation within the rigid system of regulation under gilds typical
of the rest of France. In the end, the state was forced to yield to Lyons
because of its strategic importance near the frontiers of Savoy and Italy.
The appeals to patriotism made by the advocates of a 'national economy'
were forced to yield to the interests of a city whose traditions were
those of an open and liberal welcome to foreign merchants and capital,
and whose wealth was generated largely at the expense of a large trading
deficit with the Italian cities. It was more than half a century before
France began, under the rule of Colbert, to divert its economy towards
the ideal of self-sufficiency. The plans of his precursors had foundered
because they failed to take account of the underlying structures, and
attempted to force the economy into channels which were insufficently
prepared.[21]

The same is true of the notorious project of Alderman Cockayne to
undertake to export only fully finished and dyed cloth from England to
the Netherlands. However perfectly it fitted the theories of full industrial development, its characteristic of a sudden *coup d'état* ensured its
failure, since the capacity of the English finishing industry was
inadequate to meet the demand. The state had made the mistake, so
common at the time, of combining its own short-term interest in financial profit from the fees paid by the projectors for their monopoly with
a half-comprehended understanding of the fashionable doctrines of
economic writers.

The ideal of self-sufficiency within a national economy, embracing a
colonial system which provided deficient raw materials or precious

metals, or both, remained at the heart of economic thinking in the seventeenth century. It had proved unrealisable in the sixteenth century because the states with the largest overseas empires lacked the domestic industrial and commercial capacity to enforce in practice the monopoly of trade with their colonies. It remained a distant dream even in the seventeenth century, and we are left with a fundamental paradox that an age which strove to achieve national autarchy in the interests of defence saw wars in which the commercial factor became more and more prominent, and in which international trade continued to expand.

Notes

1. H. van der Wee, *The Growth of the Antwerp Market*, I, p. 306.
2. R. Gascon, *Grand commerce et vie urbaine au xvie siècle—Lyon et ses marchands (environs de 1520—environs de 1580)*, pp. 240-2.
3. Quoted from Savary's *Le Parfait Négociant* (1675) by H. Sée, 'Quelques aperçus sur le capitalisme commercial en France au xviie siècle', *Revue d'histoire économique et sociale*, XII (1924), p. 166.
4. N. Salomon, *La campagne de la Nouvelle Castille*, pp. 119-20.
5. M. Bresard, *Les foires de Lyon, passim.*
6. J.-C. Bergier, *Genève et l'économie de la Renaissance*, pp. 363-89.
7. R. de Roover, *Money, Banking and Credit in Mediaeval Bruges*, pp. 19-29.
8. M. Basas Fernández, *El consulado de Burgos en el siglo xvi, passim.*
9. State Papers Foreign, 1575-77, quoted by E. Lipson, *Economic History of England*, II, pp. 231-2.
10. R.W.K. Hinton, *The Eastland Trade and the Common Weal in the Seventeenth Century*, Ch. IV.
11. D.O. Wagner, 'Coke and the Rise of Economic Liberalism', *Economic History Review*, VI (1935), pp. 30-42.
12. A. Friis, *Alderman Cockayne's Project and the Cloth Trade in the Reign of James I, passim.*
13. H. Taylor, 'Price Revolution or Price Revision—the English and the Spanish Trade after 1604', *Renaissance and Modern Studies*, XII (1968), pp. 5-32, esp. 11-12.
14. Ibid., p. 9; Cornwallis to the Privy Council.
15. Dollinger, op. cit., *passim.*
16. T.S. Willan, *The Early History of the Russia Company, 1553-1603, passim.*
17. A.C. Wood, *A History of the Levant Company, passim.*
18. See E.F. Hecksher, *Mercantilism,* and for recent developments in the discussion of the concept, D.C. Coleman (ed.), *Revisions in Mercantilism.*
19. J. Pérez, *La révolution des Comunidades de Castille*, pp. 102-7.
20. J. Larraz, *La época del mercantilismo en Castilla*, pp. 106-10.
21. H. Hauser, *Les débuts du capitalisme*, Ch. VI, 'Le Colbertisme avant Colbert', pp. 181-222.

3 MONEY, BANKING AND CREDIT

In considering the money supply in relation to trade in the sixteenth century we are faced with a paradox. The fifteenth century, or at least the greater part of it, is usually regarded as a period when a shortage of the precious metals as a circulating medium helped to inhibit trade and to keep prices and levels of activity stagnant. The sixteenth, by contrast, is classically viewed as a period of general inflation during which the increase in the money supply outpaced the volume of goods and services available. Yet, according to one recent specialist, Europe suffered from 'a growing dearth of monetary resources.'[1] The early satisfaction of demand for more of the precious metals generated rising expectations among governments and private individuals, and there is little doubt that the scale of state expenditure, especially the rapidly escalating scale of warfare, was a leading force of acceleration in the economy.

Medieval Europe had not lacked its own sources of the precious metals, especially silver. The slackening of production in the mines of central Europe which occurred in the early fifteenth century reflected the stagnation of trade, the exhaustion of many seams, and a shortage of capital and techniques for the exploitation of more difficult ones. Later in the century the slightly more buoyant economic climate linked with the beginnings of an expansion in population provided a stimulus to increased output, but more important was a combination of the indebtedness of the Habsburg Emperors and the financial genius of Jacob Fugger of Augsburg. From 1487 Jacob Fugger increased his grip on the production of silver in the Habsburg lands under licences granted in return for substantial credits granted to the Archduke Sigismond, ruler of Tyrol. In the 1490s Fugger increasingly turned his personal attention to the exploitation of the mineral resources of Hungary. This still-independent country was already under heavy pressure from the Turks, and was showing signs of internal disintegration as a consequence. The times seemed inauspicious for the revival of Hungarian mining, but the infusion of Fugger capital and enterprise led to a programme of rapid modernisation with the use of new German techniques. In association with Jan Thurzo, the Fuggers soon established a virtual monopoly of Hungarian silver and copper production. These operations were the more rewarding because the value of the copper produced was sufficient to cover the cost of mining and separation, the silver being both a

bonus and free of all taxes. It has been estimated that between 1494 and
1526 the Fuggers, apart from their associates, made some 750,000 to
800,000 Rhenish florins in profit from their Hungarian enterprise alone.
The accumulation of such capital explains how the Fuggers were able to
lend more than half a million florins to Charles V at the time of his
election to the Imperial throne in 1519.[2] The mines of Hungary, the
Tyrol, Bohemia and Germany were probably producing as much as three
million ounces of silver a year at their peak in the 1530s, possibly four
times as much as in the mid-fifteenth century, and about four times as
much as the annual imports of silver from the Spanish Indies as late as
the 1540s.[3] The addition from all these sources to the stock of silver in
Europe, allowance being made for 'wastage' through export and for that
proportion which was not monetarised, was nevertheless insufficient to
maintain the ratio of value between silver and gold, so that the former
continued to appreciate in terms of the latter at least until the 1540s.

The European monetary system remained bimetallic, and the continuous process of adjustment of values between gold and silver created
serious tensions in the economy. What was a further complexity of a
complex system for the merchant engaged in international trade was an
opportunity for profit to the financier who specialised in exchange
transactions.

The search for a more adequate supply of gold went back far into
the fifteenth century. Commercial contacts with North Africa had been
prized by the Genoese in the later middle ages as a source of gold. The
Portuguese had always known the importance of Moorish gold, and
their coinage reflected Moorish occupation long after the reconquest
was completed. In 1415 they occupied Ceuta, and within twenty years
were again issuing gold coinage in quantities which implied a considerable success in drawing African gold away from Italy.[4] They pressed
further south along the African coast in search of more direct access to
the gold produced south of the Sahara, and succeeded in attracting a
part of the trans-Saharan caravan trade to their base at Argain, where
they sold horses, wheat and cloth in exchange for slaves and gold. From
1456 Gambia became the principal Portuguese route of penetration to
Timbuktu and its hinterland, until in 1475 the site of their future principal base of São Jorge da Mina was discovered, far to the east on the
shores of the Gulf of Guinea. By the turn of the century, over 100,000
cruzados of gold were annually entering the coffers of the Portuguese
Crown from Guinea, without taking into account the profits of the
private individuals who held the monopoly of the trade by royal licence.
A large part of the profits made by the Crown was ploughed back into

further voyages of discovery, and by 1497 the way to India lay open to the fleet of Vasco da Gama. From this time onwards, the gold which flowed into Portugal from West Africa became the means by which the empire in the Indian Ocean was launched and maintained.

Though neither the Portuguese nor their later competitors were able to sell enough European goods in the East to pay for the spices and cloths which they purchased, the drainage of precious metals from Europe by this route should not be exaggerated. It has recently been argued that for most of the first half of the sixteenth century, the quantities of bullion exported to the East by the Portuguese averaged less than half of the royal income in gold in the early years of the century. The price advantage initially gained by the Portuguese over their Venetian competitors, who obtained spices from the Levant, meant that only a fraction of the quantity of bullion left Europe for each pound of pepper and spices which the Portuguese imported compared with the Venetians. It is therefore likely that Portuguese imperial expansion, at least down to the middle of the century, led to a net increase in European stocks of gold.[5]

From 1492, the voyages of Columbus led to the development of some of the Caribbean islands followed by that of mainland Mexico and Peru, and the rapid exploitation of their enormous reserves of the precious metals. Initially, imports of treasure into Spain were entirely of gold. Only after 1519 did silver begin to arrive, and not until after 1560 did it begin to exceed the imports of gold in value.[6] At least as late as 1550 the value of gold imports into Spain was nearly double that of silver, totalling about 8 million ducats between 1551 and 1555, or roughly 1,000,000 ounces.[7]

About the middle of the century, there are signs that the European economy was still starved of the precious metals, despite the apparently huge additions. Political and military factors were undoubtedly of prime importance in the worsening of this crisis. The last years of the reign of the Emperor Charles V saw him at war simultaneously on three fronts— against France, the Turks and the Protestant princes in Germany. His indebtedness, like that of his enemies, grew rapidly, and though the Fuggers remained loyal to his cause, if only in the vain hope of recovering what they were already owed, he was forced to turn elsewhere for financial support. Already in 1552 Italian, mainly Genoese, contractors undertook almost half the business of the transfer of monetary resources to the theatres of war, and in 1554 they undertook it all.[8] More important, from the 1540s the syndicates who signed the *asientos* with the Castilian Crown began to demand and obtain permission to export treasure to meet at least a part of their obligations. In this way American gold and silver began to circulate more widely in the European economy. Together with the direct exports of treasure by the government, the drainage of the precious metals from Castile into the rest of Europe between 1551 and 1556 approached 5,000,000 ducats. This figure, which of course covered only legally authorised exports, exceeded the royal share of imports from the Indies, and was not far short of half the total imports, which reached a peak in these years not exceeded until 1561-5.

When imports of treasure to Spain began to rise again after 1560, silver was clearly playing the major role. The richest silver mine of all, at Potosí in Peru, had been opened in 1545, and was followed by others in northern Mexico. In the 1560s the proportion of silver by weight in the treasure fleets had risen to 97 per cent, or perhaps 70 per cent by value, whilst the share of gold continued to fall steadily to little more than one per cent by weight, or around 15 per cent by value in the early decades of the seventeenth century. The imports of gold nevertheless remained at much the same levels as before, and the rapid change in the relative position of silver in the total is a measure of the enormous increase in its output. The new mines in Mexico and Peru rapidly adopted the technical revolution originating in Germany of the use of mercury in the extraction of silver from the ore. The quantities of mercury used are revealed by the export of no less than 15,000 tons from the mine of Almadén in Spain between 1559 and 1660, in addition to that produced at Huancavélica in Peru, which was considerably more.[9] At their peak in the 1590s, imports of American treasure into Spain averaged 7,000,000 *pesos* a year, or rather more than 8,000,000 ducats, and of this over 80 per cent by value was in silver.

Silver thus became the dominant currency medium in later sixteenth-century Europe, and its infiltration throughout the continent became more rapid. Relatively plentiful, its value in relation to gold began to decline, reversing the earlier trend. In Castile, amongst the first areas to feel its impact after Andalucía, where it entered Europe, silver was drastically devalued in relation to gold in 1566, the ratio moving from a little over 10:1 to 12:1. As gold became relatively more valuable, it tended to be withdrawn from circulation. It grew more attractive to hoard it, especially in the form of older coins. A Jewish merchant of Prague had a treasury at the end of the century which consisted largely of gold coins, mostly a hundred years old.[10] As early as 1537 Charles V had substituted a lighter slightly less pure coin for the gold *excelente* of Granada, the *escudo*, but both became worth more in terms of silver *reales* than their official valuation in terms of the 'money of account', the *maravedí*. As early as 1553, when large quantities of silver had found their way to Antwerp from Spain, Sir Thomas Gresham noted that whilst silver was very plentiful on the Bourse, gold was unobtainable:

> here is no kind of gold stirring, which is the strangest matter that ever was seen upon the Bourse of Antwerp, having no other payment but silver Spanish reals; as for angels and sovereigns here is none to be gotten, for that the exchange is so high.[11]

Spain had become more than ever the source within Europe from which the monetary stocks of other areas were fed. The silver mines of Central Europe fell into decline, through exhaustion and the 'dearness' of the silver they produced.

The official needs of the Spanish government abroad remained the largest single means by which the silver was exported, and even England benefited from the arrival of the future Philip II in 1554 to an extent which assisted an upward revaluation of the English coinage after the debasements of the later years of Henry VIII and the reign of Edward VI.[12] Spain's need for money in the Netherlands grew to even higher levels after the outbreak of the Revolt, but after 1568 the dangers of the English Channel forced her to seek an alternative route. Silver had the disadvantage compared with gold of greater bulk. Less easy to smuggle in quantity, but much more demanding in transport and protection, it could hardly be carried through an unfriendly and unstable France, and the new route lay to Barcelona and Genoa, and then overland through Milan, Savoy and Lorraine, along the same route as that used by the Spanish armies. Already during the early 1570s between 2 and 4 million *escudos* a year were being spent on the army in the Netherlands, and this was to grow in some years of the 1580s and 1590s to the equivalent of over 20 million *escudos,* far more than was being received from the Indies.[13] A large proportion of this money was of course not sent in the form of bullion or coins. The Genoese, exploiting their financial strength and their new strategic position on the major route between Spain and the Netherlands, extended their control over the royal finances of Castile, especially after 1575. It has been suggested that a principal reason for their success was their better access to gold, still necessary for transactions in many areas, and particularly favoured by Spanish troops in the Netherlands for their pay. Through the fairs of 'Bisenzone', the Genoese gained control of the major exchange transactions in Europe, and exploited the high value of gold to secure additional profits on their conversion operations.[14]

The capacity of major bullion flows to attract trade was a permanent phenomenon of the times, but the second half of the sixteenth century provides the most striking examples. The economic life of the western Mediterranean received a much-needed stimulus from the new routes taken by Spanish treasure. The port of Leghorn in the Duchy of Tuscany, and to some extent the whole area from Barcelona to Naples, saw a revival of activity. Italian ports became attractive to English merchants in the 1580s when Spanish ports were being closed to them, and silver obtained from the sale of metals and cloth was used for their purchase of currants and spices in the eastern Mediterranean. Though, like others, the Spanish government prohibited the export of bullion and coinage by merchants, the regulations were evaded on an ever-increasing scale. As Spain's need for northern European grain and timber increased, the government was compelled to allow payment in cash, the demand for Spanish products being insufficient. The presence of large colonies of foreign merchants in Seville, the nerve-centre of Spain's American trade, bore witness not only to the growing attractions of engaging illicitly in that trade, but also of the demand of their compatriots in Portugal, France, England and the Netherlands (both 'loyal' and 'rebel') for silver. As it became clear that the monetary resources of the Portuguese empire were inadequate under the changed conditions, Lisbon merchants were among those who flocked to Seville in the wake of fishermen from the Algarve. The export of Spanish *reales* to the Near and Far East in large quantities in the second half of the sixteenth century gave them such familiarity that they were much preferred to other western money. It became necessary for the English and the Dutch to use them when they developed their own direct trade with the Orient in the early seventeenth century. The English East India Company set up a 'Committee for rials' which searched far and wide for Spanish 'pieces of eight'. They found them with difficulty at home, apart from occasional small quantities obtained from West Country traders and privateers, and looked to the Breton ports and Rouen, whose merchants and sailors were in close contact with Bilbao, Seville and Cadiz. That the volume of the East India Company's trade with the Orient was governed by the availability of the right medium of exchange is a striking example of how not only the money supply in general, but its specific character, could influence the scale and direction of trade.[15]

The trade of the Dutch and, on a much smaller scale, that of the English, in the Baltic area, was possible only by the export of currency to make up its deficit. The Dutch sales of grain in the Iberian peninsula and the Mediterranean were purchased in the Baltic ports with Spanish silver as well as Dutch cloth. In these two principal directions, therefore, a proportion of the additional stock of silver left Europe, making possible the extension of its trade on a world basis, and at the same time mitigating the inflationary effects of the silver imports. These outflows are more difficult to quantify than the imports, but have a further importance. They were, in effect, an illustration on a world scale of a phenomenon which was equally applicable within Europe. Nor was the changing relative value of gold and silver consistent, either between the regions of Europe or between Europe and the outer world with which the European economy was coming into increasing contact, or indeed between the countries of Asia themselves. Just as the Genoese exploited their access to highly valued gold in Europe, the Portuguese, Dutch and English exploited the relatively high value of silver in the Far East (except Japan) and the further Baltic hinterland, inclusive of Muscovy.

Though the trend was towards an equilibrium between the values of gold and silver in the bimetallic currency system, it was never achieved within western Europe, even though the economies of north and south and east and west were becoming more interdependent—or at least less autonomous. The domination of silver in the system during the later sixteenth century had a long-term inflationary effect, and perhaps had a greater impact on retail prices than the increase in gold stocks earlier, but we know that the long-term change of trend in European prices between the fifteenth and sixteenth centuries had its origins in other factors as well as the money supply, notably in a demographic upsurge which put particular pressure on agricultural prices, and in the general acceleration of commercial activity. We are also in a better position than we were when Earl J. Hamilton published his *American Treasure and the Price Revolution in Spain* to put the gentle inflation of the sixteenth century into perspective, and even to suggest that those contemporaries who established the view that American bullion was the major cause of price inflation did not win all the points in their debate with those who thought that 'debasements' of the currency by government action were more important. Writers of the Salamanca school reached the conclusion that the treasure of the Indies had caused the rise in prices thirty years before Jean Bodin lent it his authority in his *Réponse à M. de Malestroit,* and before it had made its major impact. Yet a recent writer has argued that Malestroit had a better appreciation than Bodin of the importance of the increasing ratio of the value of gold to that of silver, especially as it affected France. The French government, with its relatively weak currency system, starved of metallic reserves, was compelled to order severe devaluations of its money of account, the *livre tournois,* in face of the flood of Spanish silver and of its own internal political problems after 1560.[16]

From the point of view of the merchant community, the short-term tensions in the relative value of gold and silver, the efforts of governments to adjust to them or to resist them, and the short-term fluctuations in prices, from season to season, from year to year, and from place to place, were of greater importance than the long-term trend. The merchant who engaged in a trade over a relatively short distance might turn his capital over once or twice a year. An English merchant trading with Antwerp or an Augsburg merchant trading with Venice might achieve this. It mattered very much more to him whether the exchange rates varied seasonally than whether the long-term trend was towards rising prices, whether in terms of gold or silver.

From the end of the sixteenth century Europe began to enter a period when the influx of silver began to slacken, slowly at first, with the steep decline in Spain's imports coming at the very end of the period we are concerned with. First in Spain, more because of her heavy re-export of silver than of the absolute decline of imports, and somewhat later elsewhere, the quantity of silver in circulation ceased to be adequate. A process similar to that which had affected gold from the middle of the century began to affect silver. The consequences, for Spain most of all, but for other countries also, were to be far more serious. Copper, which had tended to appreciate in value relative to silver, was brought in as a substitute for silver not only in the coinage which affected the poor man, but also that used by the merchants and the government. The first stage in the process was the result of a decision taken in 1599 to re-issue the *vellón* coinage of Castile as pure copper after extracting the silver content which it had contained throughout the sixteenth century. Whilst this measure in itself, with the coining of additional pure copper money, was not too harmful, and indeed cured a shortage of coins of small denominations, it was rapidly followed by others which reduced the weight of the coins without altering their face value, or increased the face value without altering the weight. Instead of appreciating because of its metallic content to values above its face value as the old mixed *vellón* had done, the new coinage was immediately recognised as merely token money, and confidence in it was virtually nil. As the Crown made an immediate profit of 100 to 250 per cent on each operation, it was tempted, in the desperate need for any source of revenue, to repeat the dosage of this dangerous medicine, despite the protests of the *Cortes* and its own promises to desist. A new kind of inflation hit a Castilian economy which was already in crisis, and great instability followed the equally drastic attempt to reverse the policy in 1627. Worse, in addition to its own discredited copper coinage, the government was faced with an influx of counterfeit copper coins minted abroad, which even the death penalty and the jurisdiction of the Inquisition could not prevent. Amongst the most serious consequences was a rise in the value of silver so that by 1626 it stood at a premium of 50 per cent compared with the beginning of the century. It was thus driven almost completely from circulation in Spain, and all payments which had to be made abroad in silver were that much more costly. The government suffered doubly, as the largest spender abroad and as the importer of the copper (largely Swedish) for the vastly increased *vellón* circulation.

It is a sign of the basic unity of the European economy, despite its regional diversity, that within a few years the Spanish experience was echoed elsewhere. In France copper coinage was minted in 1607, and by the 1630s the premium of silver over copper had also risen to 50 per cent, as it had in parts of Germany, whilst in Sweden it doubled between 1626 and 1630.[17]

The opening of the Thirty Years War from 1618 helped to accelerate these processes. In Poland and many of the German states a wave of devaluations accompanied the raising of troops. War conditions always deeply affect trade, but though these deliberate debasements altered the terms of trade sharply against the devaluers, the Dutch and the English suffered because their over-priced exports dropped steeply in volume. Exports of English cloth to the Baltic declined by nearly half between 1618 and 1622 in the wake of devaluations of the Polish *groschen*. As the English writer Edward Misselden put it:

If the money rise in denomination above its true worth in valuation and the exchange also rise accordingly, if this merchant do not raise the price of his commodity in due proportion answerable thereunto, he shall be sure to come home with a weeping cross, however he make his return, whether by exchange, or in money, bullion or wares.[18]

Silver began to flow out of England, attracted by its higher valuation abroad, and for a whole year in 1619-20 no silver was coined at the English Mint. The 'scarcity of money' in England was a further depressant to industry and trade, and new, more sophisticated explanations of the outflow of bullion were born of the urgent controversy which raged during the crisis. Thomas Mun's theory of trade balances and bullion flows, seeing exchange rates as an expression of the mechanism of the commercial system, rather than the result of deliberate manipulations of bankers, was evolved in these years. As he expressed it:

> the gain or loss which happeneth to merchants' exchange by bills is ruled by the plenty or scarcity of money in the places where it is delivered out and taken up, and this plenty or scarcity of money is caused only by the over or underbalance of our commodities in the respective places of foreign trade.[19]

The period ended as it began, in the sense of the apparently widespread shortages of the metallic basis of the currency system, but with the additional element of greater instability. The metallic currency was, however, only one dimension of the financial structure, and it is appropriate to begin the transition to a discussion of its other elements by dealing briefly with the question of 'money of account'. Basically, money of account was a unit employed as a common denominator in terms of which metallic coins were given a value which coincided with their intrinsic worth at the time when they were struck. The unit of account might or might not coincide with an actual coin, but commonly it did not. It frequently had its origin in an actual coin which had fallen out of use, and it might be either a small or a large unit. In Castile the *maravedí* was very small, and in course of time was often replaced, especially at state level, by the ducat or the *escudo*. The *maravedí* had however the advantage that it was possible to express almost all coins, gold, silver or *vellón* in whole numbers of *maravedís*, whilst the absence of a single multiple between the silver *real* and the ducat or *escudo* caused inconvenience. In most parts of western Europe however, variants of a duodecimal system were employed, in most of which the pound, or *livre*, formed the basis of the money of account, with twenty shillings or *sous* to the pound and twelve pence or *deniers* to the shilling.

Whilst the system of money of account was essential to financial life, in the course of time it created difficulties of its own. The constantly changing relative values in intrinsic terms of gold and silver coins of various denominations and dates of issue theoretically demanded an equally constant review of their values in terms of the money of account. In practice these readjustments were delayed, and since in the sixteenth century the trend was towards the appreciation of silver in terms of gold, later followed by the reverse, and since governments did not readjust the values of the coins together, there were always differences between regions in close commercial contact with each other, so that a coin which was 'undervalued' in its country of origin would tend to be exported to an area where its intrinsic value was better recognised. After 1531 gold was overvalued in Sicily, at a ratio to silver of no less than 15:1. Consequently, silver coins were exported from the island to purchase gold, which was recoined in Sicily at a profit, especially to the government.[20] In other words, the ratio between the value of gold and that of silver was not changing at an even rate throughout Europe, and an undervalued coin in one area might be overvalued in another. This gave rise to considerable opportunities for speculation. Some Jewish merchants of Ancona in the early 1550s had bought gold in Lisbon, converted it into silver in Antwerp at a profit, and then transferred it to Rome where silver was still at a ratio of only a little above 1 to 10 to gold, thus making a second profit.[21]

Money of account nevertheless helped the development of the banking system, which became an increasingly important and specialised activity. The image of the merchant of the later middle ages, voyaging with his goods and money bags, was never appropriate to the wealthier members of the class, and the most highly developed economies, especially in the north Italian cities, had developed banking systems not only for the management of relations between local citizens but also for the settlement of debts between distant places. Banking, as we understand it, had reappeared in Italy as early as the twelfth century. In the thirteenth century local laws, under the reviving influence of Roman law, certainly recognised the validity of the transfer of debts from one person to another. In practice the early banks evolved from the activities of money-changers who began to keep records, and gradually took on a wider range of economic functions. They were sometimes made responsible for the withdrawal of unsound or worn coins, and acted as agents for the mints, but their essentially banking function lay in the acceptance of deposits of surplus cash. Regulations were evolved to compel them to offer sureties against default, and they began to allow overdrafts to favoured customers. Most private banks were owned by families who also carried on trade, though the most successful tended to concentrate more on banking as they grew richer. A further stage came when banks came to hold accounts with each other, either in the same city or elsewhere, or else established branches in other places. The way was thus opened for their customers to settle debts by transfer in the bankers' ledgers instead of in cash, whether locally or through the network which soon covered the major cities of the western Mediterranean and the great fair towns of France, Germany and the Netherlands. The settlement of debts became associated with the periods of the fairs, each fair being followed by days set aside for the clearing of accounts, settlement sometimes being postponed until the next fair. Credit was therefore inevitably required and given. It was an essential characteristic of the banking and payments system, giving rise to a long controversy in which the Church authorities tried to resist as usurious the taking of 'excessive' interest in return for credit, and in which the commercial and financial communities devised more sophisticated methods of disguising interest under the cloak of the provision of a service.

It was in the field of settlement of mercantile accounts involving different currencies, that is to say involving exchange, that the Church's resistance was first broken. Long before the sixteenth century, the letter of exchange had become the most usual way of transferring money from one currency to another, and had evolved into a virtually stereotyped form. A merchant who owed money abroad normally did not settle directly with his creditor, the letter of exchange normally involving four parties, two of them intermediaries, who though usually themselves merchants, had evolved as specialists in exchange matters because of the regularity of their dealings with correspondents abroad. The merchant who owed money drew a letter of exchange on his local specialist, settling his debt with him in local currency. The specialist sent it to his correspondent abroad, who paid the creditor in the other local currency. The time which elapsed between the drawing of a letter of exchange and its eventual settlement represented the period of credit, varying according to the distance involved and also according to the relationship of the date of the letter to the settlement dates at the fairs in both places. The letter of exchange was acceptable to the canon law of the Church because it was easy to show that the risk involved in offering a fixed sum in settlement in another currency after the lapse of some months, during which the relative values of the two currencies might alter, justified any profit which the specialists might make. The merchant-banker who specialised in exchange transactions kept the records of his customers' accounts, so that again periodic settlement meant that cash payments were either completely eliminated or reduced to the difference between credit and debit totals. It is also important to emphasise that many quite important commercial centres did not act as clearing centres for letters of exchange, and that merchants trading from them drew their letters on major financial centres, the number of which was quite restricted. Only the very largest had a network which put them into relationship with all the others, so that settlements between Bordeaux and Burgos, for example, would be effected in Lyons or Medina del Campo.

The basic principles of a banking and exchange system were clearly not innovations of the sixteenth century, but the period was one of further developments and the more widespread use of existing techniques. The increased quantity of surviving documentary evidence has its dangers, tempting historians to see it as proof of a quantitative increase in the use of written instruments of credit. The chance survival of large collections of mercantile papers from the fourteenth and fifteenth centuries, such as the Datini archive at Prato, should make us cautious. Nevertheless, when due allowance is made for this factor, it seems certain that resort to written and increasingly stereotyped instruments did spread during the sixteenth century. It is equally clear that many conservatives still hankered after the old times when verbal agreements had greater force than the written word. In Medina del Campo it was still normal in the middle of the sixteenth century for a depositor to give a verbal instruction in a bank which entered his transaction in its ledgers in his presence,[22] and in cases of disputes concerning commercial contracts in the courts great emphasis was still placed on the oath of the parties. The spread of written instruments had disadvantages which tended to increase as the world of commerce became larger and more impersonal, and for which solutions began only slowly to be found.

It has recently been argued that there were two parallel streams of development of financial techniques during the sixteenth century.[23] The first represented a straight evolution of devices and institutions which had their origins in medieval Italy, spreading through the fairs of Geneva, Lyons and Castile, and eventually reaching their fulfilment in seventeenth-century Amsterdam. Essentially, this development reduced itself to an increasing sophistication in the handling of letters of exchange. Before the end of the fifteenth century the practice of immediate 're-change' was spreading in the most advanced centres, which increasingly detached speculation on the exchange from real transfers of money, and enabled credit to be given without any intention of transfer. 'Interior' or 'dry' exchange took the process a step further, by enabling even the fiction of transfer to be dispensed with. At the same time the practice spread of converting all real moneys into an entirely fictitious money of account which had a greater stability than normal moneys of account because it was expressed in terms of a fixed quantity of fine gold. In Lyons and the Genoese fairs of Besançon at least, the further step was taken of declaring a rate of exchange for all currencies in terms of the money of account used at the fair at the moment when payments were about to commence. Alongside the system of current accounts and deposits, it became easy for international settlements to be integrated in turn by the payment *in banco* of letters of exchange. From this it was but a short step to the reinforcement of the private banks by the restoration or introduction of public banks.

Public banks were no innovation in southern Europe. The bank of San Giorgio at Genoa was centuries old, while Barcelona, an early imitator of Italian commercial and financial institutions, had established a bank under municipal control in 1400.[24] Both of these, and others in the Mediterranean area, were created to remedy the deficiencies of the smaller private banks, and especially to provide a stronger basis for the city's own credit. The Bank of Barcelona was specifically prohibited from lending money to private individuals, but as elsewhere the prohibition was almost certainly evaded from an early date. The conditions of the late sixteenth and early seventeenth centuries led to a revival of public banking in the Mediterranean and to its introduction in the north. In 1587 the Venetian Senate established the Rialto Bank, which at its origin simply continued the functions of the private deposit banks. There was no interest on deposits and the transfers from one account to another required the presence of both parties. The bank was soon successful in attracting deposits which passed a million ducats without being called upon to pay out large sums in cash. In 1593 the Senate ordered that in future all payments by letter of exchange were to be made only through the bank's accounts. The motive behind this order was almost certainly to limit the spread of endorsement of letters of exchange, and disobedience was punishable by a fine of 500 ducats. It is doubtful if this conservative measure had much effect however, and later decrees of 1605 and 1607 compelling all payments for the purchase of goods in excess of 100 ducats to be made in the bank were hardly more successful. The bank ran into difficulties with the state by carrying on speculative and credit operations beyond its legal powers. The continuous appreciation of gold and silver in the early seventeenth century lowered the real value of the depositors' accounts, and it was only by engaging in these extra activities that the bank could protect its customers.

In 1619 the state set up another bank, the giro bank, originally intended as a short-term expedient, but which developed into a more important institution than the Rialto bank. It originated from the demand of a single dealer in precious metals who had provided the Venetian mint with a large quantity of silver, that he should be paid half in gold and half either by a credit in the Rialto bank or a 'new giro'. The giro bank thus came into existence for the settlement of a state debt over a period of years. Once established, the giro bank became attractive to the government for extending its own credit facilities. By 1630 the new bank's debt had risen to five times the limit originally envisaged, and under the pressure of war and plague the government had often not provided it with the sums promised for cash payments to its creditors. Again the bank had only survived by overstepping the original purpose of its found-ation—private citizens who were not creditors of the state had started accounts with it, and effected transfers with each other in its books. It thus took over similar functions to the Rialto bank, which was suppress-ed as superfluous in 1638. By 1630 the value of the new bank's depos-its exceeded those of the Rialto bank by more than a hundred per cent. It had evolved into a state institution which was founded on the state debt, and virtually issued fiduciary credit.[25]

In 1609 the city of Barcelona decided to set up another bank to operate alongside the bank of deposit, to be known as the 'Bank of the City of Barcelona'. The motives of the municipal authorities were made perfectly clear in the preamble to the order, and lay in the increasing monetary disorder which was infecting Catalonia from Castile, with the entry of lightweight and false coins. The bank of the City was intended to protect the deposit bank against losses of good quality currency, and to enable commercial life to continue on the basis of the poor quality coinage in circulation.[26] It became an essential part of Barcelona's com-mercial life, as Catalonia was forced to accept the lower Castilian stand-ard for silver, and a return to 'sound money' proved impossible.

The Bank of Amsterdam was also founded in 1609, and was also a response to monetary confusion.[27] Although the United Provinces were rapidly becoming the most important commercial power of northern Europe, this very fact was laying them open to the influx and circulation of foreign coins, the quality of which was lower than that of the new coins of the Republic. It was found impossible, despite regulations, to control the activities of mint-masters and money-exchangers, and it was decided to establish a municipal bank in Amsterdam. It was rapidly copied in Middelburg, Delft and Rotterdam, though that of Amsterdam retained a pre-eminence which matched that of the city in financial affairs. All letters of exchange worth more than 100 Flemish pounds, or 600 florins, were to be payable only through the bank, thus forcing merch-ants to open accounts with it, but they could not overdraw. The exchange bank of Amsterdam was successful in keeping a cash reserve which at most times was equal to or greater than the deposits. In this respect the bank prevented the expansion of credit, and restricted growth in the money supply. It was unsuccessful, however, in putting the metallic currency system into greater order. The forces which were increasing the value of gold and silver in terms of the money of account were too strong, and as we have already seen, the premium of silver over copper had increased to 50 per cent by 1630. It must nevertheless be counted amongst the factors which gave the Netherlands their pre-eminent position in seventeenth-century trade. Though silver was 'tight' in Amsterdam, it was because the Dutch did not endeavour to retain the considerable percentage of Spanish silver which reached them, but allowed its free export in the interest of a trade which had become world-wide.[28] After their establishment in the Far East, the Dutch soon made contact with Japan, where they found supplies of silver essential to their spice trade, which, as in the case of the Portuguese a century before, lessened their dependence on European sources.

The second stream of development of financial techniques, perhaps more fruitful in the long term, originated in Antwerp, and was to form the basis of further innovations in seventeenth-century London.[29] Though the letter of exchange came into increasing use in Antwerp and other northern centres in the sixteenth century, it remained essentially an instrument for the transfer of money, and its credit and speculative aspects were relatively neglected. The letter obligatory, or 'inland bill' as it came to be called in seventeenth-century England, was the principal means of settling debts among merchants. It was particularly fitted to a society in which the development of private banking facilities was surprisingly weak in view of the importance of Italian merchant colonies in its development. There had been a development of private banking in Antwerp in the fourteenth century, which had fallen into decline in the fifteenth, and had almost completely collapsed during the financial difficulties of the 1480s, when the normally small houses lacked sufficient strength to ride the storm. The remarkably rapid development of Antwerp's commerce in the early sixteenth century therefore took place against a background of a relatively primitive financial structure, in which the relatively small demand of the state for credit had not encouraged greater sophistication. These deficiencies were remedied by merchants by a variety of methods. The postponement of payments, supported by widespread use of the letter obligatory, was of some assistance, but by far the most important development was the practice of making the letters payable to bearer, so that they began to pass from hand to hand, as a form of fiduciary money, until the point was frequently reached when the original debtor received his own letter as a credit from another party.

Though the system allowed trade to function without recourse to banks, it produced many difficulties. In many places, including the Netherlands, neither local customary law nor ancient Roman private law as interpreted locally favoured the transferability of debts. Medieval law had argued that only the original creditor could sue for recovery. Only in the sixteenth century was it accepted that the death of the debtor did not take away the rights of the creditor. On the other hand, the fourteenth and fifteenth centuries had seen the development of law relating to business partnerships which included acceptance of the principle that a company was a juridical entity distinct from the persons who composed it, so that the problems created by the death of a partner were at least mitigated. Resistance to the spread of transferable instruments of credit came also from the legal obstacles which stood in the way of an ultimate recipient recovering money in disputed cases, of which there were many, both concerning letters of exchange and letters obligatory. Legal protection for the bearer had been dependent upon the existence of a formal *cessio,* but as early as 1507 the group of citizens whose sworn opinion determined legal customs in Antwerp stated that such a formal proxy was not necessary for a bearer to take proceedings. A royal ordinance of 1537 made this principle applicable to the whole of the Netherlands, and the practice of circulating letters payable to bearer expanded rapidly. It was realised, however, that legal protection was in itself not enough. The recipient of such a letter gained little unless he could either pass on the letter to another creditor, or obtain cash, since the intermediate cessor of the letter was relieved by the law of all further liability. The solution lay in the adaptation of a practice dating from the later middle ages for the transfer of cash debts by assignation to a named third person who was himself a creditor of the creditor of the original debtor, who was not liberated from his own debt until his creditor had actually received the money. The further difficulty of proof of such assignation of a debt still remained, but legal practice in Antwerp was firmly on the side of the bearer in forcing the burden of proof of final and absolute transfer of the debt represented by the letter upon the creditor who passed it to the bearer. Formal proofs of transfer therefore became more common, at first on a separate document, and later by endorsement of the original.

Growing confidence in these safeguards paved the way for a great expansion of the transfer of debts by assignation, and by 1607 a new edition of the customs of Antwerp included a paragraph on the question which referred to such assigned bills passing to 'as many as four or five persons or even more'. Writing in England in 1622, Gerard de Malynes suggested that an official register of assignations of commercial debts should be kept, as it was in Rouen and Lisbon, but it does not seem that such a register was kept in Antwerp. It is possible that the influence of the English Merchant Adventurers on Antwerp practice had been strong, as they had led the pressure in Antwerp for explicit proof of assignations, and were themselves used to drawing up a separate document for the purpose. The final step to the entering of the assignation on the original document was apparently not taken in Antwerp during the sixteenth century, though it became common practice during the next.

Endorsement leading to full negotiability instead of transfer seems to have developed earlier for letters of exchange than for letters obligatory. Examples have been found from southern Europe in the late fourteenth and fifteenth centuries, but it is unlikely that the practice was widespread, transfer through bank being much more common there even in the sixteenth century. The generalised use of the letter of exchange in northern Europe probably dates from the last third of the sixteenth century, coinciding both with the beginning of political troubles in the Netherlands and with the domination of the Genoese in international payments. Its spread to England may well have followed the return of English merchants in force to the Mediterranean in the last quarter of the century. The purchase of both letters of exchange and letters obligatory for cash was a further development of the sixteenth century. It was in fact a symptom of the more widespread use and circulation of these instruments. As more and more credit bills circulated, and approached the character of fiduciary money, it became more and more difficult for a creditor to obtain cash. Those with surplus cash were therefore in a position to offer it in exchange for bills at a discount. This practice began with matured bills at their payment date. Later it was applied to bills which were not yet due for settlement, and naturally at a discount rate which took into account the unexpired period of credit. That it was more commonly applied to letters obligatory than to letters of exchange was a recognition that the former normally envisaged a shorter period of credit than the latter.

Such financial techniques undoubtedly helped the European commercial system to free itself in part from immediate dependence on the supply of metallic currency, and it is significant that they came into widespread use in periods when there was a *strettezza* or tightness in the supply of the precious metals. It is virtually certain, however, that they contributed greatly to the expansion of trade and increased the velocity of circulation of money in the economy. This factor was undoubtedly important in the rise in prices, even if it cannot be measured as accurately as the increase in the stocks of the precious metals. Although it could be said that in Lyons at the end of the century 'as much as a million livres could change hands in a single morning without a single *sou* being disbursed',[30] it is arguable that the economy was still very dependent upon the short-term availability of metallic currency.. Ultimately, the supply of credit was dependent upon adequate flows of gold and silver, and although at any one time this varied sharply from place to place, it depended in the last analysis on the regularity of the shipments from the New World, upon which the credit of the Spanish monarchy rested. Great crises were relatively infrequent, but when years of excessive expenditure were followed by a drop in the imports of bullion, the Spanish government failed, as in 1557, 1575 and 1596, to meet the obligations on its short-term debts, and was forced to convert them into long-term debts with interest secured largely on the internal revenues of Castile. The reverberations were immediately felt as far away as Antwerp and Genoa. The 'bankruptcy' of 1575 offers a particularly important example which throws light not only on the fragility of the Spanish government's own credit, but on that of the economy of western Europe.

The early 1570s had seen a great increase in the military and naval expenditure of Spain, both in the Netherlands and the Mediterranean, and this coincided with a drop in the imports of treasure to 11 million *pesos* from 1571 to 1575 compared with 14 million in the preceding five-year period, the royal share showing a proportionately steeper decline. The declaration of 'bankruptcy' of 1 September 1575 took the form of a decree that denounced all the short-term contracts signed with financial syndicates for the transfer of money to the Netherlands and Italy, on the grounds that they had been inequitable to the Crown, pending a thorough investigation of their terms. Most of these contracts had been concluded by Genoese groups, and it is likely that the 'bankruptcy', although forced on the government, was exploited by it as a means of freeing itself from the increasing hold which the Genoese had secured on the Crown finances, and indirectly on the Castilian economy. If this was indeed so, it was a total failure. The resources of Castilian financiers, including Simón Ruiz of Medina del Campo, proved an inadequate alternative. The Genoese took vigorous steps to prevent others from being able to transfer money to the Netherlands, and used their great influence all over western Europe to prevent the Castilians from obtaining letters of exchange. The consequences were disastrous both for Philip II's policy in the Netherlands and for the already shaky economy of Antwerp. The more than usual backlog in the payment of Spanish troops in the Netherlands led to a general mutiny and the sack of Antwerp in 1576. Many Spanish, Portuguese and Italian commercial concerns in Antwerp went bankrupt, and many others left for Cologne and elsewhere. It was hardly surprising that several banks in Seville had to close their doors. By 1577 Philip II was forced to patch up his relations with the Genoese, who retained their domination over Castilian public finance until 1627.[31] Their grip, which had become stronger since their intervention in the last years of Charles V, was a proof of a wider strength which had been built up over the preceding half-century.

Always of great importance in the trade of the Mediterranean, the Genoese had begun to turn towards financial transactions in their own right. The existence of a tax on all letters of exchange issued in Genoa makes it possible to calculate roughly the volume of business, which rose from half a million *lire* a year in the 1490s to over two and a half million by the mid-1520s, and much more if the profits of the farmers of the tax are allowed for.[32] Among foreign financial centres, Lyons was of prime importance to the Genoese as to other Italian cities. Though the Florentines were the most numerous among the Italians who dominated the financial life of Lyons from the later middle ages, the Genoese were of increasing importance in the first quarter of the sixteenth century, during the period of French political control of the Republic. In 1528, however, Genoa moved permanently into the Habsburg camp, and her bankers and merchants were forced to abandon Lyons as a centre for their operations. Though the government of the Republic did its best to protect existing Genoese investments in France, the following year saw various attempts to find an alternative to provide a link for their vital dealings with south Germany and the Netherlands. In 1534 the Duke of Savoy expelled Genoese merchants who had settled in his territory after leaving Lyons. They decided to move to Besançon, in the centre of the Habsburg-controlled Franche-Comté, and well situated with easy access to the Rhine valley, and through Geneva, to Switzerland and Italy.[33] Just under half a century later, with the massive flows of silver from Castile reaching Genoa, they moved the fair from Besançon to Piacenza, where it continued to be held under the name of the fair of Bisenzone until 1621. Significantly, the move came also after the decline of Lyons as a major financial centre of France and the Alpine region had begun. Genoa was vital to the Spanish monarchy since here alone bankers seemed able to command both sufficient resources to cope with the enormous credits required to handle the transfer of money to the Netherlands on the scale reached in the 1590s, and also to convert the silver they received from Spain into the gold which was essential for the payment of troops. The fairs of Bisenzone were tightly controlled by a relatively small inner group of men who fixed the exchange rates, which had an influence on those of the whole of Europe. They also enjoyed an even greater ability to effect settlements on other centres, or to postpone them to a later fair, than Lyons had shown in its hey-day. According to contemporaries, in 1588 the total payments settled at Piacenza were more than 37 million *scudi,* and as high as 48 million a few years later.[34]

The increased supply of the precious metals during the sixteenth century had assisted in the general expansion of the economy, and the currents of gold and silver had created a series of changing focal points to which trade was attracted. It had enabled western Europe to look outwards towards the Far East, the Baltic and Muscovy. Towards the end of the period a new instability resulted from a renewed dearth of silver. By that time the development of credit and of paper methods of settlement had so evolved that, if not without stresses, the more dynamic areas were able to surmount the crisis. The first decades of the seventeenth century were decisive in establishing the supremacy of the Dutch, despite the difficulties they encountered as a consequence of the renewal of war with Spain after 1621, and of the permanence of war conditions in the Baltic. For the Mediterranean economies on the other hand, these years were equally decisive in turning societies which had struggled to adapt to new conditions towards a permanent decline. It was no accident that the partial withdrawal of the Genoese from the business of Spanish public finance in 1627 coincided with the final industrial and commercial stagnation of Italy.

Notes

1. F.C. Spooner, *The International Economy and Monetary Movements in France, 1493-1725*, p. 2.
2. L. Schick, *Un grand homme d'affaires au début du xvie siècle—Jacob Fugger*, pp. 27-119, 175. See also R. Ehrenberg, *Capital and Finance in the Age of the Renaissance*, pp. 64-8. For further discussion of the Fugger family see below, pp. 106-11.
3. J.U. Nef, 'Silver production in Central Europe, 1450-1618', *Journal of Political Economy*, XLIX (1941), pp. 575-91.
4. V. Magalhães Godinho, *L'économie de l'empire portugais au xve et xvie siècles*, pp. 178-9.
5. Ibid., pp. 199-218.
6. Earl J. Hamilton, *American Treasure and the Price Revolution in Spain, 1501-1650*, p. 40.
7. Calculated from figures in Hamilton. The ducat, or more properly the *excelente* of Granada, was coined from 1497 onwards, with 65½ struck from the mark of gold, 23¾ carats fine, roughly equivalent to 8 ducats per ounce. The percentages of gold and silver imports given by Hamilton are by weight, and have been converted to value using a ratio of 11:1.
8. R. Carande, op. cit., III, Tables, pp. 472-97.

9. P. Chaunu, *Séville et l'Atlantique, 1504-1650,* VIII, i, i, p. 1119.
10. Spooner, op. cit., p. 28.
11. Ibid., p. 23.
12. F. Braudel, *La Mediterranée et le monde méditerranéen a l'époque de Philippe II,* I, p. 437.
13. G. Parker, 'Spain, her Enemies and the Revolt of the Netherlands', *Past and Present,* No. 49 (1970), pp. 72-95, especially pp. 85-90.
14. F. Ruiz Martín, *Lettres marchandes échangées entre Florence et Medina del Campo,* Intro., pp. liii-lv. For the fairs of 'Bisenzone', see below, pp. 69-70.
15. N.K. Chaudhuri, *The English East India Company,* pp. 124-5.
16. Spooner, op. cit., pp. 82-6. For the Spanish writers, see M. Grice-Hutchinson, *The School of Salamanca—Readings in Spanish Monetary Theory, 1544-1605.*
17. Spooner, op. cit., pp. 50-1.
18. E. Misselden, *The Circle of Commerce* (1623), pp. 16-17, quoted by B.E. Supple, *Commercial Crisis and Change in England, 1600-1642,* p. 75.
19. Thomas Mun, Memorandum of 1622, quoted from British Museum, Additional Mss. 34,324 by Supple, op. cit., p. 214. Mun's work, *England's Treasure by Forraign Trade,* was written in the 1620s, although not published until after the Restoration.
20. Braudel, *La Méditerranée,* I, p. 421.
21. Spooner, op. cit., pp. 23-4.
22. H. Lapeyre, *Une famille de marchands—les Ruiz,* p. 260.
23. H. van der Wee, 'Anvers et les innovations de la technique financière aux xvie et xviie siècles', *AESC,* XXII (1967), pp. 1067-89.
24. A.P. Usher, *The Early History of Deposit Banking in Mediterranean Europe,* especially pp. 269-300.
25. G. Luzzato, 'Les banques publiques de Venise (siècles xvi-xvii)', in J.G. van Dillen, *History of the Principal Public Banks,* pp. 39-78.
26. Usher, op. cit., pp. 433-58.
27. J.G. van Dillen, 'The Bank of Amsterdam in the Seventeenth Century', in van Dillen, op. cit., pp. 79-123.
28. V. Barbour, *Capitalism in Amsterdam in the Seventeenth Century,* p. 53.
29. H. van der Wee, 'Anvers et les innovations', loc. cit.
30. Gascon, *Grand commerce,* I, p. 248, quoting Claude de Rubys, *Histoire véritable de la Ville de Lyon* (1604).
31. Ruiz Martín, *Lettres marchandes,* Intro., pp. xxxiii-v and xli-ii.
32. D. Gioffré, *Gênes et les foires de change—de Lyon à Besançon,* p. 107.
33. Ibid., pp. 115-19.
34. Braudel, *La Méditerranée,* I, p. 461.

4 TRADING CENTRES

The complex and changing currents of trade cut new channels along which commercial cities blossomed, leaving others to silt up and their prosperous centres to wither. In a study of the growth and decay of some of the greatest commercial centres we are analysing a dimension of economic life which transcends not only the experience of the individual but carries us outward from the city itself to the life of its region, and beyond. Some examples have been chosen for detailed study as representative of various regions with a varied experience.

Lyons

Lyons evolved during the last decades of the fifteenth and the early decades of the sixteenth century from a centre of purely regional importance into a commercial and financial metropolis not only on the national but the international level, with a population which by 1520 was between 60,000 and 70,000 persons. Its geographical advantages are obvious: easy communications with the Mediterranean by the Rhône valley, with Switzerland and the Rhine, with central France by the Saône or the Loire and thence to Paris, and by the Alpine passes to the cities of north Italy. Lyons' commercial life had centred on its fairs since 1420, but it was not until the 1460s that they began to attract foreign merchants and financiers in large numbers. The political support of Louis XI, the restoration of peaceful trading conditions in France after the end of the Hundred Years War, and the transfer westwards of the principal trade routes of the Italians combined to give Lyons the opportunity to develop its latent geographical advantages. After a decade of difficulties between 1484 and 1494, during which the jealousy of the Provençal towns succeeded in persuading the young Charles VIII to suspend the privileges of the Lyons fairs, a period of steady expansion returned.

During the sixteenth century, Lyons' trade was based squarely on textiles, which averaged over 70 per cent by value of the goods entering the city, largely due to the predominance of expensive Italian silks. In 1569 the value of Genoese velvets alone was between 8 and 9 million *livres.* The variety of silks was great, and became greater as Lyons became a centre for the redistribution of silks over an area which extended to Spain, and even to the Spanish empire in America. The famous black satin of Lucca was worth 11 *livres* the *aune* (of one-and-a-quarter yards) around the middle of the century, the equivalent of a month's wages for a building worker, or three months' supply of bread in 'normal' years for a family of four. Genoese velvets were worth between 7 and 10 *livres* the *aune*, the cheapest being the taffetas, those of Florence fetching nearly 4 *livres*, and those of Lyons itself only one *livre*. Woollen cloth did not compare with these values: the most expensive Dutch woollens could be worth 1 *livre* 19 *sous*, whilst those of Orleans barely made 10 *sous*. At first dealing exclusively in Italian silks, Lyons began to develop its own silk-weaving industry from 1536, relying on raw silk from Spain as well as Italy, and by 1569 was importing 450 bales in three months.[1]

Lyons exported relatively little raw wool, but its cloth exports were an essential complement of its imports of silks, estimates of their value being around 3½ million *livres* in 1568, at least double that of the late fifteenth century. Italy was its major market, especially Naples, Milan and Venice (probably for re-export to the Levant), and Frankfurt-on-Main in Germany. Linen was also a principal export, raw linen being sent to the weaving areas of Bresse, the Dauphiné and the Beaujolais, the finished cloth returning to Lyons for sale. In this way, its commercial importance enabled it to stimulate regional industry. Later, it was exerting an influence much further afield, pulling in linen goods from the manufacturing centres of the west and north: from Brittany, Châtellerault, Lorraine, Rheims, the Champagne region, from Hainault and Flanders in the Netherlands, and from Constance. Especially for Flemish linens, as for English cloth, the trade of Lyons enables us to detect their expansion in European markets. Most of these linens were re-exported from France. In the 1550s Gérardin Panse, one of the leading merchants in the trade, had markets in Paris, Montpellier, Toulouse, Thiers, Le Puy, Piedmont, Genoa, Catalonia (including Barcelona), and even in Antwerp. The Spanish market expanded rapidly after the peace of Cateau-Cambrésis in 1559. Lyons benefited especially because the increasing insecurity of the Bay of Biscay made it an important point on the trade routes between Spain and the Netherlands.

The position of Lyons in the spice trade reflected the fundamental changes in the European distribution network following the Portuguese use of Antwerp, but it had grown originally as a consequence of the decision of the Italians to make it their principal distribution centre for France. The merchants of Lyons argued that this could enable spices to be sold up to 20 per cent more cheaply than if they were imported through their rivals the ports of Languedoc, which had in any case failed to maintain their direct trade with the Levant. Lyons and its old Languedocian rivals at first united against the threat of the entry of spices from

Portugal into France through the Gascon ports, but Lyons' economic strength enabled it to attract these supplies, not directly, but through Antwerp, from 1508. Only eight years later Portuguese spices began to enter Lyons from Marseilles. In 1525-6, 386 bales of pepper entered Lyons by the Saône route, and since they paid the tax levied on goods coming from abroad, they presumably came from Antwerp. They accounted for 11 per cent of the spices entering Lyons from all sources, and though more may have come from Antwerp through Geneva, it is clear that the proximity of Venice meant that the Italians were still dominating the Lyons spice trade, despite the allegedly enormous advantage in price of the Portuguese spices. Later the 'direct' route made a stronger challenge to the Antwerp route. In 1533-4, 149 bales of pepper came from Bayonne, rather more than came down the Saône. In 1540 Francis I, in a measure of economic warfare against Charles V, banned the import of spices except through the maritime ports of France, so that between October 1543 and October 1544 only 66 bales of pepper entered Lyons from Antwerp, compared with 391 imported from Venice by special licence. The position of 'Mediterranean' spices on the Lyons market had undergone a crisis, but they seem to have recovered their almost complete domination by the 1540s. The route by which they came was, however, changing substantially, with the emergence of Marseilles as the point of entry into France. In the short run this did not represent a challenge to the position of the Italians in the trade, and indeed the choice of the Marseilles route as opposed to the overland passage of the Alps was the result of their initiative. In the longer term, the combination of the maritime expertise of Marseilles and the financial resources of Lyons was to provide the basis for the revival of direct French trade with the Levant after 1570.[2]

Lyons was perhaps its own most important customer for the spices, with Paris, Troyes, Tours, Orleans, Limoges and Toulouse following behind. The apparent absence of the Atlantic ports and Marseilles is notable, since all were open directly either to the Portuguese or Mediterranean supplies. Nor is there much evidence of the re-export of spices from Lyons, though occasional references to trade with Nuremberg are less surprising than those to Spain. Despite their interest, spices formed a relatively modest part of Lyons' total commerce. In 1569 they accounted for only 11 per cent of customs receipts, less than one-fifth of the value of textiles and raw materials, and only about a quarter of the value of silks alone. On the scale of the European spice market its position was equally modest. The 500 bales or about 1,000 quintals of pepper which entered Lyons in 1570 were only about 4 per cent of the pepper trade of Alexandria, and only about 8 per cent of Venetian purchase there.[3]

It is clear that Lyons had an unfavourable balance of trade with Italy, reflecting that of France as a whole, and the same was true of its relations with the Netherlands. Imports of Hondschoote says were exceeded in value by those of linens from Holland, Cambrai and Hainault, with a wide variety of miscellaneous goods and spices making up a total compared with which exports to these areas were a mere 6 per cent in value. With Spain on the other hand, Lyons enjoyed a favourable balance, importing relatively little wool and some silk, but exporting knives and paper, and especially books from the growing publishing and printing industry of the city, as well as re-exporting Italian silks and Netherlands woollen and linen goods. The total value of its imports probably reached 10 or 11 million *livres* a year around 1569, perhaps a third of all imports into France.[4]

Lyons' trade was relatively highly concentrated in the hands of the largest firms—ten or so companies of the first rank, supported by a score or so of others. Of the 552 merchants registered in 1569, ten imported over a third of all goods and the top 33 firms accounted for no less than 74 per cent of the total, the remaining 26 per cent being shared among 499 smaller traders, of whom the vast majority were little more than pedlars, or peasants from the neighbouring region. The Luccan firm of the Bonvisi paid 6 per cent of the total import taxes, followed by a group of other Italian companies paying between 3 and 4 per cent each. The domination of the Italians in the import trade is very clear from these figures, and of course they completely dominated banking and finance. Only one native French firm paid more than 2 per cent, with another nine exceeding one per cent.[5] It is less easy to analyse the export trade, but the picture could well have been different. Some French firms were important in the export of cloth and books, but on the whole they seem to have limited themselves to trade with the rest of France. The domination of the Italians was of course based on control of the import of silks, in which concentration was even more marked. Five firms handled nearly half of the business in 1569, whilst in the most expensive Luccan silks three firms did over half of the business. The very largest firms tended to specialise less than some of the smaller, and some of the Italians succeeded in penetrating the interior markets of France. The Salviatti, a Florentine firm who were important from 1505 until the opening of the French religious wars, had factors in Toulouse, Marseilles, Montpellier and Rouen, as well as Bruges, Venice, Rome, Bologna, Naples, Salerno, Medina del Campo and Zaragoza. They sold French and English cloth in Italy, brought in 17 per cent of the spices to Lyons in 1538, and 22 per cent in 1548. They penetrated the trade in metals, sending German silver to France, Italy and even Spain, and Spanish copper to Italy. The Bonvisi traded in Lyons from 1504 to 1629, when they went bankrupt, but in their best years around 1569 their trade was probably worth 1 million *livres*. They sent English cloth and Flemish linen to Italy, imported silks from Naples, Messina and Vicenza for sale in Lyons or in Tours, where they had a virtual monopoly. The principal branch of their trade was, however, between Spain and Italy through Lyons.

Monopolistic tendencies reached their peak in the spice trade, though concentration was probably less after Antwerp entered the market. In 1507 at the All Saints Fair, the Genoese Johano brought in all of the total of 234 bales of pepper which paid the special tax (the *garbeau*), and during the whole of the financial year 1507-8, he and the Florentines Dati and Bartolomeo Panchati imported 90 per cent of the total. The Venetians seem to have left the distribution of spices in Lyons, as in many other centres, to other Italians, especially the Florentines.

The progress of the city was dependent on the close union of trade and financial dealings. Trade itself still reflected the cycle of the fairs, that of Easter being the busiest, nearly equalled by the August fair, with the All Saints and the *Foire du Roi* in December coming well behind. The interval between the fairs varied, and consequently the length of time between settlement dates. Merchants were therefore compelled either to remain in Lyons, to leave a factor or agent, or to use a resident merchant or banker to look after their affairs. Traditionally, the consul of the Florentine merchants called the merchants together to announce the dates for payment, which differed for various groups. The Milanese, Genoese and Venetians formed one group, the Bolognese, Florentines and Luccans another, the Neapolitans and Sicilians a third. On the date fixed, the merchants assembled to assign debts and credits on other centres, postpone them until the next fair, or settle them in cash, sometimes by loans from the bankers at rates of interest varying from 2¼ to 3 per cent from fair to fair. It does not seem that the pressure of public borrowing often forced up the commercial interest rate to harmful levels. Even during the so-called *Grand Parti* in 1556 when large numbers of citizens participated in huge loans negotiated on behalf of the Crown, the rate of interest between fairs did not rise higher than an annual equivalent of 10½ per cent, and it soon fell back to about 8 2/3 per cent by 1561. The use of surplus mercantile capital for the purchase of *rentes,* land and urban property does not seem to have starved commercial life, whilst its investment in industry was equally important and economically more fruitful. This was particularly true of the silk-weaving and printing industries. Silk-weaving required especially heavy capital investment over a considerable period, normally beyond the reach of the artisan. A bale of silk could cost as much as 1,200 to 1,500 *livres*, or as high as 10 *livres* a pound, with prices rising rapidly later in the century. The *marchand-fabricant* stepped in to fill this gap, by purchasing the raw silk from the Italian importers. Men like René Laurencin and Claude Gapaillon might have several thousand *livres* worth of silk out for weaving and dyeing, and much more owing to them from customers in other parts of France for the woven cloth they had already sold.

For Lyons the outbreak of civil wars in France from 1562 was to have very serious consequences. The receipts from the *ad valorem* customs of 6 *deniers* in the *livre* fell progressively from 1559 to 1563 by 50 per cent. The first crisis was temporary, and in the later 1560s the levels of 1559 were exceeded. From the 1570s another fall began which continued until 1589, when receipts were only one-third of those of 1559, and recovery in the 1590s was only slight. Since these were also years of more rapidly rising prices, the real fall in traffic was probably much greater. The tax was farmed out and even between 1564 and 1569 the contractor, Louis Dadiaceto, repeatedly complained that he was losing money on a rental of 70,000 *livres* a year. Bankruptcies had been rare in Lyons before 1562. The effects of the royal bankruptcy of 1557 which paralleled that of the Spanish monarchy, were relatively short-lived, but in the 1560s the payments of the fairs began to be increasingly disrupted. By the seventies bankruptcies multiplied: there were eight in 1572, nine in 1574 and eleven in 1577. Bankruptcy was of course only the extreme symptom of a general restriction of credit. Many merchants were forced to arrange moratoria or concordats with their creditors who agreed to accept only a fraction of what was due to them. The important firm of Panse among the natives, Obrecht and Minquel and Manlich the Elder among the Germans, Bernardin and Guinigi among the Luccans, were forced into bankruptcy. Sometimes extra-commercial considerations were involved, as in the case of Obrecht, who had lent large sums to the Huguenots. Mutual aid helped members of the various 'national' groups to weather the storm. In 1566 the Luccan banking firm of Francote was bailed out by its fellow-countrymen with over 120,000 *livres* of support. Many other foreign merchants withdrew from Lyons during these years. Among the greatest, the activity of the Bonvisi suffered a sharp decline after 1586, although some very sharp 'lows' had already been experienced in 1576 and 1580. It must be remembered that Antwerp too was suffering badly in these years, and the Bonvisi's crisis of 1576 was perhaps a distant reflection of the Spanish monarchy's bankruptcy of 1575, just as their crisis of 1585 coincided with the siege of Antwerp.

By the 1590s Lyons was cut off from Marseilles by the royal army. To the decline of French cloth production which accompanied the worsening of the civil wars had now to be added the threat of direct English competition in the cloth trade as the Levant Company expanded its markets in the Mediterranean. The spice trade fell away from the greatest boom of the century in the early 1570s, when Marseilles had exploited the war between Venice and the Turks to penetrate the Levant. From 1586 to the end of the century, and beyond, Lyons almost reverted to the position of a centre of local and regional trade which it had been more than a century before. When general recovery came in France, Lyons benefited only partially, as financial activity came to be increasingly concentrated in Paris.

Seville

Since it is not one of the principal aims of this book to discuss in detail the evolution of Europe's trade with the Americas or the Far East, it might seem inappropriate to take the growth of Seville as a main example. However, Seville's position as the major link between the Indies trade and that of Europe makes it an essential one. Unfortunately, its trade with the Indies has alone been the object of minute study,[6] and the records of its European trade are by no means satisfactory, at least in comparison with the exceptional detail and continuity of those of the *Casa de Contratación* which controlled the Indies trade. The Sevillian monopoly of trade with Spain's American empire was founded as much on geographical and economic realities as on its legal foundations. 'Was not Seville and all Andulusia the furthest point and the end of all land, and now it is the middle to which come the best and most esteemed of the Old World. . . to be carried to the New?'[7] So wrote Tomás de Mercado in the second half of the sixteenth century.

It is important to emphasise that its monopoly was not as narrow as might be supposed. Not only the ports at the mouth of the River Quadalquivir, such as San Lúcar de Barrameda, but also Puerto de Santa María and Cádiz further south formed part of its commercial and legal entity. Columbus had sailed from Cádiz on his second voyage in 1493 and from San Lúcar on his third in 1497. A royal decree of 1503 established the administrative centre of this complex at Seville, but it did little more than register an existing state of affairs. Seville was already the leading port of Andalucía, important in the fifteenth century for its trade with the Mediterranean, the Barbary coast and the Canaries, and for the size of its Genoese colony, established since the fourteenth century. It enjoyed easy access to the Castilian interior, and its immediate hinterland could provide a surplus of agricultural produce. The temporary lifting of its monopoly (for outward voyages only) in favour of the Cantabrian ports in 1529 only served to provide further proof of Seville's natural advantages as the centre of the Indies trade. Not only had it a running start over any competitors, but its more southerly position was decisively superior in offering the fleets the advantages of the winds and currents of the Atlantic over a longer season of the year in both directions. The route which Columbus had taken via the Canaries proved to be the ideal commercial route to the Caribbean, offering a convenient intermediate base for taking on supplies before the direct crossing of the Atlantic in the latitude of the steady north-east 'trade winds'.[8] In view of the development of relations with England and France during the sixteenth century, Seville offered considerably better security than the northern ports.

In 1492 Andalucía, and hence the region of Seville, reached the end of a long period of internal colonisation which had culminated in the fall of the Moorish kingdom of Granada, and forces of social expansion were poised to turn outwards. Emigration to the Indies was heaviest from Andalucía, but the outward movement was more than compensated by migration southwards from Castile. There is ample evidence of the settlement in Seville of Cantabrian and Basque sailors, sea captains and merchants, and the city grew more rapidly in size during the sixteenth century than almost any European port. Recent research suggests that in the early 1530s Seville had a population of more than 50,000 persons, including a substantial number of transients, and was already the largest town of Castile.[9] By 1561 it had 19,000 households, and a probable minimum of 95,000 inhabitants, with a further rise to nearly 26,000 households, or 130,000 persons in the early 1590s, despite a series of epidemics of plague in the 1580s.[10] Immigration, and perhaps a birth rate in excess even of the high average for towns in the early modern period, enabled Seville to recoup its human losses with relative ease at least until the great plagues of 1599 to 1601. In the second half of the sixteenth century it was not only by far the largest city in Spain, but in Europe was surpassed by very few, such as Naples, and in the seventeenth century only by such capitals as London, Paris and Madrid.

Its power of economic attraction was certainly no less than its capacity to draw in humanity. The economic and financial tides began to flow more and more strongly between Seville and Old Castile. The fair-

town of Medina del Campo and the wool centre of Burgos both felt its
pull, especially as it was increasingly colonised by northern Spaniards.[11]
Its hinterland was the broad valley of the Guadalquivir, rich in agriculture, especially to the south, and it had been as an agricultural capital
that Seville had developed after the reconquest in the thirteenth century.
Its own food supply was thus well assured and the region's surplus available for export to the Indies. Later, the relatively easy communications
for bullock carts proved even more valuable in the transport of large
quantities of mercury from the mine of Almadén for use in silver-mining
in America, whilst its supplies of pine-wood for construction and fuel
were floated down the river. Its deficiencies in harder woods and the
large trees essential in shipbuilding meant that its trade depended on an
expansion of the shipbuilding industry of the Cantabrian coast, and it
has been estimated that as many as 80 per cent of the vessels engaged in
the transatlantic trade were obtained there.

The emphasis which Seville's position in the Indies trade has received
has obscured the fact that much of its agricultural exports—as well as its
import trade—were to Europe. There is evidence that wine was being
exported not only to America but to Biscay, Galicia and Portugal.
Around 1580 the *alcabala* on wine in Seville reached 40,000 ducats,
compared with 22,000 for that on wood, and 32,000 for olive oil.

The physical arrangements in the port of Seville were very simple,
and compared unfavourably with those of such centres as Antwerp. A
single bridge of boats linked it with the thriving suburb of Triana across
the river. Its warehouse facilities were poor, and no great construction
of suitable stores was undertaken, possibly because the active season of
the transatlantic fleets was short. It is possible that the obstructiveness
of speculators, who profited from the high prices of provisions and naval
stores during the periods when the fleets were being prepared, was a
more important obstacle to the extension of warehousing than lack of
space. The difficulty in repairing ships was partly solved by the use of a
suitable site a few miles down river, but as the tonnages of vessels increased, it became increasingly necessary to develop the facilities of the
ports at the mouth of the Guadalquivir as far afield as Cádiz, and to
resort to the trans-shipment of goods for conveyance to Seville. Since
at least four-fifths of the convoys made a call at Cádiz on the outward
voyage, an increasing quantity of goods was loaded there. As the proportion of goods from other European countries in the exports to the
Indies continued to rise, especially after the middle of the sixteenth century, the inaccessibility of Seville became even more inconvenient. The
state of the river seems to have deteriorated and the number of vessels

lost through grounding rose steeply. In 1611 a contract was placed for the clearing of the river bed of hidden wrecks, after several years of above-average flows of water had increased the alluvial deposits. Galleys, withdrawn from the fleet employed in the defence of the coast against Barbary corsairs, were used to transport particularly valuable incoming cargoes, especially treasure, and were one of the means by which Seville staved off the day when it ceased to have physical control over the trade which it administered.

Seville became notorious for the greed of its citizens. The prices at which its municipal offices were sold (the post of *venticuatro,* or councillor, could be worth 7,000 ducats), is evidence not only of the intense competition for honours, but of the likely profits which could be made from them. Membership of the city council was reserved for men of noble status, and the Crown profited greatly from the sale of *hidalguías.* In Seville the practice of trade was not incompatible with nobility. The entry into commerce of nobles of old stock was paralleled by the ennoblement of merchants risen from the 'middle' classes, and intermarriage between noble and mercantile families was hardly cause for comment. The greater nobility invested especially in shipping, though some put their capital into goods. Don Alvaro Bazán was perhaps the first to use his own ships in the Indies trade, of which he was Captain-general for fifteen years in the middle of the century. The Ponce de León, Dukes of Arcos, invested in trade, especially Luís, Lord of Villagarcía and Rota, who maintained factors in the Indies from the early years of the century. The lesser nobility were not above accompanying their goods to America, no doubt with the hope of extending their landed estates by investing their mercantile profits there. Such were not strictly merchants, but serve to show that in Seville everybody exploited trading opportunities. There were many converted Jews among the lesser nobility, often boasting superficially impressive genealogies, the falsity of which was sometimes discovered when they had the temerity to apply for admission to the jealously guarded Old Christian preserves of the Military Orders.

Merchant wealth in sixteenth-century Seville was naturally great. Juan Antonio Vicentelo de Lera provided his daughter with a dowry of 240,000 ducats when she married the Count of Gelves—well within his capacity, since on his death in 1597 he was worth 1,600,000 ducats. Whilst this was an exceptional case, there were many whose fortunes ranged between 200,000 and 400,000 ducats. Some of the richest were *indianos,* men who had lived in the Indies and probably retained property there when they returned.[12]

As the imports of silver from America expanded so did the attractions of Seville to the merchants of northern Europe. As Spain became progressively less able to supply the needs of the colonists from her own industry, through a combination of uncompetitive prices, low quality, or simple inability to produce what was in demand, so the flow of northern goods increased. Since Andalucía could not offer enough of her own produce in exchange, the balance was exported by the northern merchants in silver. What they could not export legally, they took illegally with the connivance of native merchants and even of some royal officials. This process gained pace from the 1560s, when the character of the goods in demand in America shifted from agricultural produce and raw materials towards more valuable luxury items. Though the size of the fleets continued to expand until after 1600, they were increasingly filled with goods brought especially by merchants from both the northern and southern Netherlands. Around 1570 a group of Spanish merchants expressed their concern in a memorandum to the Council of State which foresaw the ruin of Spain's trade with the Indies, and serious losses to the treasury. They pointed to the fact that the Genoese had become progressively less interested in the trade in goods in Seville as they obtained increasing numbers of licences to export silver in return for their loans to the crown, and that the Netherlanders were taking their place. Whilst it may be some exaggeration to say that the 'Dutch had conquered Seville without firing a shot' by 1570,[13] the trend was clear. Nor was it easy for the Spanish government to distinguish between loyal Flemings and rebel Dutch, even at times when they felt able to try to enforce a prohibition on rebel commerce. Often, when Spain's need for Baltic grain was acute, it was compelled to bow before the supremacy of Dutch shipping in the carrying trade and formally open its ports to them.

Gradually, the role of the resident merchants in Seville was changing to that of intermediaries and commission agents, preferring to invest their capital in *juros* and land with which to establish entailed estates. They allowed their names to be used as cover for the trade of the Netherlanders, and great personal profit was made by grandees like the Duke of Medina Sidonia, from whose town of San Lúcar much of the silver was shipped by the northerners. In 1595 Philip II decided to strike at the clandestine commerce of Seville. The king's agents visited 63 merchant houses in the city, belonging to Castilians, Portuguese, Flemings, French and Germans (suspect because of their relations with England, Holland and Zeeland), but found no English or Dutch, 'because it is well known that they only trade in Spain through intermediaries whom they can trust.'

If it was difficult for Philip II's officers, it has so far proved impossible for the historian to find evidence with which to quantify this process. Yet it is important to recall that the total volume of trade registered in the books of the *Casa de Contratación* continued its long-term expansion in volume until it reached a peak in 1608-10. If the peak values were reached slightly earlier, it was because the silver imports, so important in the values, reached their peak in the 1590s. From then onwards the attractions of Seville for the northern merchants, though still important, began slowly to decline, as they gained the confidence to penetrate the defences of the Spanish Caribbean and develop direct trade with the colonists, whose collusion in the breach of Seville's monopoly was as eager as that of the Sevillians in welcoming the traitors within their gates. Again, it is difficult to measure the extent of this illegal traffic, except through the reverse mirror of the declining official traffic of Seville and its outports, in which it was only one of several factors.

Foreign merchants were also important in the equipment of the fleets of the *Carrera de Indias* in arms and munitions, as well as providing credit for goods sold for export, thus helping to increase the total volume of business. Frequently the city authorities took the side of the foreigners against the Sevillian merchant *Consulado* when it wished to secure postponement of repayment until the arrival of the next fleet.[14] The city's concern was a clear indication of a growing dependence on foreign capital, and of its recognition that the consequences of frightening it away would be worse for both Seville and Spain than the disadvantages of its presence.

Evidence of the legal trade of northern merchants in Seville is not systematically available, and it was of course dependent on the state of political relations. In a week of March 1605 San Lucar de Barrameda saw the arrival of 59 foreign vessels, of which the majority were French (39), 11 Flemish, 5 English and 4 Scottish. Their average tonnages varied, that of the French being the lowest, that of the Flemings the highest. During the last week of April in the same year 27 French vessels arrived in Seville, as well as 19 English, 6 Scottish, 2 Dutch and 1 Flemish. Locals noted with surprise and admiration the skill of the northern captains in negotiating the river with ships of high tonnage at least as well as the natives. In 1606 no less than 229 ships left for France, particularly for Calais and Rouen, 87 for England, mostly for London, 52 for Spanish and Portuguese ports, 34 for Italy and Sicily, 14 for the Canaries, 7 for Madeira, 4 for Angola, 3 for Palma Mallorca, 1 for Brazil and 1 for the Azores. The goods the incoming vessels brought usually included

French linen cloth, and in years of dearth Baltic grain. Of the 39 French ships entering San Lúcar in the period referred to above, 18 were carrying grain, 14 of them exclusively. Norwegian timber was to be found in Flemish or French vessels, and a Lübeck ship of nearly 300 tons arriving in March was fully loaded with timber. Sometimes the secret import of artillery from Holland was authorised and vast quantities of needles were imported for re-export to the Indies. England provided tin and lead, and even beer was brought from Lübeck.[15] The foreigners exported local produce, especially wines and olive oil, together with some products of the Indies, such as indigo or cochineal. Of 61 vessels leaving Puerto de Santa María in 1606, three went empty, 16 had a cargo of wine only, 6 more of wine and salt (that of the coast south and east of San Lúcar being particularly prized), and 10 more were fully loaded with salt.[16] Wool, too, was exported, though not apparently in large quantities.

The problem created by the adverse balance of Seville's European trade was never solved. The Duke of Medina Sidonia recommended that the export of silver should be legalised, but this realism found little favour with the monarchy. Ships which brought the bulkier low-value cargoes could probably find enough local goods of a similar value for their return voyage, but those which brought the more expensive goods could never do so—a cargo of cloth could be worth 100,000 ducats. The maintenance of trade was therefore impossible without the illegal export of silver. As the seventeenth century proceeded, and more direct trade between northern Europe and the Spanish Indies developed, it was the smaller fry of European merchants and ship captains who continued to collect in shoals around the outports of Seville for the pickings of the surviving Indies fleets. The inducements to evade the rules of the *Casa de Contratación* were increasing on all sides. The duties levied on goods entering Seville on their way to and from the Indies were rising to levels at which fraud was very tempting, especially as goods destined for re-export were not exempt in either direction. After 1543 all goods entering from the Indies paid not only the *almojarifazgo* or customs but also the *alcabala,* and later the level of the *avería* paid for the expenses of naval protection further increased costs, whilst the *Casa de Contratación* from time to time levied special dues on goods to recover the successive loans it was forced to make to the Crown.[17]

Seville began to go into commercial decline early in the seventeenth century, reflecting not only the factors discussed above but the general decay of Spanish commerce and society. After 1620, its decline accelerated and by 1640 was catastrophic. Its official trade had long ceased to be a measure of the real levels of trade between Europe and America, and its illicit attractions were much diminished as the stream of bullion dwindled.

Antwerp

Antwerp entered the sixteenth century already in a powerful economic position. During the fifteenth century the fairs of Brabant had become the meeting place of exporters of growing quantities of English cloth and German merchants, especially from Cologne. Bruges, the rival Antwerp was to supplant, had pursued a policy of rejection of English cloth, because of the competition it threatened for the Flanders industry. Geographical factors also helped Antwerp. Tidal changes were slowly improving its access to the sea, whilst that of Bruges was deteriorating with the silting up of the River Zwin. Antwerp was also coming to rival Bruges as a centre for the distribution of spices brought by German merchants in rivalry with the Italians who still concentrated on Bruges. The rise of the Breton merchant marine in the second half of the fifteenth century led to the triumph of French salt in the Netherlands and assisted the growth of the herring-curing industry in Antwerp and the surrounding region, whilst industrial development had been generally stimulated by monetary devaluations in the 1460s and 1470s, especially in the towns of Brabant.

The political factor was nevertheless of prime importance. The aggressive policies of Charles the Bold led in his later years to a financial crisis from which Bruges, and some of its Italian colony including the Medici bank, suffered severely. On Charles's death in 1477 there were risings in many towns, followed by French invasion, and throughout the 1480s the Netherlands were deeply troubled. Flanders was the worst hit, and in 1483 rose in rebellion against the new ruler Maximilian, who only succeeded in restoring his authority in 1492. Bruges took part in the rebellion and was blockaded for a time. The Venetian galleys were temporarily diverted to Antwerp and Middelburg and in 1488 the Hanseatic, Spanish, Portuguese and Italian colonies moved to Antwerp.[18] Though they returned to Bruges in 1492, from this point onwards, Antwerp's commercial future was assured. Bruges complained that the Brabant fairs were lasting longer than their legal limit. In 1496 the Alderman of the Hanse wrote to Lübeck that the commercial significance of Bruges had become negligible and that the majority of commercial transactions in the Netherlands were concentrated around the Brabant fairs.[19] It is dangerous to exaggerate the rapidity of the decline of Bruges, however, and it has been shown by the standards of the tax on property and goods that although Bruges was outclassed by Antwerp, as late as 1569 it was still second in the Netherlands as a trading centre. Bruges continued, for some decades into the sixteenth century, to possess a superior structure of financial techniques, though Antwerp was rapidly replacing it as the quantity of its commercial capital increased. Antwerp was nevertheless changing fast as early as the turn of the century. The Bruges complaint concerning the Brabant fairs had substance, while Antwerp was becoming a place of residence for large numbers of foreign merchants. Perhaps too much emphasis has been placed on the growth of the colonies of south European merchants as a factor in the development of Antwerp into the commercial metropolis of north-west Europe.[20] Numerically, at least, the Germans remained predominant during the early decades of the sixteenth century, and the west German merchants, long since established, especially so.[21] Their economic importance was, however, less than their numbers would suggest, and it remains to a large degree true that the creative force in Antwerp's development in these years was the combination of the south Germans, trading in metals, the English in cloth, the Italians in silks and spices and the Portuguese in spices. There were other factors as well. Antwerp was well placed to benefit from the Baltic grain trade now that it was falling into the hands of the north Netherlanders. The war with France in the 1480s had cut off supplies from Beauce, and both Antwerp and Amsterdam later gained the privilege of free trade in grain from Philip the Fair, posing a threat to the grain staple of Ghent. Antwerp dealt in grain not only for its own rapidly growing demands, but for re-export, and it succeeded in maintaining its right to export even after the bad harvest of 1521 caused a general embargo.

The Portuguese choice of Antwerp as their staple for the distribution of Asian pepper and spices after 1500 was no accident, since they had been selling west African 'pepper' (*malagueta*) in the late fifteenth century. The arrival of the first Asian spices from Lisbon in 1501 nevertheless had a dramatic impact in Antwerp, important psychologically as well as economically. It expanded the trade of the south German merchants in silver and copper, and by 1508 the trade in precious metals had risen to 60,000 marks a year. In the same year 3,000 quintals of spices reached Antwerp, rising to 8,000 yearly after 1510. After that year there was an interruption in the sailings of Venetian galleys to Antwerp, and they did not re-appear until 1518.[22] Spices from Antwerp began to penetrate the markets of Germany and France, first reaching Lyons in 1508.[23] The south Germans expanded their capital investment very rapidly. That of the Fugger rose by an average of over 50 per cent a year from 1511 and 1527, that of the Welser by 9 per cent between 1502 and 1517, and that of the Imhof by nearly 9 per cent a year from 1484 to 1522.[24]

As far as spices and metals were concerned, the role of native merchants in Antwerp was largely confined to that of intermediaries between the great foreign houses and the retail trade, though they played a much larger part in the trade in cloth and grain. English cloth exports rose to 80,000 pieces a year during the first decades of the sixteenth century, much being re-exported to Germany, Poland and Italy. Its importance to Antwerp was industrial as well as commercial, since most of it arrived unfinished and undyed, and the finishing industry of the Antwerp region became an essential link between the Netherlands and the English economies which helped to maintain Antwerp's position as a major English cloth-staple even during troubled times later in the century. The increased activity of the port benefited the contractors, and a great building boom not only provided a profitable field for investment but ensured high wage rates even for unskilled workers.[25] Antwerp's boom carried with it the outports of Walcheren, Bergen-op-Zoom, and places as far afield as s'Hertogenbosch. Much of the revived wool trade of Bruges went to supply the cloth industry which found new markets through Antwerp.

Behind the commercial and industrial expansion Antwerp's financial position was strengthening, but its techniques were still relatively undeveloped. As late as 1513, the Rechtegen and the Fugger made loans to the government in the form of pepper sold on credit. There was as yet little interest in government or municipal finance, but after 1515 government borrowing began to expand at a pace which drove up interest rates to 28½ per cent a year in June 1517.[26]

Most of the 1520s and the early 1530s were to be a critical period for Antwerp. The foundations of its prosperity were gradually eroded, inaugurating a period of disturbance from which it did not emerge until after 1535. Political events were again of decisive importance in this reversal of fortune. Though most of the military operations in the wars between France and the Habsburg Charles V took place in Italy, the economic effects were widespread. Embargoes and interference with seaborne trade meant that no Spanish, Portuguese or Italian ships reached Antwerp in 1522 or 1523, whilst the overland trade to Lyons was also interrupted. Dependence on French salt meant a severe shortage; dearer herrings coincided with dearer bread, cutting into the living standards of the poorer classes. By the 1530s Venice had recovered from the shock of the Portuguese competition in the spice trade, and the Portuguese themselves were finding alternative outlets. Though Antwerp continued to export Portuguese spices, even to Italy as late as 1543-4,[27] the decline of the Portuguese factory at Antwerp was already well advanced, so that it was finally abandoned in 1549. The reaction of the cities of the Hanseatic League to the growing threat of Dutch capital and commercial enterprise in the Baltic was sharp. For a time the Sound was closed, and privateers operating from Lübeck remained a threat to Dutch navigation even after it was re-opened. It was not until after the Treaty of Speyer in 1544 that the Dutch advance in Baltic trade began again. Whilst it lasted, this crisis had its repercussions in Antwerp, but the situation in central Germany was even more serious because the disruption caused by the Reformation crisis, leading to the war of the Schmalkaldic League from 1546, was to have permanent effects. At home the government's insistence on a strong currency further inhibited expansion as cloth exports were priced out of the Baltic market. Antwerp's fairs never recovered commercially, but became of greater financial importance, as Charles V's great reliance on the Antwerp money market was leading to an increase in the quantity of silver reaching the Bourse, its financial operations having been transferred to new premises in 1532.

Already in the troubled years of the early 1530s the scale of trade with Spain and Portugal was growing fast. The size of the Spanish colony was expanding, despite the maintenance of official headquarters in Bruges, their *de facto* privileges in Antwerp being if anything more extensive than those of other nations. By 1550 at least 200 Spanish merchants were operating from Antwerp.[28] Native merchants were also beginning to penetrate the Iberian trade, reaching as far south as the Canaries and the Portuguese sugar colony of São Tomé, where Jacob Groenberghe and Pauwel van Dale provided capital for the expansion of production. By 1550, Spanish wool was reaching the Netherlands in quantities as high as 40,000 sacks a year, as its greater suitability for the lighter 'new draperies', combining with the decline of English wool exports, made it the principal source of supply for the Netherlands cloth industry.[29] Spain was also providing an expanding market for exports, as Spanish price levels rose faster, and the quality of her own manufactures was surpassed. The commercial revival of Italy also helped Antwerp's recovery, especially as it formed a stable part of the Habsburg political system, and provided a growing market for overland trade with Antwerp, taking over 40 per cent of all its overland exports from 1543-5.[30] English cloths, especially kersies, were particularly important in this trade, followed by Flemish linen, Hondschoote says and luxuries

such as tapestries. Among imports, Italian silks and gold thread found
an expanding market in Antwerp, especially through Genoese merchants.

Trade with France also began to expand again, with increased quantities of Breton and Norman canvas and sail-cloth as well as wines among
the imports. The English devaluations of the 1540s stimulated cloth
exports to record levels, with a peak of over 135,000 pieces reached in
1554. Antwerp was almost the sole beneficiary of this in the Netherlands, since most other centres could not face the competition in traditional cloths, whereas the effect in Antwerp was further to stimulate
the finishing industry.

The boom of the 1540s also saw a further increase in the importance
of native merchants in Antwerp's foreign trade, some approaching the
great foreign colonists in stature, whilst the money market finally reached a pre-eminent position in northern Europe. The commercial slump
of the 1520s and 1530s had paradoxically stimulated investment in
government and municipal loans, which offered a better return than
trade for surplus capital generated in the previous boom. The later
return of better trading conditions did not end this process, particularly
as the needs of Imperial finance were approaching a peak.

The 1550s saw a crisis which was of European, or even world-wide,
dimensions and brought Antwerp's renewed expansion to a halt. Largely
political in origin, it was the consequence of the disasters which befell
the Emperor Charles V from 1552 onwards: his defeat in Germany at
the hands of the Protestant princes, the French occupation of Metz,
Toul and Verdun, their presence in Hainault and the defeat of the Genoese fleet by the Turks. The truce of Vaucelles with the French was of
brief duration, war again breaking out in 1557. The economic factors
were in some degree independent: a decline in the volume of Spain's
trade with the Indies, a fall in the imports of treasure in the later fifties,
bad harvests in 1556 and 1557 (which meant that Antwerp could not
even obtain grain from Amsterdam) and the petering out of the English
cloth boom. Though Antwerp recovered from this crisis, its position was
more fragile, and in two areas the consequences were irreversible. The
decay in the prosperity of south Germany was now clearly reflected in
the customs revenues of south-east Brabant. The balance of economic
power in Germany began to shift back to the ports of the North Sea
and the Baltic and by now Amsterdam was in a position to benefit most
from the expansion of the Baltic grain trade which gained pace in the
second half of the century. Also, the effects of French invasion and
famine on the economy of the southern Netherlands were severe. Workers began to emigrate from the fear more of starvation than of the

activities of the Inquisition which had intensified after 1550. Though
the moneyed classes were untouched by this and were able to enjoy the
benefits of a new industrial expansion in the 1560s, Antwerp's position
as a financial centre was threatened. The growing importance of the
Genoese in the public finances of the Habsburgs, together with the
lesser use by the English Crown of the Antwerp money market, inaugurated a trend towards a return to the conditions of the early years of the
century, financial transactions again being dominated by the needs of
commerce.

Antwerp was still well placed to benefit from the revival of trade after
the peace of 1559. Now almost the sole marketing centre for the products of south Netherlands industry, it was concentrating more than ever
on the trade with Seville. Native firms like the della Faille shifted the
emphasis of their trade from Italy to Seville, with profits as high as 100
per cent. Trade with France recovered, and there is evidence of some
Spanish wool reaching France through Antwerp, profiting from the 50
per cent reduction of the duties on wool exports to the Netherlands.[31]
Nor was Antwerp entirely excluded from the Baltic. Some merchants
formed 'eastland' companies, others began to trade with Norway and
Sweden. This resurgence took place against the background of an unfavourable trend in commercial relations with England. The revaluation
of sterling by Elizabeth I in 1560 was followed by a further fall in English cloth exports and the Merchant Adventurers caused several provoc-
ative incidents in Antwerp with Netherlands and Hanseatic merchants.
The Regent Margaret of Parma imposed a ban on English cloth imports
in 1563, and a mutual embargo on Anglo-Netherlands trade followed.
Though relations with the Merchant Adventurers were patched up in
1565, things were never the same again. The experience of 1563-4
proved to the Merchant Adventurers that they still needed Antwerp, but
the search for alternative centres for the English cloth trade was intensified in the years that followed.

In the mid-1560s political and social troubles broke out in the southern Netherlands which were to be the prelude to revolt against Spanish
rule. Discontent bred of dearth was coupled with Calvinist agitation
amongst the lower classes, whilst members of the nobility protested
against the religious policy of Philip II, and popular disturbance was
stilled neither by a promise that the Inquisition would operate more
mildly nor by the fall in the price of bread in the spring of 1566. In the
summer came the Iconoclastic riots, spreading from west Flanders, and
reaching Antwerp in August. For the whole summer, trade was virtually
at a standstill, with merchants joining the stream of emigrant workers.

The defeat of rebel forces and the flight of William of Orange led to a partial recovery, but it was now the turn of Calvinists to emigrate. Though many Catholics returned, foreign shipping did not do so in quantity and in 1569 new embargoes on Anglo-Netherlands trade followed Elizabeth I's seizure of treasure on its way up-Channel for the payment of the Spanish troops of the Duke of Alba. English privateers and the rebel Sea-Beggars destroyed the security of the route from the northern Netherlands to the Baltic. From 1567 the Merchant Adventurers began to experiment with a new cloth staple at Hamburg, which was developing facilities for finishing English cloth.

From 1572, when the Sea-Beggars inaugurated a new phase of the revolt by seizing Brill and a succession of other towns in Holland and Zeeland, the Scheldt was blockaded. Maritime trade was only possible because of the development of a system of licences permitting the citizens of Holland and Zeeland to trade with Brabant and other loyal provinces, as well as directly with Spain and Portugal, on payment of a tax. Antwerp was also able to maintain contact with the west through the use of other ports and overland routes. The sack of the city by mutinous unpaid Spanish troops in 1576 had, however, a much more devastating effect than the blockade. The Portuguese colony moved to Cologne, followed temporarily by many Spaniards. In 1577 Antwerp decided finally that its interests compelled it to throw in its lot with the rebels. The Pacification of Ghent of 1576 had inaugurated a brief period of 'national' revolt against Spanish rule, and until 1579 the whole country was out of Spain's control. Though the Pacification had guaranteed freedom of trade to the southern provinces, Zeeland continued to exact convoy dues for access to Antwerp, and commercial capital continued to flee the city. A period of brief optimism after 1580, which saw the setting up of a Turkish 'nation' in 1582, was soon followed by the beginning of the successful military operations of the Duke of Parma in the southern provinces. In 1585 the siege of Antwerp itself followed on the second sack of the city in 1584, this time by French troops of the Duke of Anjou. Antwerp capitulated to Parma in August 1585, and though it remained inside the political frontier of the Spanish Netherlands, continued to be denied access to the sea by Dutch control of the Scheldt estuary, and its population fell from over 80,000 before the siege to around 55,000 in 1587, and to only 42,000 by 1589.

Yet Antwerp still had an important role to play, both commercially and financially. Its proximity to the Dutch border made it an attractive centre for the essential trade with the enemy which Parma himself had authorised as early as 1587. Spanish, Portuguese and Italian firms, as well as native concerns, continued to use it as a base for their north European trade. Contacts were kept up with the many who had emigrated to the north and who played an important part in the development of Amsterdam and other northern centres. Financially, Antwerp continued to be the main centre for the waging of the war against the Dutch, though the money came almost entirely from Spain. Commercial activity could still cause surges of demand for credit which caused 'tightness' of money on the exchange and high interest rates, particularly in 1591 when exceptionally large contracts for Baltic grain were negotiated. Antwerp's dependence on the industries of the north became greater, despite the political barriers, since the revival of the economy in the south, though significant, was not entirely to Antwerp's benefit. The manufacturing towns of the south-west became increasingly important centres for the sale of their own goods, either through the ports of the far west of the Netherlands, or through France. Antwerp's economic future was to be largely confined within 'national' limits.

Marseilles

At the beginning of the sixteenth century Aigues Mortes was still the principal outlet of the trade of the Rhône valley to the Mediterranean, its harbour was already threatened with silting up and Marseilles, although it stands to the east of the Rhône delta, was to be its heir. A proper quay was talked of as a necessity in Marseilles from 1493 and work was begun within a decade or so. The political importance of the enterprise, undertaken during the wars in Italy, encouraged the Crown to offer a subvention for the continuous dredging operations necessary to keep the port clear.[32] Marseilles had already taken part in the premature and abortive plans of Louis XI for the capture of a share in the Levant trade from the Venetians, and from the beginning of the reign of Charles VIII had benefited from the construction of naval vessels and the supply of food and munitions for the Italian wars. Merchants of Italian origin were already active in the town, dealing in spices brought by the Venetians and engaged in a variety of trades with Spain. At this period its trade was clearly dominated by foreigners, mostly Italian, but with some Spaniards and Savoyards.

By the 1520s the population of Marseilles was about 15,000 persons, and went on rising to some 35,000 by the 1580s,[33] despite severe outbreaks of plague, for example from 1580 to 1582. With the political troubles of the early 1590s, when the town was under the dictatorship of Casaul and the Catholic League and cut off from the rest of France by the forces of Henry IV, its population probably dropped steeply. It rose again during the period of reconstruction to about 45,000-50,000 in 1610, not counting the considerable floating population typical of a port town. Despite these resources of manpower, during the first half of the sixteenth century at least, Marseilles lacked a merchant class with sufficient capital to develop its merchant fleet and the deficiency was made good by Lyons. As late as 1589 it was noted by a merchant supplying Marseilles with wheat that it was necessary to change money at Lyons. Even for the work of maintenance and improvement of the port, it was indebted more to the French Crown than to local capital. In the 1560s the government gave 120,999 *livres,* using the income from the customs on spices for half of the sum.[34]

An important step in the growth of Marseilles came in 1536, when agreements were first signed giving French merchants liberty of commerce in the Turkish empire. In the short run, it did not do much for the merchants of the town, as in 1541 Francis I made the import of spices from the Levant a royal monopoly. This was lifted, at least for Syria, in 1545, at the price of a 4 per cent duty. Trade with Barbary was also expanding and in 1552 the *Compagnie du Corail de Bône* was established. Despite fluctuations due to the renewal of war with Spain and the beginnings of political troubles in France, expansion continued and in 1566 an agent sent to the royal court was instructed to say that goods imported from Alexandria and Tripoli (Syria), 'which are spices, drugs, cottons, gall-nuts, leather goods. . . cause many foreign merchants to come daily, bringing a great quantity of gold and silver to have the said goods' for which 'in the past they had to go to Venice, Flanders and elsewhere. . . now the Kingdom's provision of the said goods is made by way of Marseilles'.[35]

In 1569 the privileges of French merchants in the Turkish empire were extended to cover foreign vessels. All except Venetian ships were compelled to fly the French flag whilst in the Levant, while the French consuls tried to exploit this concession by seeing to it that such ships unloaded in French ports. The outbreak of war between Venice and the Turks from 1570 to 1573 gave the Marseillais a further opportunity, as virtually the only neutrals in the Mediterranean. With the support of a Lyons banker, P.P. Nobili, and of a Venetian refugee, C. Dura, the *Compagnie d'écarlate* was founded for the export of cloth to the Levant. The effects of the war on the levels of trade in Marseilles were dramatic. The revenue of the 1 per cent port tax rose from an average of around 7 to 8,000 *livres* to 12,000 in 1570, to 13,200 in 1571, 15,000 in 1572 and 19,000 in 1573. Customs on spices rose from 20,000 *livres* in 1560 to 164,000 in 1571. Drawn by this prosperity, an agent of the Lyons banking firm the Bonvisi obtained citizenship in 1571, and the Augsburg firm of Manlich set up a factory in the same year. At the same time Marseilles began to capture the market in silks, hitherto channelled through Lyons by the overland routes from Italy. The League of Blois signed by Charles IX with England in 1572 further helped Marseilles by encouraging the English vessels returning in increasing numbers to the Mediterranean to use French ports.

Though this boom was generated by temporary political factors, its effects were longer-lasting. Though the Venetians rapidly recovered their position in the Levant after peace with the Turks was restored in 1573, the levels of trade at Marseilles remained above the levels of the 1560s until 1580.[36] Sugar-refining began in 1574, and a second cloth-exporting company was established in 1576, followed by a soap-boiling factory in 1578. Plague between 1580 and 1582, the activities of Barbary corsairs and, to a lesser extent, new export duties imposed by the government combined to bring this phase of Marseilles' expansion to an end. The 1590s, with the troubles of the *Ligue*, were worse. In 1590 the English ceased to trade at Marseilles and all the benefits of their growing trade with the Levant and Italy now went directly to England. Though there was a slight improvement after 1596, by 1600 Marseilles had regained no more than half of its previous trade.

Several factors retarded recovery during the early decades of the seventeenth century. Privateering and piracy in the Mediterranean were causing difficulties for the merchants of all countries. In 1599 the town council of Marseilles saw it as a main reason for the decay of trade. Shortly before, a vessel containing 20,000 *écus* of goods had been seized within sight of the port and another with a cargo worth 14,000 *écus* at Aleppo. In 1623 the St Jean was captured on its way home from Anatolia with goods estimated at the enormous sum of 300,000 *écus*, or more than a million *livres*. From 1610 to 1628 a state of official war existed between France and Algiers, during which hundreds of French vessels were taken, and 8,000 sailors sold into slavery. Hardly had peace led to a reduction in these losses when further serious outbreaks of plague struck the northern Mediterranean, including Marseilles, and after 1635 war with Spain led to the prohibition of trade with the enemy. The success of the English and the Dutch in trade with the Levant, thanks to the superior quality of their goods, and the initiative of Armenian merchants in bringing their silks to France for sale at such places as Toulon were further sources of grief to the Marseillais. The port's greatest days lay in the future, beginning with the stimulus of Colbert's administration after 1660.

During most of the period, the importance of foreigners in the trade of Marseilles remained great. They tended to trade with their home countries rather than with the Levant, and set Marseilles on the road to becoming an important entrepôt. The Genoese were the largest exporters, trading in Egyptian cotton, Barbary skins and Spanish wool, with their principal markets in Italy, Nice, and even as far east as Chios. The Florentines concentrated on Leghorn, where they sent wool, leather, paper, anchovies and figs. From 1590 onwards the role of the foreigners began to decline, not only absolutely but relatively to Marseilles' declining total trade. On the other hand, the motives for foreigners to seek citizenship grew stronger as higher customs duties increased discrimination against them. It is therefore not surprising that growing numbers were assimilated after 1577 when citizens were exempted from the 4 per cent tax on spices. Some of them married poor Marseilles girls to their factors so as to use their names in trade and in 1585 the government reacted by limiting the grant of citizenship to two men a year.

It is not easy to measure the growth and fluctuation of Marseilles' trade in statistical terms. The farming of the various taxes gives us only a very rough idea, as the percentage profit the farmer made could vary greatly, and they were very quick to demand a reduction in the rent in times of poor trade. Some of the taxes were levied only on foreign merchants, so that another indefinite variable must be allowed for. Until 1585 the only suitable tax for this purpose was the *Table de la mer*, theoretically 2 per cent of the value of goods. It suggests a value of overseas trade of 300,000 *écus* a year as early as 1515, rising by the 1540s to double this figure, with a high point of over 1,500,000 *écus* in 1543, not reached again until 1560. In effect, allowing for inflation, this hardly represents a significant real increase, but contemporary estimates for 1580 suggest that it was as high as 1,800,000 *écus*. Allowing for fraud and the fact that the figures applied only to the trade of non-citizens, it is likely that such an estimate was conservative. It has been suggested that the trade may have been as much as six times as great as the taxed element, which would give a total value of 4,800,000 *écus* in 1590, plus the tax-free trade in grain and wool worth possibly another million *écus*. Calculations based on another tax of 1 per cent levied on all goods entering the town by sea or land from 1584 give an even higher total of 7 million *écus*. On a national scale, this would mean that Marseilles received nearly 20 per cent of all French imports.[37]

Leghorn

Like Marseilles, Leghorn came into prominence in the last quarter of the

sixteenth century, but on the basis of a quite different policy. It was the
only port of the Duchy of Tuscany, the heir of the Florentine Republic,
after its recovery by Florence in 1543, and following the silting up of
Porto Pisano. Its communications with Florence were not easy, as Leghorn lies away from the mouth of the river Arno. In the sixteenth and
seventeenth centuries there was no real road because of the barrier created by the marshes, so goods were trans-shipped on to boats of five or
six tons, which could ascend the river. Cosimo dei Medici was to
improve the situation by constructing a canal, completed in the 1570s.
Whilst Leghorn was developed as a port it was never an important
residential centre for merchants, who continued to stay in Pisa, and an
attempt to develop its fairs as a financial exchange centre to rival the
Genoese fairs of 'Bisenzone' was a failure.[38]

Leghorn therefore remained small in size, despite its rapid expansion
as a port. A census of 1601 suggests it had a population of only 5,000,
including a substantial garrison of 750 men, 700 sailors and a good
supply of 76 prostitutes, but only 9 merchants, the 100 Jews probably
belonging to the artisan class. Its importance as a port grew much faster
and a series of foreign consulates were established; the French in 1579,
the Venetian in 1585, the Ragusan in 1588, the Genoese in 1596, the
Dutch about 1605, the Portuguese and Swedish in 1609 and the English
in 1634. The records enable us to reconstruct the phenomenal development of its maritime activity in the late sixteenth and early seventeenth
centuries, though there is a serious gap at a crucial period between 1593
and 1607. In the former year 219 vessels entered its harbour, recently
provided with new deep-water channels and a new fortress to guard it
which was allegedly built in five months in 1590. By 1607-8 the number
of ships had risen to 1,437 and by 1609-10 to 2,454.

The great dearth of wheat in Mediterranean countries in the 1590s
seems to have marked the turning point in Leghorn's fortunes. Before
that the sparse records suggest that it was a staging-point in the carrying
trade of the Mediterranean, importing some Sicilian grain and Sardinian
cheese. It was frequented mostly by Ragusan vessels, with occasional
visits from Spanish, Portuguese, English and Flemish ships trading within the Mediterranean and by a larger number of small vessels engaged in
purely local traffic. This pattern was maintained during the period from
1573 to 1593, with evidence of a growing number of vessels, mostly
Genoese, carrying Sicilian wheat, but doing little business in Leghorn.
Gradually, new elements began to appear. Quantities of pepper came
from Alexandria, in ships from Marseilles or Ragusa. North Africa
assumed some importance after the *détente* with the Turks in the later

1570s. The Iberian peninsula also emerged as the most important zone of trade, with 30 to 40 vessels arriving from Spain in most years, especially from Alicante. The absence of Barcelona is striking, but accountable for by its strong connection with Genoa. From Portugal came an average of 7 to 10 ships a year, mostly from Lisbon, with a few from the Algarve ports of Lagos and Faro. Wool, silks, leather, cochineal and some sugar were the principal cargoes from Spain, much of the bulkier goods coming in large Ragusan ships from Alicante. The Lisbon vessels brought spices, dye-woods, porcelain, slaves, saffron, fish, pearls, parrots, kersies and tin. Some of these goods were clearly of northern origin, and were probably trans-shipped in Lisbon, or picked up *en route*.

The most significant development was the arrival of vessels whose home port was in northern Europe. *La Rondine,* despite its name apparently an English ship (and certainly English-owned), arrived in June 1573 with a cargo of tin, lead, wool, kersies and some traditional broadcloths. In 1573-4 there were as many as 12 English ships, the number fluctuating around this level until 16 were recorded in 1592-3. At least half of these vessels were from London, the rest in small numbers from Southampton, Bristol, Yarmouth and other ports whose names are garbled beyond recognition in the records. The continental ports of the English Channel, the North Sea and the Baltic sent a few ships, until in 1590-1 there were 33, rising to 102 in 1591-2, and 67 in 1592-3. Clearly these brought large consignments of wheat. The Dutch were already very prominent, sending 63 ships during the three years, but with the Hanseatics as strong rivals. Hamburg alone sent 59 ships, Danzig 29, outclassing Lübeck with 11 and Emden with 5.

The Medici Dukes of Tuscany had been interested in the grain trade for a long time, and special stores were constructed in Leghorn to deal with the increased quantities. Duke Fernando (1578-1609) took the initiative in sending agents to Poland, Danzig and Hamburg to negotiate purchases, and personally invested large sums. Once again, 'political' initiative was of decisive importance in the transformation of a port. The records show total grain imports of 35,000 tons during the period 1590-93. Using a calculation made by Braudel of 4-5 Venetian ducats as an average price for a *fanega* of wheat[39] (about 1 cwt) at the end of the century, it can be presumed that the value of Leghorn's imports was at least 3 to 3½ million ducats. Grain occupied a great tonnage of shipping, but the value of other imports was considerable. In these three years no less than 900,000 lb of silk were handled. If the price was anything like that in Lyons somewhat earlier, it was also probably worth 3 to 3½ million ducats. Imports of wool totalled 9,600,000 lb, or

over 4,000 tons, the vast majority of it from Spain. It represented also
the bulk of Spanish wool which reached Italy. Its quality and its price
were high, and taking the Old Castilian price for 1601 as a rough basis
gives a minimum value of 200,000 ducats for Leghorn's wool imports.

In 1593 Leghorn was made a free port for entrepôt purposes, and it
is a pity that the immediate impact of this important innovation was
followed by a gap in the records of the movement of the port until 1607.
The dramatic change in its trade by then did not simply consist in an
increase in scale. The Ragusans still came from Alicante and Marseilles,
but not apparently from Sicily. Northern vessels were carrying more
general cargoes, except for the Hanseatics who still brought mostly
wheat. More and more large ships were to be seen, from Marseilles, Cor-
sica and smaller Provençal ports such as La Ciotat and St Tropez, more
Catalan ships and more Genoese. Luxury goods such as spices, pepper
and silk had become more important, some of the pepper now arriving
from England and the Netherlands. The *Fortune* of Amsterdam was the
first Dutch vessel recorded bringing spices from the Netherlands as early
as 1605. The English and the Dutch were using Leghorn more and more
to the exclusion of Venice, no longer caring to make the long detour
into the Adriatic on their voyages to or from the Levant. Undoubtedly,
Leghorn benefited from the easy access to the centre of the Italian peninsula; in 1628 it was stated by Venetians that one bale of goods for
Vicenza cost 1 dollar for unloading and transit at Leghorn and 8 more
for land transport to Vicenza, whilst it cost 30 to 40 dollars for transport from Venice. Leghorn later enjoyed great prosperity from the trade
of the English and Dutch.

Amsterdam

The commercial life of Leghorn was not closely linked with that of
Amsterdam and their importance was unequal, yet they had some things
in common, so it is appropriate to take Amsterdam as the last example
for detailed discussion. At first sight, the situation of Amsterdam does
not seem favourable to its development as a port. It faced the Zuider
Zee rather than the North Sea, its port lay well back from the sea, and
was shallow, involving the frequent use of lighters, whilst the town itself
had to be supported on piles because of the marshy ground. Its strength
lay in its relatively strong defensive position against attack whether
from sea or land. It lay at the centre of a rich agricultural zone, and also
of the main fishing industry of North Holland.[40] By the middle of the
fifteenth century it was already the principal port of the province, and
its access to the great estuaries of the Rhine and Maas was assured

through a network of waterways which led through Gouda and Geervliet. This route was already used by the smaller ships of the Hanseatic cities on their way to the southern Netherlands.[41] Amsterdam was already trading in its own right with the Baltic and with England, France, Spain and Portugal. By 1500, the north Netherlands merchants were penetrating the Baltic to an extent which was already challenging the supremacy of the Hanseatic cities. Unwelcome in the major centres, Dutch ships had found a friendlier reception amongst the smaller towns of the Baltic coast and amongst the landowners anxious to expand the market for their grain and timber. At the same time, it was the ports of North Holland which enjoyed the major share. As much as 78 per cent of all Netherlands vessels passing through the Sound had captains domiciled in the area around Amsterdam, in towns such as Enkhuizen, Hoorn and smaller places in the Waterland region.[42] Merchants of Amsterdam provided an important part of the capital needed for the commerce of the region, though recent research suggests a greater independence of the smaller centres than was formerly believed.

Though small, Amsterdam was growing rapidly, expanding from under 2,000 households in 1494 to nearly 3,000 in 1514. The decline in the relative strength of the Hanseatic League in western trade was accompanied by a vigorous effort on the part of the Dutch to expand their markets in Denmark and Norway, assisted by a political connection with the Danish Crown, which controlled the Sound. During the first half of the sixteenth century Amsterdam continued to develop as the commercial centre of an expanding trade in grain, timber, pitch, tar, flax, hemp and metals from the Baltic, exchanged for fish (principally herrings), wine, and particularly salt, obtained from western France and later also from Spain and Portugal. Its industrial development was modest but steady. Though its cloth production did not rival that of Leyden or Naarden, in 1514 it was already producing 5,000 to 6,000 pieces a year, as well as being the centre for the marketing of its neighbours' cloths. Brewing, rope-making, oil-refining, soap-boiling, candle-making, the manufacture of artillery and the building of ships were already being carried on. Towards the middle of the century Dutch commerce to the Baltic steadily expanded. The surviving registers of the Sound Toll are not an entirely satisfactory source for this period, and inferences drawn from the crude figures of shipping movements they provide can be misleading. Paradoxically, though their absolute numbers rose, the proportion of Dutch vessels passing to and from the Baltic seems to have declined, but this is in most probability the result of the inclusion in the Toll Registers of previously exempt Hanseatic ships. In

any case it appears that around 1540 more than half of the vessels paying dues at the Sound were Dutch. The war with Lübeck caused a serious
disruption in the early 1540s however, and in 1543 no Dutch ships were
recorded. The Treaty of Speyer of 1544 permitted a resumption of the
long-term trend and henceforward the Dutch were guaranteed freedom
of access to the Baltic.

The share of Amsterdam in the trade was also rising in proportion to
the Dutch total. It is possible to analyse at least its export trade in great
detail for the years 1544 and 1545. Trade with the rest of the northern
Netherlands accounted for just over 25 per cent of the total, with
Groningen, Friesland and Kampen occupying the principal positions.
Its trade with the outside world is revealed to be more far-reaching than
is often supposed. If Denmark took little more than 1 per cent of its
exports, Norway took 7 per cent. Amsterdam's trade with the western
Hanseatic cities was even more important, Emden taking 2.8 per cent,
Bremen 4.2 per cent, and Hamburg no less than 13.2 per cent. In the
Baltic, Danzig already stood out with 5.4 per cent, Riga coming well
behind with only 1.4 per cent. Surprisingly, Lisbon was in the prime
position, taking no less than 14.2 per cent of Amsterdam's exports. Textiles were especially important in the trade with Hamburg, with herrings
coming close behind, whilst grain was especially important in the trade
with the eastern Netherlands and with Portugal. The outlines of Amsterdam's commerce thus remained traditional, but its growing control over
the exchange of the staple products was reflected in the growing wealth
of its merchants. According to the tax register of 1543, a total wealth of
£194,125 Flemish was shared among 92 of them. Nearly all the larger
commercial fortunes of the north Netherlands belonged to citizens of
Amsterdam, surpassing any in South Holland or Zeeland.[43]

The progress of the Dutch and of Amsterdam in particular continued
steadily during the third quarter of the century, with an average of over
1,300 vessels passing the Sound annually during the 1560s, but the beginning of the new phase of the revolt against Spain had serious consequences from 1569, when only 469 Dutch ships passed through the Sound,
the number recovering only to an average of 1,000 or so a year during
the 1570s. In 1578 Amsterdam belatedly joined the revolt. Her trade
continued to expand, the 1580s seeing the levels of Baltic trade of the
sixties re-established, to be surpassed in the nineties, with a climax of
1,953 passages in 1596.[44] Undoubtedly Amsterdam benefited enormously from the difficulties experienced by Antwerp. The migration of Protestant merchants from Antwerp to Amsterdam accelerated after 1576 and
more from 1584. Many of them were able to escape with their capital

and their role in both the expansion of Amsterdam and in the modernisation of its commercial techniques was of the greatest importance.

Hitherto Amsterdam's organisation, especially on the financial side,
had been conservative. The development of banking and credit was well
behind that of Antwerp. This was partly accounted for by the nature of
trade with the remoter Baltic regions, where the exchange of goods by
barter was still widely practised, sometimes even without a notional
monetary value being placed on the items exchanged. Dutch merchants
often continued to regard barter as preferable to the sale of goods on
credit. The use of the letter of exchange was restricted, especially in the
Baltic, though it was being used more widely in greater centres like
Danzig.

The contrast between conservative and advanced commercial techniques is well illustrated by the firms of Cunertorf-Snel and the Van
Adrichem. The former operated from Lisbon, but originated from Kampen. With its factors at Antwerp and in the Baltic, it traded on a simple
basis in which each transaction was self-contained, the capital being
invested in goods which were sold for the purchases of other goods at
each end of the route employed. The inflexibility of this method was
revealed when the partners tried to extend it to the sale of spices in
Danzig. Because the Danzig market could not absorb a sufficient quantity their factor was unable to purchase other goods for return to Lisbon.
The Cunertorf-Snel failed to take account of a fundamental aspect of
the Baltic trade, that it was necessary in the end to use money in the
Baltic to purchase grain or timber, because, like the Far East, it could
not absorb enough western goods to balance western demand. The Van
Adrichem, of Delft, on the other hand, displayed a more sophisticated
and 'capitalist' approach. Concentrating on the corn market, they were
quite willing to supply their factor in Danzig with money, either in cash
or by letters of exchange, leaving him freedom of manoeuvre in choice
of the appropriate moment for purchase, and even the choice of the
grain. At both the purchasing and the selling ends of their trade the Van
Adrichem used a knowledge of the highly fluctuating market in grain
to the best effect possible in given circumstances, even, by the 1590s,
to the extent of permitting their Danzig factor to return his capital by
bills of exchange rather than in goods if the rate of exchange was particularly favourable. The realisation of a money profit, by whatever means,
had thus taken prime place over an exclusive concern with trade in
goods.[45]

The influx of new men and capital from the 1580s enabled Amsterdam to revive and extend its control over the Baltic grain trade and its

European markets. The times were highly favourable, a growing shortage of corn in southern Europe forcing even Spain to permit the Dutch
entry to her ports. The last vestiges of competition had been crushed
with the failure of Antwerp. Geography, combined with the failure of
local competition, enabled Amsterdam to dominate the corn trade by
establishing itself as the indispensable intermediary. The amassing of
stocks increasingly enabled the market to be manipulated in the interests
of the entrepôt.

The early decades of the seventeenth century were to see more
violent fluctuations in Amsterdam's trade with the Baltic. Years of
depression coincided with difficult years in the war against Spain, but
the Twelve Years Truce from 1609 to 1621 saw another boom, the
number of passages through the Sound reaching a new high average of
over 2,000 annually between 1618 and 1620. They again fell dramatically under the pressure of the conditions created in the Baltic by war between Sweden and Poland, the opening of the Thirty Years War and by
the heavy pressure placed on the Dutch in the first few years of the renewed war with Spain. Between 1625 and 1630, Dutch passages through
the Sound averaged less than 1,000 ships, but recovered again in the
1630s.[46]

The trade was again rapidly changing in character as Dutch commerce
penetrated to the Levant and the Far East. Spices, now brought directly
by the United East India Company, began to rise in relative value in the
Baltic trade, overtaking herrings between 1625 and 1635. There was
also a boom in the exports of Dutch cloth, which comes to equal the
value of French wines, but was severely hit by the crisis of the 1620s.
Amongst exports from the Baltic, grain retained its pride of place, averaging as much as 100,000 tons a year, and timber a steady 10 per cent
in value, with flax and hemp increasing. Most dramatic of all was the
expansion in the trade in metals, especially Swedish copper and iron
which expanded from 2 per cent to 16 per cent of the total between
1600 and 1625. Here, as in the corn trade, the Dutch, led by Amsterdam, established a dominant position.[47] Yet the balance of the trade
remained unfavourable. Though perhaps the number of ships sailing in
ballast into the Baltic fell proportionately, it remained at over 50 per
cent, because of the smaller bulk of the inward cargoes. Nor did the
trade produce a favourable monetary balance, the deficit being made up
by the silver obtained from Amsterdam's grip on the trade of the Iberian
peninsula and growing direct contacts with the colonists of Spanish
America.

In these years the character of Amsterdam's commercial and financial life underwent rapid changes. Now a metropolis of 100,000 inhabitants, it had doubled in size after the influx of southern immigrants. In the more exotic atmosphere following the formation of the East India Company, speculation became almost feverish. Dealings in the shares led to violent fluctuations in their value, which often bore little relation to the real state of the eastern trade. At times, as in 1609 when the Directors complained to the government in the Hague, speculators were combining to force down the share values with the object of taking control.[48] The belated development of marine insurance was also giving rise to the gambling spirit, as it did elsewhere. At the same time, opportunities for the investment of capital both in urban building and in the development of polders (drained land recovered from the sea) expanded greatly. In 1615, of the fortune of 256,000 florins left by the merchant Alent ten Grootenhuis, lands and farms in the Beemster polder alone were worth 140,000 florins, as well as land, a house and a brick factory at Naaesen worth 18,000 florins, 32,000 florins of shares in the East India Company, 25,000 florins in stocks of spices and 11,000 in shares in ships and credits due. Thus the tendency of the rich to invest in real estate was no less strong in seventeenth-century Amsterdam than elsewhere, though in this case it was often in land which had been won from the sea, representing an increase in the area available for cultivation by the intensive methods for which the Dutch were already renowned. The largest fortunes now grew very fast. In 1624 Jacob Poppen left nearly a million florins, of which nearly half was also represented by land in the Beemster polder, and another 100,000 in houses. In the tax registers of 1631, 98 persons were listed with fortunes of over 100,000 florins, over 200 more had between 50 and 100,000, and nearly 600 had between 20,000 and 50,000.

Through the multiplication of individual wealth following the increased scale of operations rather than through any radical change in techniques, Amsterdam became a capitalist centre on a new scale. The development of a credit system led to the creation of private banks alongside both the municipal Exchange Bank and the state Credit bank, which seems to have supplied credit to smaller traders and retailers. Private banks evolved naturally from the surplus capital of private merchants. By these means, the general level of interest rates was brought down to levels which were not matched elsewhere in Europe, further increasing the competitive advantage of Dutch traders. Cheap transport was made possible by the low capital cost and small crews of the *fluits* constructed in huge numbers by semi-standardised methods in the yards of the area around the city. Self-confidence amongst both individuals

and groups led to attempts to establish monopolies and cartels in specially favoured trades. The example of Elias Tripp and Louis de Geer in
Swedish copper is studied below. Whale fishery was another example,
where two Amsterdam companies joined forces together with one in
Zaandam, to form the 'Northern Company' which extracted privileges
from the Estates General in 1614. The individual enterprises retained
their identity, but agreed to operate under the general direction of an
assembly, which meant that by 1622 a virtual monopoly had been
established in favour of those who had been engaged in the trade since
1617. It prevented over-fishing and fixed the selling price of whale
blubber, but failed to obtain the approval of the Estates General for the
prohibition of imports into the United Provinces by outsiders.

Amsterdam was yet to see the greatest period of her ascendancy in
world commerce and finance. Behind it lay the power of an Estates
General which was penetrated by the commercial ethos, and which saw
that the vital interest of the Republic lay in the maintenance of its trading advantages. Almost instinctively, Amsterdam operated on doctrines
of foreign trade, especially concerning the free export of currency in an
effort to achieve an overall favourable balance of trade, without necessity for the bitter controversy which was simultaneously raging in the
merchant community of London.

Notes

1. Gascon, *Grand commerce, passim.*
2. For the expansion of the trade of Marseilles, see below pp. 92-5.
3. Braudel, *La Méditerranée,* I, p. 500.
4. Gascon, *Grand commerce,* pp. 108-28.
5. The German merchants were exempt from import taxes, but it is unlikely that
this alters these figures in a substantial way.
6. H. and P. Chaunu, *Séville et l'Atlantique.* The main text, by Pierre Chaunu, is
in Volume VIII, itself in three parts. There are excellent tables and diagrams in Vol.
VI. A useful summary of the work can be found in P. Chaunu, *Conquête et exploitation des nouveaux mondes.*
7. Tomás de Mercado, *Suma de tratos y contratos de mercáderes,* quoted in R.
Pike, *Aristocrats and Traders–Sevillian Society in the Sixteenth Century,* p. 1.
8. Chaunu, *Séville et l'Atlantique,* VIII, i, p. 165.
9. Pike, op.cit., p. 11.
10. Ibid., p. 13. Cf. M. Drouhet, *Une grande ville d'ancien régime–Séville dans la
seconde moitié du xvie siècle* (unpublished thesis quoted by P. Chaunu, *Conquête
et exploitation,* p. 270.)
11. Chaunu, *Seville et l'Atlantique,* VIII, i, p. 252.
12. Pike, op.cit., pp. 116-17.
13. Braudel, *La Méditerranée,* I, p. 573.
14. M. Moret, *Aspects de la société marchande de Séville au début du xviie*

siècle, pp. 67-8.
15. Ibid., pp. 75-6.
16. Ibid., p. 80.
17. A. Girard, *Le commerce français à Séville et Cadix au temps des Habsbourgs,* p. 30.
18. Van der Wee, *Growth,* II, p. 104.
19. Ibid.
20. A. Goris, *Les colonies marchandes méridionales à Anvers, passim.*
21. W. Brulez, 'Bruges and Antwerp in the 15th and 16th Centuries—an Antithesis?', *Acta Historiae Neerlandicae,* VI (1973), pp. 1-26.
22. Van der Wee, *Growth,* II, p. 127.
23. R. Gascon, 'Le commerce des épices a Lyon', *AESC,* XV (1960), pp. 638-66.
24. Ehrenberg, op.cit., pp. 119, 195, 237-8.
25. Van der Wee, *Growth,* II, p. 127.
26. Ibid., II, p. 141.
27. W. Brulez, 'L'exportation des Pays Bas à l'Italie par voie de terre au milieu xvie siècle', *AESC,* XIV (1959), pp. 461-91, at pp. 483-6.
28. Goris, op.cit., p. 69.
29. P.J. Bowden, 'Wool Supply and the Woollen Industry', *Economic History Review,* 2nd Ser., IX (1956-7), pp. 44-58, at p. 48.
30. Brulez, 'L'exportation', loc.cit.
31. Van der Wee, *Growth,* II, p. 224, quoting Lapeyre, *Les Ruiz,* p. 384.
32. J.R. Collier and J. Billioud, *Histoire du commerce de Marseille,* III, pp. 32-3.
33. Ibid., III, p. 181.
34. Ibid., III, pp. 187-8.
35. Ibid., III, pp. 196-7.
36. Ibid., III, p. 199.
37. Ibid., III, p. 549.
38. F. Braudel and R. Romano, *Navires et marchandises à l'entrée du port de Livourne, 1547-1611.*
39. Braudel, *La Méditerranée,* I, p. 517.
40. V. Barbour, *Capitalism in Amsterdam,* p. 13.
41. O. Nübel, *Pompejus Occo, 1483 bis 1537—Fuggerfaktor in Amsterdam,* pp. 22-30.
42. A. Christensen, *Dutch Traffic to the Baltic around 1600,* pp. 39-41.
43. N.W. Posthumus, *De Uitvoer van Amsterdam, 1543-45,* pp. 186, 189.
44. Christensen, op.cit., p. 87.
45. Ibid., pp. 383-400.
46. Ibid., pp. 87-8.
47. Ibid., pp. 360-1.
48. A.E. Sayous, 'Le rôle d'Amsterdam dans l'histoire du capitalisme commercial et financier', *Revue historique,* CLXXXIII (1938), pp. 242-80.

5 THE MERCHANTS

The status of merchant in the sixteenth century was usually, though
not exclusively, restricted to men who engaged in trade above the
retail level. We know the names of thousands, but we cannot follow
the careers of more than a small number in detail. We are here, perhaps
more than in other areas, at the mercy of the chance survival of the
sources, and must beware of assuming that those we can study in close-
up were either typical, or more important than others. Fortunately
modern research has produced studies not only of some of the greatest,
but also of some of more modest means and capabilities, and where we
cannot know them in detail, we can sometimes study the activities of a
group by the use of statistical information. Rather than categorising
them in general terms, it seems preferable to single out a few individuals
and families for discussion in the context of their varied commercial
environments.

The Fugger of Augsburg

To begin with the Augsburg family of Fugger is to begin with a dynasty
whose position was perhaps more outstanding in their time than any
other. The first half of the sixteenth century has often been described
as the 'age of the Fugger', and whatever distortion results from this, it
reflects contemporary opinion, and contrasts with the later part of the
period when no single family seems to stand out to put their stamp on
the age, though there may have been several as rich. Their pre-eminence
depended on the close association which they formed, and loyally
maintained, with the Imperial Habsburgs, and hence on their increasing
concentration on government finance. In that sense, they transcended
the world of commerce, though they never left it, and were to be found
at the end of the century as at its beginning, in the negotiation of large-
scale deals in pepper as well as of government loans.

From rural origins, in which agriculture had been mixed with a
little cloth-weaving, a Hans Fugger had migrated as a weaver to Augsburg in 1367 and set up in a small way as a merchant dealing in wool
and cloth. Less than a century later Jacob Fugger the Elder was engaged in foreign trade, and by his death in 1468 his fortune was reckoned
for tax at a level which made him seventh in rank among the rich merchants of Augsburg. His widow and sons carried on the business in wool,

cotton, fustians, silks, Mediterranean fruits, spices and drugs. It was the youngest son, Jacob (1459-1525), who was to emerge as the leader of the firm in the late fifteenth and early sixteenth centuries as it grew into international fame.[1] As the youngest son he had entered the priesthood, but renounced a canonry in order to join the business in 1478. After a year's apprenticeship at the *Fondaco dei Tedeschi* in Venice, he returned to Augsburg, there inaugurating a period of expansion in the firm's Venetian business which led in 1484 to the acquisition of larger premises in the *Fondaco*. It was around this date that Jacob took the decisive step of entering the metal trade of Tyrol, which rapidly led to the beginnings of the Fugger's relations with the Habsburgs. The Archduke's need for money had led him to pledge his future receipts from the tax on silver paid by the producers to merchants who provided ready cash, but local resources of capital were inadequate for his needs. Other Augsburg firms, as well as some from other Bavarian towns, had already interested themselves in the profits to be made in Tyrol, but Jacob Fugger rapidly established his position in competition with them. By 1487 he had ousted his rivals the Baumgartner by offering a sum to the Archduke which was in excess of the firm's capital at the time, but proved to be well within its resources, since the money had only to be provided in monthly instalments, easily covered by the receipts from the sale of the silver. From the moment in 1490 when control over Tyrol passed into the hands of the future Emperor Maximilian, Jacob Fugger found himself in an even more powerful position to dominate the Tyrolean silver market. The revenues of the silver tax had risen to 150,000 florins a year, and total production to 400,000 florins.[2]

In the 1490s Jacob Fugger turned his attention to the exploitation of the mineral resources of Hungary, where, in association with Jan Thurzo, a programme of modernisation was carried out, using the latest German techniques. Within a few years the Fugger established a virtual monopoly of Hungarian silver and copper production. Copper was the commodity which played a crucial role in extending the Fugger's international commercial empire. Copper and silver were intimately associated in the ore, and preliminary refining left a quantity of silver (about 2 per cent) mixed with the copper. The latter was not subject to any special tax in Hungary, and by exporting the percentage of silver contained in the copper the tax on it was evaded, and the silver separated in modern factories set up for the purpose in Thuringia and Carinthia. The latter factory was very well placed for transport to Venice where silver was in heavy demand for meeting the deficit in the trade in

Levantine spices. Copper from Hungary was sent not only to Venice but also to central Germany, and by extending this route the Fugger were able to recover from the collapse of the Venetian silver and copper markets during the war with Turkey and the competition of 'Portuguese' pepper and spices which immediately followed. The power of the Fugger was now such that they succeeded in gaining a complete control over Tyrolean copper production on a falling market. A tighter grip on Imperial finances was again a key to this operation, whilst the rewards they received included partial exemption from Habsburg tolls on the transport of Hungarian copper through Austria, further improving their commercial competitiveness.

The decline of the Venetian market for metals was thought by many to be a permanent one, and the rise of Antwerp as a key point for the distribution of pepper and spices brought there by the Portuguese created an expanding demand for copper to feed the Portuguese trade with Africa. The Tyrolean copper producers demanded that the Emperor should prohibit the sale of any copper but Tyrolean in Antwerp.[3] The position of the Fugger was too strong, however, and by 1514 they had succeeded in gaining entry to the Netherlands market for their Hungarian copper, whilst permitting the sale of Tyrolean copper in Italy and southern Germany. The Fugger had already responded to the call of Antwerp. Between 1497 and 1504 more of their silver went to Frankfurt-on-Main and Antwerp than to Venice, and soon after, the whole of their silver production was reaching Antwerp.[4] The Fugger accounts from 1497 to 1504 reveal that south German copper was already reaching Antwerp through middlemen.[5] From 1504 they sold Hungarian copper directly in Antwerp, shipping it through Danzig and Stettin. As early as 1510-11 over 50 per cent of the Hungarian copper was sent there, compared with only 3 per cent to Venice and Trieste, and representing the highest absolute total recorded until 1540, though the percentage passed 60 around 1530.[6] The Fugger also joined, perhaps in rivalry with their competitors the Welser and the Imhof, in financing a Spanish voyage to the spice islands by the Pacific route.

By the 1520s the Fugger had established the mature form of their European and commercial network. Their earliest 'factories' or dependencies were naturally in Germany, at Nuremberg from 1486 and at Breslau from 1494, as well as the original one at Venice. That of Ban Bistrica was responsible from 1494 for the administration of their Hungarian mining enterprises, as those of Schwaz (1522), Hohenkirchen and Fuggerau were for mining in Germany and Austria. As the network of their metal trade expanded, factories came into existence along its principal routes—at Cracow, Breslau, Leipzig, Vienna and Bolzano, whilst the Antwerp factory greatly increased its importance after 1505, the year in which the Fugger also established themselves in Lisbon. By the 1520s Milan, Frankfurt-on-Main, Cologne, Budapest, Danzig, Innsbruck, Halle and Rome had been added, in addition to the extremely important agency at the Spanish Court. From that time also the revenues of the Spanish Military Orders, including the mercury mine of Almadén, came under the Fuggers' administration, as part of the repayment of the loans granted to the Emperor Charles V for the Election of 1519.[7]

The construction of a network not only covering Europe but looking beyond it to the growing commerce of the Portuguese and Spanish empires was undoubtedly the work of Jacob Fugger. The firm had been run as a partnership following the death of Jacob the Elder, and on the younger Jacob's entry in 1480 it seems still to have been on the basis of a purely verbal agreement. The serious disadvantages of this were made evident when it became necessary to reconstruct the firm as Jacob's elder brothers died, first George in 1506, and then Ulrich in 1510. The widows were in each case paid out in cash, and a new partnership formed in which Jacob's nephews participated. Jacob seized the opportunity to establish a greater concentration of control in his own hands. Instead of an agreement between equals, the arrangements completed in 1512 fully recognised the uncle's seniority in experience over his nephews. Hitherto the firm had enjoyed the good fortune of a sufficient supply of male heirs competent to assist in the running of the enterprise, but after 1512 Jacob reserved to himself the right to determine whether and when the partnership should be dissolved. Since 1502 the firm had also been protected by a special capital fund for the Hungarian mining enterprise, the heavy capitalisation of which could otherwise have proved embarrassing when a partner died or withdrew. Thus by 1512 Jacob had established both the security and permanence of the firm's capital and his own control over it.

The death of Jacob 'the Rich' in 1525 involved a complete assessment of the firm's assets, and the final balance was not struck until 1527, as control passed into the hands of his nephew Anton. The gross assets were no less than 2 million Rhenish gold florins, and after the deduction of debts, over one and a half million. Goods in stock were worth nearly 400,000 florins, over half of the value being in copper. Clearly by this date the major part of the assets were in the credits of the loan business, amounting to 1,650,000 florins.[8] The accuracy of this assessment is undoubted, and is a testimony to the tight financial control maintained over all the factories from the headquarters in Augsburg. Here the accounts of all the dependencies were checked annually against each other, after reduction to a common accounting unit, the Rhenish gold florin, and after the adjustment of the complex differences between local weights and measures.

Between 1480 and the death of Jacob the Rich the capital of the firm had expanded about forty times, and though business continued to prosper under Anton's direction until the 1540s, its expansion was nothing like as rapid. Increasingly dominant were the loans made to the Emperor Charles V and his brother Ferdinand, as well as considerable sums lent to Henry VIII of England. The company's assets reached their peak in 1546, but some very difficult years followed, as the political fortunes of Charles V changed for the worse. Anton thought of winding up the firm around 1550, but as he put it,

> on account of long wars, matters have gone right heavily, so that not only were we unable to bring our own business to an end and collect the monies owing to us, but we have been constrained, in order to serve the Emperor and the King, to make fresh loans, ourselves borrowing money and getting into debt.

In fact the Fugger made further large loans to the Emperor in 1552, although this was probably from the partners' private funds rather than those of the firm, and followed this by further loans secured on the revenues of the Netherlands, those of Spain being anticipated until 1557. Between 1552 and 1554, within less than two years, they had lent the Habsburgs more than ever before in an equivalent period. So they were badly caught by the declaration of bankruptcy by the Spanish monarchy in 1557.

Anton Fugger died three years later, having found great difficulty in finding any of the younger generation of the family fitted and willing to take charge. Finally affairs were placed under the direction of his nephew Hans Jacob and his own eldest son Marx, with a recommendation that affairs be wound up as soon as practicable. Anton's advice was ignored and business went from bad to worse. Hans Jacob was forced to leave the firm in 1563. It took over his personal debts in Augsburg, but he was forced to hand over all his personal property to creditors. Further blows were dealt to the firm by the Spanish bankruptcy of 1575, and its position was worsened by the grip which the Genoese were establishing on the European credit system. Yet they struggled on into the seventeenth century, with large sums still recorded as assets in Spain in the

1620s, but which were soon to be overtaken by liabilities. It has been estimated that most of the firm's earnings over the course of a century were lost in Spain by the middle of the seventeenth century. Over-commitment to the public finances of the Habsburgs brought its eventual penalty. The Fugger are an example of a dynasty which survived in the world of high finance for a century after they had reached the peak of their eminence. The tenacity of some members of the family was quite remarkable. Others took the classical path into the ranks of the cultured nobility, amongst whom even the great Jacob the Rich was to be counted from the early years of the sixteenth century.[9]

The Ruiz of Medina del Campo

The age of the greatness of the Ruiz family of Medina del Campo in Castile lay in the second half of the sixteenth century. Though its leading member, Simón Ruiz, engaged from time to time in the business of government loans, the Ruiz remained deeply involved in the trade in commodities. Based in the principal financial centre of Castile, their network of correspondents linked them with Lisbon, Italy and Antwerp.

The first generation of the Ruiz to achieve prominence was a triumvirate of brothers, Andreas, Vitores and Simón. Andreas was settled in Nantes from his youth, certainly from 1537 onwards, and remained there until his death in 1580, becoming a naturalised Frenchman in 1546. Together with his brother Vitores, who remained at Medina del Campo, Juan de la Presa and the latter's cousin Francisco de la Presa of Burgos, Andreas formed a company engaged mainly in the cloth trade. He also acted on a commission basis for many merchants of Lyons and Rouen, using the Bonvisi as his correspondents in the French financial capital. He was also attracted by state loans and tax-farming, especially towards the end of his life, though not always to great profit.[10] These dealings with the French monarchy did not exclude similar contacts with the King of Spain, and he was in practice the consul of the Spanish merchant community in Nantes.

Simón Ruiz moved from his birth-place at Beldorado to Medina del Campo, where his brother Vitores was already established, around 1550 and began trading in Breton linens. His early partnerships were relatively short-lived, often concerned only with one enterprise, until in 1556 he contracted one with Yvon Rocaz and Jean Le Lou of Nantes which lasted until Rocaz's death in 1569. It was around this date or a little later that some unfortunate experience in Franco-Spanish trade led him to try his skill and luck in speculative activity on the money exchanges. Complaints of inadequate profits from the import of cloth

for Seville in the 1560s, and the series of bankruptcies there, which had
echoes as far away as Bruges, were followed by actual losses in the early
1570s. Fortunately he was making substantial profits on the exchanges,
from a mere four hundred ducats in 1570 to over four thousand in
1572.[11] At the same time he was diversifying his commercial activity,
exporting saffron and salt and importing wheat, making contact for the
first time with Antonio and Luis Gomes d'Elvas of Lisbon. This link
was to be very important during the rest of his career, since he was
able to offer the Lisbon firm a connection with the financial market of
Lyons, the lack of which had been a remarkable defect in the Portuguese
capital's commercial network. He also developed his links with Antwerp
through men who included Alessandro Bonvisi. He capped this phase
of his career in 1576, when he stepped in during the aftermath of the
state bankruptcy of 1575 to provide Philip II with letters of exchange
for the payment of wages to troops in the Netherlands, forming a part
of the group of Spanish men of affairs who attempted to free the Crown
from the grip of the Genoese syndicates.[12] Simón Ruiz was too cautious
to commit himself deeply in such dealings, and soon reverted to the less
risky private financial market, always balancing it with trade in goods.
Between 1574 and 1581 he saw profits on his Breton trade alone of
over 13,000 ducats, at a time when this trade was past its best, and his
attention was turning more towards Rouen and Antwerp. The latter,
despite the increasing insecurity of the English channel and the closure
of the Scheldt, had still a considerable trading capacity, using the overland route to Rouen, and by the Loire to Nantes. From 1574 to 1581
Ruiz made a profit of nearly 14 thousand ducats on his Flanders trade,
mostly by the import of cloth.

   In 1585 he decided to associate his nephew Cosmo and his employee
Lope de Arziniega with his business, the latter taking day-to-day charge
of the traditional trading activities, freeing Simón to concentrate on
financial deals and new experiments such as trade in Swedish and Hungarian copper. In 1592 there was a further reorganisation, with his
nephew forming a new company 'Simón and Cosmo Ruiz', the latter
increasingly running the business, soon to fall on hard times. Simón
Ruiz virtually retired, to found the hospital in Medina del Campo which
bore his name. He died in 1597, leaving a fortune estimated to have
been as high as 378,000 ducats, some of it invested in the *juros* of Castile (the long-term government debt), in the *censos* (agricultural loans)
of the region, and in the *tercias reales* (the royal share of the ecclesiastical tithe) of nearby Zamora, which were payable in wheat. By far the
major part of his fortune was in the state debt and the credits he held

on the exchanges of Piacenza, Lyons and Lisbon.[13] His wealth did not compare with that of the Fugger, and was perhaps only a tenth as much, but that of the Fugger firm was much more subdivided, and his fortune compared well with that of the second rank German financiers of the middle of the sixteenth century.

Simón Ruiz was fortunate in his withdrawal from business at the peak of his prosperity. Medina del Campo had been shaken by the bankruptcy of 1575, and was to be finally ruined by that of 1596, a few months before his death. The financial centre of Spain was moving to Madrid, rapidly growing as the fixed capital and centre of the administration, and Medina ceased to be a commanding place for the conduct of either commercial or financial affairs. Under Cosmo's direction the Ruiz enterprise became increasingly concerned with financial transactions, to the exclusion of the traditional trade with France, weakened since the late 1580s by the last and most destructive phase of the French wars of religion, and later by the open war between Spain and France. A brief incursion into the slave trade with the Indies was a fatal exception. Cosmo was imprisoned on charges of defrauding the government, an experience which virtually ended his career as a businessman, and the following years were full of interminable law suits. The second generation of the Ruiz, both in Spain and in France, were of lesser calibre and the Spanish branch displayed the prevalent desire to withdraw from commerce and live as gentlemen. The early years of the seventeenth century were particularly unfavourable to Spanish trade, and individual character apart, the attractions of the still relatively safe investment in *juros* and *censos* was greater than those of the market place or the exchanges.

The Hermite of Marseilles

The temptation to invest trading profits in local or national loans, or in tax-farming, was not resisted even by merchants who never achieved the wealth of the Fugger or the Ruiz. The example of the Hermite brothers of Marseilles is typical of hundreds. Antoine and Gilles Hermite were the sons of a Marseilles lawyer, of origins in Toulon. It is not known when they set up in partnership, but it was probably before 1570, and it may well have been that the death of their father, leaving them little cash but some land, enabled them to start in business in a small way.[14] If this is so, we have an example of a movement into trade and away from land ownership which runs contrary to the conventional view of the social aspirations of the middle and professional classes of Europe, at least outside England and the Netherlands. In 1572 Antoine represented a maternal cousin, married to a merchant-draper of Aix-en-Provence, in a small transaction involving three English kersies, and the brothers invested the modest sum of six hundred *livres* in kersies for sale in Syria. From May to October 1573 Antoine sailed on a voyage to Alexandria as scrivener, carrying a small quantity of goods for trade on his own account as was customary at the time, bringing back some linen and a little pepper and ginger. The brothers' appeals to their cousin for money were answered with a loan of 535 *écus,* and the sale of their father's vineyard at Mont-Jusieu brought another 190 *écus.* The year 1575 saw further sales of land for 500 *écus,* and further borrowings of money from their sister and cousin. These ways of raising capital seem to have enabled them to carry on a modest level of trade, with a turnover of around 2,500 *livres* a year in 1574 and 1575. The Hermite entered the Levant trade at a favourable moment for Marseilles, during the Turko-Venetian war of 1570-73. They were among many relatively small Marseilles firms who benefited, and seem to have been more successful than some in maintaining their position after normal relations between Venice and the Turks were restored.

During 1575 and 1576 the brothers successively voyaged in the Levant. Their surviving correspondence begins in 1578, and reveals a widening scale of business with several larger Marseilles firms, some of whom used Gilles as an agent in the Levant. After 1585 they had their own agents there, including a nephew of Gilles. Between 1585 and 1588 Antoine was selling Egyptian cotton and muscats to Italy, Spain, Brittany and England, as well as cotton and silks to Lyons. The year 1589 began a period of great difficulty in the trade of Marseilles. Following the accession of Henry IV to the throne, the last phase of the French civil wars saw Marseilles taken over by the forces of the Catholic League, and for a time isolated from the rest of France. As commander of the castle of Cassis, Antoine Hermite became deeply involved in political and military affairs, whilst Gilles only found a limited amount of time for a few not very successful attempts to establish a trade with Genoa. The Levant trade fell into the background, but horses, wheat, sugar and oil from 'Barbary' were sold. In 1596 Gilles died of wounds, and after his return to Marseilles Antoine took sole charge of the business. His Levant trade seems to have picked up, as his correspondence reveals a consignment of twelve bales of silk bought as late as 1609 for 3,800 *écus.*

The Hermite brothers had begun to diversify their activity quite early. In the late 1580s Antoine had taken an interest of twelve *quirats* (carats or 24th parts) for 4,000 *écus* in the form of the one per cent duty levied by the Marseilles authorities on goods entering the port. Though this did not prove very profitable, it reveals that he possessed a considerable surplus of capital, and was free from the need to borrow for the conduct of commerce. Later, Antoine became involved in the financing of maritime loans to ship-owners, and it seems to have become an important branch of his activity. In 1601 no less than 10,000 *livres* were invested, rising to a peak of 34,000 in 1605, then declining apart from 1610-12 until his death in 1616. In his later years Antoine was also investing heavily in land, purchasing the *seigneurie* of Cerriste in 1607, and making further additions in 1612 and 1613. Commerce seems to have been the exclusive activity of the Hermite for only a part of one generation. The aspiration to 'live nobly' was strong, and their use of a small inheritance in land for commerce, as a means of returning to the land as true gentlemen may not have been untypical. Their activity as *rentiers* and tax-farmers may, for all we can tell, have contributed more to their fortune than the profits of trade.

The Danse and the Motte of Beauvais

The Danse and the Motte of Beauvais operated in another region of provincial France, rising from obscurity to a position of some local distinction in the first half of the seventeenth century, against a background of generally more difficult commercial conditions.[15] Beauvais was a town of about 13,000 inhabitants in the mid-seventeenth century, the centre of an important cloth-weaving region; the production and sale of cloth occupied a large part of its population. Conveniently situated for both Paris and Rouen, it was also well placed between these markets and Flanders, which supplemented locally produced linen, the bleaching of which was carried on in the town. During the decade before France entered the Thirty Years War in 1635, the cloth industry of Beauvais prospered, and although the war cut off its contact with Flanders and Artois, linen which had previously been exported for weaving could be woven on the spot.

The Danse, of rural origins, had been established in Beauvais since the mid-sixteenth century, with a business as merchant-drapers, and became increasingly prosperous. The Motte came from much further afield, possibly from Lyons or Savoy and were certainly less deeply rooted in the Beauvais area. Lucien Motte was born in 1592 and died in 1645. An inventory of his estate in 1650 revealed a fortune of 175,000 *livres*, plus two houses. Of this total no less than 42,000 *livres* was in merchandise, 22,500 in credits due from sales, and 46,750 in *rentes* (interest-bearing bonds). The small proportion in real property, less than seven per cent of the total, was remarkably low for the time. Of the goods in stock the vast majority was linen cloth, much of it 'demi-Hollande', a superior quality worth up to three *livres* the *aune* (slightly less than a yard), three or more times as expensive as ordinary qualities. The credits due to him give some indication of the geographical spread of his trade in the last months of his life. Lyons came at the head of the list, followed by Paris and Rouen, whilst the towns nearest to Beauvais came last. This distribution was novel for the cloth merchants of Beauvais, and it is possible that the family's origins had influenced Lucien in breaking into new markets. The size of the individual consignments also suggests that the customers were merchants in large-scale business, and since Lyons was a principal centre for the export of French goods to Italy, it is likely that a proportion of his sales there found their way abroad. The total of credits due also suggests that the annual value of Motte's trade was approaching 100,000 *livres* a year, equivalent to several thousand pieces of cloth. It is the more remarkable that this was achieved in war time, in the midst of the Fronde and of an economic crisis. The relatively small amount of cash recorded in the inventory also suggests that most transactions were settled on paper, though none of these documents appears to have survived. The letter of exchange was a relatively unimportant instrument for Motte, as his trade was almost entirely within the French monetary area, and use was normally made of letters obligatory. Lucien Motte's singularity amongst his contemporaries in Beauvais or elsewhere lay in his apparent reluctance to invest his commercial profits in land or houses, yet he did invest considerable sums in private *rentes* (mortgages) to produce an annual income of over 2,000 *livres,* mostly from members of the lesser nobility of the region who needed to raise money, like La Dame de Meux, who used Motte's cash to purchase a commission in the army for her son.

Nicolas Danse was born in 1597 and died in 1661, and our knowledge of his affairs is improved by the survival of family papers, including both an inventory of his estate at the time of his death and a statement of the method of its partition among his heirs. He owned 26,000 *livres* worth of houses in Beauvais itself, and an equal amount in houses and lands in the countryside around, the total of real property being more than double the value of furniture, merchandise and trade credits. His position as a large real-property owner also helps to account for the large debts in *rentes*—26,000 *livres.* Although his net fortune was only about half that of Lucien Motte, Danse was in partnership with a nephew, and probably in semi-retirement when he died. There is evidence that his acquisitions of land were designed to ensure that each of his six surviving children was provided with a *domaine* in the country.

Both Danse and Motte were the founders of family businesses which saw their best days in the later seventeenth and eighteenth centuries, but were established in a period of general economic difficulty. They illustrate the way in which at a lower social level than that of the great international firms, merchants played their part as lenders of money to regional society.

The della Faille of Antwerp

The example of the della Faille of Antwerp helps to show how an individual enterprise came to terms with the rapidly changing conditions and the difficulties which beset the trade of the southern Netherlands during the war against the Dutch.[16] Despite their name, they were a family of native Netherlanders, originating in Courtrai, but settled in Antwerp. The founder of the firm was Jan the Elder, who served an apprenticeship in Venice in the firm of Martin de Hane. In 1539 he was sent back to Antwerp as Hane's factor, a position which he held until 1562. With Hane's permission he soon began trading independently. This double role helped him to achieve rapid rise to prosperity, and to become a competitor of Hane whilst still his servant. He traded in woollen cloth and silk between England, Antwerp and Italy. His younger brother Jacob, also a factor of Hane, acted as his London agent, and together they also traded with Seville, Lisbon and Narva, in grain, skins, cloth, sugar and cochineal. In 1569 their partnership was dissolved, but both continued to trade, Jan confining himself to the English and Italian markets. His experience until his death in 1582 reflects the difficulties which Antwerp was feeling, but he was flexible enough to establish an agency in Hamburg when the Hanseatic city became an important staple for English cloth on its way to Italy, so that the volume of his trade suffered little. Of his two sons, Jacob the Younger emigrated to Holland, where he played an important part with other exiles in its commercial development at the end of the century. Martin remained in Antwerp, associated three of his factors with his enterprise, but retained control by providing two-thirds of the capital. Until 1594 this consortium expanded its business, re-entering the Iberian trade and trading with Italy by sea as well as by land. The overland silk trade re-assumed considerable importance, with Naples providing an additional agency from 1585. The firm played a pioneering role in the sea trade with Italy which was expanding with the supply of Baltic grain to the Mediterranean. English lead, sardines and wool were exchanged for rice, tartar and olive-oil. The trade by sea was more risky than that overland, but proved especially profitable. Relations with Seville also increased in importance, and the younger Jacob's partnership was associated with Flemings settled there.

Jan and Jacob della Faille were amongst the dozen richest merchants of Antwerp. Characteristically, it was the second generation which began to concentrate more on the purchase of land and gradually withdrew from commerce, seizing the opportunity provided by the steep decline in the price of land during the crisis in the southern Netherlands.

Antwerp remained the headquarters of the firm throughout the most difficult period. The city ceased to be of much use for the purchase of goods, though it remained a quite important market for sales especially of silk (except during the 1580s), and its recovery after 1589 was an index of the brevity of the economic crisis in the south. The headquarters dealt with business all over the Netherlands. Its purchases of linen cloth were concentrated on Courtrai until 1577, and then moved north to Haarlem and Frisia, as Flemish weavers migrated to the north. Whilst the firm's most important agency in Italy was at Venice, Verona emerged as the most important centre for purchase of silk, where the market was dominated by the della Faille and a few other firms. They purchased silk at the time of the crop and arranged for it to be spun, taking a care which gave them a high reputation for quality. The extent of trade across the military frontier with the northern provinces of the Netherlands was a striking feature of the last years of the sixteenth century, and the della Faille established the last of their series of factories at Amsterdam in 1594, in recognition of the pre-eminence which it was gaining amongst the northern cities.

The special conditions created by the siege of Antwerp from 1584 to 1585 revealed the resilience of the firm's policy. After 1584 they transformed the organisation of their overland transport, ceasing to put it into the hands of a specialist firm, but organising it themselves. Although this involved a great expansion in administrative work in correspondence with transporters all along the route through Germany and north Italy, and the disbursement of money in small quantities in many places, the savings in cost seem to have been considerable, and goods were also transported direct from the place of purchase, avoiding Antwerp.

The unusual richness of the source material for the della Faille permits an attempt to calculate their profits. They varied from 7 to 13 per cent, probably about average for Antwerp firms of the time. There was a marked difference between the profit rate on overland and on seaborne trade. The former seems to have averaged about 16 per cent, whilst the latter fluctuated wildly between nothing and 200 per cent, with serious losses which brought the average down to about 12½ per cent. This is a striking testimony to the reliability, if not the cheapness, of overland transport in the sixteenth century, and shows that the lower cost of marine transport was counterbalanced by high risks not yet adequately covered by insurance. It is also possible to calculate the velocity of turn-over of the firm's capital, which seems to have increased somewhat in the early 1590s, coming down from an average cycle of two years to about one and a half. Though this decrease was proportionately signif-icant, it is clear that the turnover was still slow by modern standards, and as might be expected from the wide geographical range of their trade, intermediate between that of firms concentrating on trade between England and the Netherlands and those engaged in transatlantic or far eastern commerce. The della Faille also remained a firm in which trade in goods was dominant over financial operations—only in one year (1591-2) did they even engage in maritime insurance. Nevertheless, they were one of the firms employing advanced business techniques which were still not universal in late-sixteenth-century Antwerp.

The Tripp of Dordrecht

With the Tripp of Dordrecht we have an example of a family which, though not so pre-eminent in its time, had features in common with the Fugger a century before them, at least in their concentration on the trade in metals.[17] In the sixteenth century members of the family had been engaged in trade along the Rhine and Maas from their home town of Zaltbommel in Guelderland. They migrated to Dordrecht before 1600, some of them moving to Sweden and Amsterdam at a later date. They dealt in a diverse range of goods, but their importance increasingly lay in trade in arms, iron, copper and tar, in all of which their Swedish connections were a key. They even reached out to Amer-ica, and were members of the Dutch East India Company. Dordrecht was an important exchange market for goods coming down the Maas, especially from the important iron and armaments-producing area of Liège, which was expanding fast during the war between Spain and the Dutch, since it was enjoying the advantages of neutrality under the rule of its prince-bishop. Elias and Jacob Tripp began salt-refining soon after 1600 and Jacob and his heirs remained active in it until 1680. Elias Tripp alone controlled 15 per cent of Dordrecht's iron trade between 1592 and 1604, while other members of the family were important in it. He began trading with west Africa, probably exporting

iron, and from 1616 was able to do so without the need to associate
with other merchants. He obtained a monopoly of trade with a small
stretch of coast from the Dutch Estates General. In 1622 a 'cartel' was
set up by the big west Africa traders of Holland on their exemption for
a year from the monopoly of the West India Company. This was possible
only because their smaller competitors had been forced to cease trading
on the establishment of the Company. Elias Tripp still revealed a wide
diversity of trade at this time, being also active in the Russian grain
trade.

It was as arms dealers that most of the Tripps gained their reputation.
The Dutch relied mostly on outside supplies for their weapons and war
materials, but during the Twelve Years Truce with Spain (1609-21) a re-
export trade flourished. About 1600 Elias Tripp began importing can-
non-balls and saltpetre from Liège, France and Germany, and around
1612 seems to have held a virtual monopoly in the import of iron cannon from England. He started iron foundries in Westphalia and Waldeck,
where he also acquired iron mines. Though he triumphed over a rival
firm which had obtained a monopoly from the Estates General for the
import of Westphalian guns, the outbreak of the Thirty Years War inter-
fered with foundry production, and Tripp rapidly associated himself
with a former brother-in-law, Louis de Geer, who secured the monopoly
of gun-casting from the Swedish Crown in 1628. The Swedish guns were
of high quality and low price, and were assured of a ready market in
the Netherlands.

The Tripp were also among the leaders in the important trade in
Swedish copper, which became of increasing economic importance in
the early seventeenth century. The Dutch managed to wrest control
over Swedish copper exports from Lübeck and Hamburg, and built up
their own copper-manufacturing industry. Under the pressure of increased demand the price of copper had doubled between 1599 and 1610,
and the Swedish Crown exploited the situation by centralising control
of the mining industry, and increased its own war potential with the
quintupling of copper exports between 1600 and 1620. The Dutch
Estates General had seen to it that most of the copper passed through
the United Provinces as a part of the terms of repayment of a loan to
the Swedish Crown. During the difficult years between 1622 and 1627,
the Dutch seem to have temporarily lost their grip on this trade, but
soon recovered it, largely as a consequence of Pieter Tripp's success in
obtaining control of large stocks of copper deposited as security for a
loan to Gustavus Adolphus of Sweden, with authority to sell it to re-
deem his credit. In 1628 the Swedes raised the official price of copper

above that of the market, and at the same time drew more credit on their deposit with Pieter Tripp than he thought safe, so he refused further loans; and in the following year the Swedes were forced to grant Elias Tripp, who had taken over the copper on deposit, a mono- poly of Swedish copper exports. He was given authority to sell the cop- per below official prices. Tripp's possession of large stocks of copper enabled him to threaten Swedish government finances by selling enough of the copper to cause a further fall in the price. Tripp was playing a dangerous game, as he ran the risk of serious loss if the price should fall too far. All the time his competitors, among whom Louis de Geer was now to be numbered, were trying to achieve their own monopoly of the Swedish copper trade. In the end a monopoly proved beyond the reach of individuals, and in 1634 they joined together to form a com- pany in which Tripp's influence was very powerful. The struggle between the Swedish government and the merchants was in the end to be won by the Swedes. Tripp was never reimbursed for his loans to the Swedes, and his heirs had to be content with an unsatisfactory settlement offering land in Sweden, which was later confiscated from the family.

The temptation to achieve monopoly control over important raw materials such as metals was copied from time to time in commodities such as pepper. Such success as was enjoyed was usually short-lived, and the long-term experience of the Tripp, as of the Fugger before them, showed that the state, despite its many weaknesses, was usually too powerful an antagonist. Yet the profits of such monopolistic *coups* were the source of great short-term gains to the greatest among the mercantile community.

The Espinosa of Seville

The Espinosa were a numerous family, some of whose branches respond- ed to the great attractions of the brilliant trade of Seville.[18] They had come originally from a small village of Old Castile, Espinosa de los Mont- eros, but were settled from the fourteenth century as traders in the fair town of Medina de Rioseco. They rose to the ranks of the most prosper- ous and by the beginning of the sixteenth century were running an important banking concern, adding to their wealth by undertaking most of the local fiscal operations. They married into other wealthy families, including that of Columbus, proved their noble status in the *Chanciller- ías* of Valladolid and Granada, became Knights of the Military Orders, and occupied ecclesiastical posts. Some members of the family left for Seville early in the sixteenth century, some migrated to the Indies. They are interesting for the wide range of their activities as they branched out from a town which was to decline by the middle of the century. Juan de Espinosa (el Romo II) was born in Medina de Rioseco but moved to Valladolid, where he ran a company with an Italian partner, Antonio Buoninsegni, and on his own account had commercial relations with Flanders, where his sons Alonso and Pedro acted as agents. Alonso was born in 1501, but went to Seville very young, and worked in conjunction with his uncle Pedro de Espinosa, combining banking and commercial activities. In 1523 he went to Flanders, and in 1524 was a shareholder for 100 ducats in a company formed by the Fugger and the Welser to finance the expedition to the Moluccas. Between 1530 and 1532 he was in Bruges, still the centre of much Castilian trade with the Netherlands. Returning to Seville he founded a company for trade with the Indies with his cousin Juan de Espinosa de Carrión, providing some 5,000 ducats of capital, which was still locked up twenty years later. In 1546 he founded a much more successful partnership with his great-nephew Gaspar, to trade with the Indies under Gaspar's name, providing 6,000 ducats of capital. This firm's capital grew to no less than 69,000 ducats, and on his death around 1560 Alonso's fortune was reckoned at 400,000 ducats. His will contained the interesting proviso that if any of his gains from interest on money either in Castile or abroad should be declared illicit according to the usury laws, the debtors should be repaid from his estate.

The Rodrigues d'Evora of Lisbon

The Rodrigues d'Evora and d'Evora da Veiga were a confusingly named group of brothers who were the heirs of a considerable commercial fortune built up by a family of Spanish origins which migrated to Lisbon in the time of King Manuel I.[19] Around 1595 four brothers, Simão, Nicolau and Lopo Rodrigues, and Rodrigo Lopes, the two former in Antwerp and the two latter in Lisbon, controlled a firm, in which Simão dominated from Antwerp. The brothers also traded through other companies—the firm of Rodrigo Lopes and Lopo Rodrigues d'Evora, Rodrigo Lopes and Sons, and the sons also traded separately as Manuel da Veiga and Brothers. The connection with Antwerp was critical, as was the movement there of younger members of the family, whilst at least one (Manuel Rodrigues da Veiga) settled in Amsterdam. Francisco da Veiga, the second son of Lopo Rodrigues, also went to Antwerp. The Ximenes of Antwerp were also related to the Rodrigues d'Evora, and together they replaced the Fugger in taking the major share in the so-called 'second contract of pepper' in 1593. The family represented a movement which was in part a consequence of the increasing pressure being placed by the Spanish monarchy, in control of Portugal since 1580, on the community of Jewish (if nominally Christian) merchants in Lisbon. At least as important a factor in the movement was the increasing attraction of trade in the Netherlands at the turn of the century. As we have seen, the division of north and south had by no means prevented trade between Antwerp and the rebel provinces, and the settlement of Jewish merchants from Portugal in Amsterdam was later to be of great importance in the maintenance of the financial system of the Spanish monarchy after the withdrawal of the Genoese in 1627. Simão Rodrigues was already making efforts to avoid dependence on the Genoese for financial transactions with the royal court, at Madrid or in Brussels. His son-in-law Pedro da Veiga withdrew from Madrid and returned to Lisbon, and the firm ceased to have any dealings in Spain except for the export of sugar from Seville to Calais, Hamburg and other northern centres. At Brussels, Simão acted on his own, enjoying good relations with the Archduke Ernest. The Brussels government turned to him in 1606 when the Genoese were short of credit. As the Archduke Albert wrote to Philip III:

> The greater part of the money which the men of affairs provide for the provisions your Majesty orders to be made does not come essentially from Spain or from Italy, but from the merchants who are natives of these states who reside in Antwerp, and if they should leave there, it would not be possible to fulfil the *asientos* which are made from Spain.

The Rodrigues d'Evora were at the point of their social evolution when they either moved away from Lisbon or out of trade and finance altogether. Simão purchased the lordship of Rodes. The stigma of Judaism was more closely attached to trade in Portugal than anywhere in Europe, and in the Spanish Indies to be Portuguese was regarded as virtual proof of Jewish race. What better way or escape from this than ennoblement, and the life of the *rentier*? Few places offered a better opportunity of achieving this than the court of Madrid, and one can hardly be surprised at the final paradox of Rui Lopes da Veiga Peretti, who became a Knight of the Order of Christ and Madrid agent of the Portuguese Holy Office from 1626.

These examples of merchant families which have been studied in some detail must serve as the basis for generalisations which also rest on the work of historians who have studied particular trades and regions. There is little doubt that at almost every level above that of the smallest, strictly mercantile activity was mixed with financial operations, whether speculation on the exchanges, tax-farming, loans to local or central government, or to local landowners or peasants. The merchants of the sixteenth century were important accumulators of liquid capital, to whom society naturally turned for credit. The state pledged its future revenues for immediate expenditure, the peasant borrowed to improve his land or tide him over years of dearth, the landowner raised money on the security of his fixed capital assets to build a grander palace in which to give grander and more extravagant entertainments, to give his daughter, often marrying into a mercantile family, a suitable dowry, or to purchase office, civil or ecclesiastical, for himself or his sons.

It is often difficult from the surviving evidence to estimate the relative importance in the construction of a fortune between trade and other activities, but it might be on balance likely that these ancillary operations were in the long term more profitable. The least scrupulous were often the most notorious. The example of Lionel Cranfield reveals the worst side of the business world and its ambitions. A London cloth merchant in the German trade who burnt his fingers with unsaleably poor quality kersies, and mixed wet and dry pepper for sale even to King James I, he graduated via tax-farming, land deals and bribery to the Earldom of Middlesex, and a career as Lord Treasurer of England which saw an attempt to impose higher ethical standards and tight budgetary control on a court from whose corruption he had profited so much, but which finally engineered his downfall. The unscrupulousness of Cranfield contrasts strongly with the tender conscience of Alonso d'Espinosa, the charitable gifts of Simón Ruiz or Jacob Fugger, or the anxieties of the Spanish merchants in Antwerp who wrote to the Doctors of the Sorbonne for guidance on the interpretation of the Church's doctrine of usury. To conclude from such a contrast that the ethics of the Catholic merchant differed from those of the Protestant is no longer tenable. It is dangerous to assert that during the course of the period that conscience weighed ever more lightly on the merchant capitalist. The variety of individual temperament counted for more even than that of local *mores* in determining the limits of professional conduct. In most areas, the Catholic Church evolved a *modus vivendi* with the world of commerce, as least as well as did the Calvinist divines. The world of commerce and finance went to considerable lengths to design its credit instruments to satisfy, rather than to evade, the scruples of the Church, which slowly diminished in face of the spread of medieval

Italian business techniques throughout western Europe.

The spread of these techniques followed from the presence of Italian colonies in the cities of the north, and the education of northern apprentices in such centres as Venice, yet it is unwise to assume that even by 1600 all merchants struck an annual balance-sheet. The prevalence of confused situations on the death of a merchant is attested by many inventories of possessions, and late into the seventeenth century there were some who seemed to manage their affairs by methods which would have seemed conservative in the most advanced areas of north Italy in the fourteenth century. It has even been argued that some English merchants of the seventeenth century traded by force of habit, at levels of profitability which rarely exceeded 5 per cent, and ignored more attractive investments.[20] We must not be so dazzled by the examples of the great innovators and merchant-princes who manipulated the credit transactions of the international fairs that we forget the immeasurable number of small merchants who continued, even in international trade, to rely mainly on barter, or semi-barter, as the basis of their commerce.

It is perhaps in the intermediate ranges that the period saw the greatest changes. It has recently been argued, on the basis of a study of south Netherlands merchants, that the spread of associations of groups of men of moderate means was the most potentially creative change in the later sixteenth century. Based on the partnership, often of relatively short life, these associations paved the way for the introduction of the joint-stock principle, but also proved adequate in themselves for the conduct of long-distance international trade. Combined with the spread of the system of commission agents, they enabled the merchants to save the expense of employing permanent factors abroad, and the inconvenience of travelling themselves. This system enabled relatively young men with a very small capital to begin trade on their own account after a period in which they traded on behalf of others for commission. The Van der Molen had carried on a substantial commission business in Antwerp as early as 1540, but the latter part of the century saw a great expansion of their number. The expansion of the number of lesser firms in the world of international trade was probably responsible for the intense competition which developed; it lies behind the complaints against inexperienced men who ruined markets, and behind the attempts of the well-established to exclude the newcomers by tightening the monopoly of the English chartered companies. The consequent instability of price structure was more important to the individual than the long-term rising trend of prices, for it was the natural desire of every merchant to

buy more favourably and sell more dearly than his competitors. The
proliferation of deals in which the intention of the parties was to cheat
each other became notorious. To sell for cash but to buy on credit was
also the ambition of the merchant of limited means, but equally he ran
the risk of being forced to sell at a loss in an unfavourable market because he could not afford to wait for better times. It was noticeable
that the greater Netherlands firms increasingly avoided those sectors
of the market which were filled by the lesser merchants, preferring the
safer competition of their equals, who though they fought hard, generally fought by the same rules of relatively low profit margins and high
turnover.[21]

In such a world, it is not surprising that the casualties were heavy.
Names which remain little more than names scattered through customs
records or notarial files disappear without trace after a few years. For
the few who rose to eminence and perhaps withdrew from trade to
join the ranks of the landed gentry or nobility, there were many who
sank with hardly a trace into the ranks of the artisans from which they
had emerged.

It is fashionable to write of the decline of the 'bourgeoisie' at the
end of the sixteenth century, even of a kind of 'self-betrayal', in which
the lessening autonomy of the great cities, faltering or declining trade
intensified the permanent social inferiority complex of the merchants,
who sought greater financial security and greater social prestige in the
purchase of land.[22] This view is applicable, with many reservations, to
most of the Mediterranean area. In Spain the social pressures were
perhaps at their greatest, and yet the economic factors were also more
powerful. The increasing burden of taxation, especially after 1575,
was not only directly harmful to trade, but intensified the attractions
of an escape into the ranks of the fiscally exempt *hidalgo* class, which
multiplied even more rapidly in the seventeenth century. In Italy there
is evidence that many individuals were investing in agriculture rather
than trade, though in the case of Venice the attractions of industrial
development in the *terraferma* of the Po valley offered an alternative
home for capital. The generalisation is certainly much less valid when
we consider the Netherlands or England, but the tendency for the
wealthier merchant to invest in land, and eventually to retire from trade,
was a permanent feature of all European societies in the sixteenth and
even the seventeenth centuries. The exceptional talents and good fortune equally necessary to the building up of a mercantile fortune rarely
continued for more than two consecutive generations, any more than
outstanding military or political talents normally appeared in successive

generations of land-owning families. Given also that land, as almost always, offered great security of capital, that its value at least kept pace with rising prices, that these qualities made it a sound basis for the grant of credit, and that its marketability was in most places increasing, it is no surprise that it formed an attractive and rational investment to a class which had the advantage of adequate liquid capital. The merchants, along with the lawyers, played an important part in the development of a more mobile market in land, especially around the greater towns.

A recent study of the substantial London merchants who made up the ranks of the Aldermen of the City in the early seventeenth century suggests, however, that the desire to retire to newly purchased rural estates, or to return to those of their ancestors, was less strong than has often been supposed.[23] Not much more than ten per cent of a sample of 140 withdrew from London, even though they purchased country estates as an investment, and those who did were not usually amongst the richest. Nor were the great majority of them the sons of gentry. Of those who were, most were from families which were hardly above the status of yeomen. This impression of a mercantile class which retained a considerable stability could be applied equally to the seventeenth-century Netherlands, where the availability of land was more restricted, and where the state was more rapidly adopting the ethos of the merchant patricians. In the north, at least, it is possible that social conservatism and force of habit operated to preserve merchant enterprises whose return on capital was low, and less than that to be obtained from safer investments.

Notes

1. Schick, op.cit., pp. 10-13. On the Fugger see also G.F. von Pölnitz, *Anton Fugger,* and Ehrenberg, op.cit.
2. Schick, op.cit., p. 33.
3. Ibid., pp. 63-7.
4. 25,559 marks of silver went to Venice, compared with 28,475 marks to Frankfurt and Antwerp. Van der Wee, *Growth,* II, p. 125.
5. Ibid., II, p. 126.
6. Ibid., III, Graph 27.
7. Schick, op.cit., map on pp. 238-9.
8. Ibid., pp. 246-7. Ehrenberg's figures for the 1527 balance-sheet differ slightly from those given by Schick, but the discrepancy is largely accounted for by Ehrenberg's inclusion of 430,000 florins in the assets for the private accounts of the partners for money taken from them after 1511. (Ehrenberg, op.cit., p. 85.)
9. Ehrenberg, op.cit., pp. 86-132.

10. H. Lapeyre, *Les Ruiz*, pp. 47-50.
11. Ibid., pp. 66-7.
12. Ibid., pp. 68-9. See also Lapeyre, *Simón Ruiz et les asientos de Philippe II*, *passim*.
13. Lapeyre, *Les Ruiz*, p. 82.
14. M. Baulant, *Lettres de négociants marseillais: les frères Hermite, 1570-1612*.
15. P. Goubert, *Les Danse et les Motte de Beauvais*, and *Beauvais et le Beauvaisis*.
16. W. Brulez, *De Firma della Faille en de internationale handel van flaamse firma's in de 16ᵉ eeuw*. There is a summary in French.
17. P.W. Klein, *De Trippen in de 17 eeuw*. There is a summary in English.
18. G. Lohmann Villena, *Les Espinosa—Une famille d'hommes d'affaires en Espagne et aux Indes à l'époque de la colonisation*.
19. J. Gentil da Silva, *Stratégie des affaires à Lisbonne entre 1595 et 1607— Lettres marchandes des Rodrigues d'Evora et Veiga*.
20. R.B. Grassby, 'The Rate of Profit in seventeenth century England', *English Historical Review*, LXXXIV (1969), pp. 236-60.
21. Brulez, *della Faille*.
22. Braudel, *La Méditerranée*, I, pp. 69-72, who writes of 'la trahison de la bourgeoisie'.
23. R.G. Lang, 'Social Origins and Social Aspirations of Jacobean London Merchants', *EcHR*, 2nd Ser., XXVII (1974), pp. 28-47.

6 THE FOOD SUPPLY

Grain

For the mass of the European population in early modern as in medieval times the supply of food was almost synonymous with the supply of bread. In times of prosperity the consumption of meat would rise, because the cost of bread was low, and there was consequently a surplus of income to be spent on other items, the consumption of which was therefore also determined by the supply of grain. Among the food grains also, the consumption of the most expensive—wheat—fluctuated according to its price in relation to that of the cheaper—rye. In times of scarcity demand for wheat dropped first, and that for rye was maintained until it too became so dear that the income of the poor was inadequate to provide the means of subsistence. At this point malnutrition weakened the resistance of the population to diseases, of which bubonic plague was only the most feared of several. Always lurking in the corners of Europe, such diseases from time to time struck on a massive scale, decimating the population and hitting especially hard the very young and the aged. The depleted population was able to feed itself and could, in certain circumstances, replenish its numbers with surprising rapidity, the birth rate rising even above the normally high levels, assisted by remarriage among the surviving adults, the death rate from plague being usually lowest amongst those of the most fertile age groups.

Such a crisis could affect the rural as well as the urban population over quite a wide area, and the mass of the European population was still rural. The peasantry, theoretically best protected as producers, could find themselves unable to produce enough for their own consumption, after meeting the heavy payments in kind or cash for rents, taxes, tithes and debts, and after retaining an essential proportion of the harvest for the following year's sowing—as much as 25 per cent in unfertile areas. The proportion of the grain crop which found its way to a market, even a local one, was small, if the proportion taken by the landlord, the state and the church is excepted, and in many cases even this was consumed directly by the enormous households of the rich. Consequently even a small fluctuation in total yield could mean a drastic fall in the supply of grain for the markets from which the larger towns and cities were fed. It is this proportion of the crop which formed the object of the large-scale trade in grain, which was therefore subject to most violent regional fluctuations in demand and even more in price.

Bulky in relation to its value, grain was exceedingly costly to transport over long distances, especially by land, and the object of all city governments was to assure an adequate supply from as close at hand as possible. The ports were naturally at a considerable advantage, and it is no accident that most of the major cities of Europe in the early modern period were close to the sea or on a major inland waterway. Madrid in the late sixteenth and seventeenth centuries was an almost unique exception, and the study of its food supply, when undertaken, will almost certainly shake the conventionally accepted generalisations about the state of Castilian agriculture. Genoa was more typical, and until the capture of Constantinople by the Turks in 1453 finally cut it off from its colonies in the Crimea, it had obtained a large part of its grain supplies from the Ukraine. Paris, at the centre of the Seine basin and not too distant from the Loire, could look to the rich grain producing regions of the Ile de France, especially to Beauce.[1] Burgos, Valladolid and the fair towns of Medina de Campo and Medina de Rioseco were close to the wheat-growing areas of the Castilian *meseta*, especially of the Tierra de Campos.

The grain trade of Venice has been well studied, especially for the second half of the sixteenth century, when the problems of the whole Mediterranean zone from Castile in the west to the Turkish empire in the east were becoming more serious and more chronic.[2] Increasing urbanisation had increased demand in relation to a production which had been held down by a general failure to improve techniques of cultivation. The extension of the cultivated area provided the only means of increasing output, such expansion being restricted both by the availability of manpower and capital and by the limited supply of fertile land. It may also be that the whole area suffered a slow climatic change which reduced rainfall in latitudes where it was already barely adequate. Venice had grown from around 100,000 persons at the beginning of the sixteenth century to about 170,000 by 1570 and despite severe plagues, which reduced it to some 130,000 between 1575 and 1577, it recovered rapidly to its peak until the renewed plagues of 1630-2. It was thus the third largest city in the Mediterranean area, surpassed only by Naples and Constantinople, which seems far to have outclassed the cities of the west. The mainland territories under the control of Venice, the *terraferma*, extended westwards beyond Verona to Brescia, north-eastwards to Udine, and eastwards to the Istrian peninsula, but contained urban centres which absorbed a great deal of local grain production. Venice was therefore one of the largest purchasers of grain in the south of

Europe. The fleets of galleys which defended its scattered trading bases along the Dalmatian coast, in Greece and its islands, and (until 1570) Crete, alone consumed as much grain as did the trading city of Ragusa for its 10,000 to 15,000 inhabitants, whilst the fleets of the Turks and the Holy Alliance which faced each other at Lepanto in 1571 could have consumed 45,000 *quintals* or over 20,000 tons of grain in the form of biscuit during the course of a year. The maintenance of its fortresses and the feeding of the populations of its trading posts absorbed more than could be produced locally. Defence and war, for both Christians and the Turks, involved great additional demands for grain in a market where war restricted the supply.

The needs of the city itself were paramount in determining the policy of the Venetian government towards the grain supply. Its population lived on wheaten bread rather than the barley or even millet which had to suffice for the peasants of the *terraferma,* which together with Piedmont, Lombardy and the Emilia formed its nearest source of supply, to the limits of the zone within which the costs of land or river transport were tolerable. Even in good years, and in the earlier part of the century, Venice's needs could not easily be supplied from these areas alone, not even with the addition of supplies brought by sea from Apulia and Sicily. These, although under Spanish control, provided additional supplies to Venice by contraband trade via the abbey of the Tremiti islands, which exploited a licence to supply its own needs to divert a surplus to Venice. Normally, therefore, Venice was forced to look further afield, to the Turkish empire, in which she normally enjoyed advantages over other Christian states because of her traditional trading privileges. Her dependence on the Ottomans for grain together with her dependence on the Levant spice trade provides an explanation of her usually peaceful relations with them. Turkey was also forced to apply strict control over the export of grain to protect the interests of Constantinople, but in practice the enforcement of the regulations was impossible, especially when, in the second half of the century, the trade fell into the hands of members of the Sultan's family, or of local officials who saw in the Venetians an excellent market for the surpluses of their own great estates.

As the century wore on, Venice was also forced to turn to Bavaria and the Austrian duchies, especially in times of dearth when the price rose to levels which justified the great cost of overland transport. This occurred for the first time as early as 1539-40, when England and Flanders as well as Provence, Languedoc, the Lyonnais and Burgundy were brought within the catchment area. Towards the end of the century the crisis in the supplies from the eastern Mediterranean reached such proportions that new solutions had to be found. In 1590 the grain harvest in Italy was universally disastrous. Supplies from the *terraferma* to Venice dropped to little more than half the normal, the export of Sicilian grain being completely prohibited in the face of local famine and the fear that little would be sown for the next harvest. High prices persisted until 1594, and a new dearth came in 1596 and 1600. In 1590 vessels carrying Baltic grain reached Leghorn[3] and Venice rapidly copied the example of the Duke of Tuscany. In September 1590 an agent was sent to Danzig, with the initial intention of ordering grain for transport overland, but the price advantages of the long sea route were soon revealed, and slowly Baltic grain began to reach Venice, with a fleet of over 30 Dutch and English ships arriving in 1594. Though Venice was more reluctant to resort to Baltic grain than were Tuscany or Genoa, during bad years in the early seventeenth century she imported up to 270,000 *staia* or over 200,000 hectolitres.

Other Italian cities were sometimes better placed than Venice. Genoa, because of its privileged relations with Spain, was allowed access to Sicilian grain, imported in quantities which averaged 6,000 or 7,000 tons a year in the 1570s.[4] Rome was a special case because it was not only a wealthy metropolis, but its population could rise greatly above the normal, both seasonally and from year to year, by the influx of pilgrims. Normally it had good resources both in the Papal States and in Sicily, but the cost of grain from the remoter areas of the March of Ancona for example, reveals the high cost of land transport. In 1555-6 the cost of grain from this region was over 80 per cent higher after the payment of administrative and transport costs than it was at the point of purchase, whilst that obtained from Sicily in 1549 only cost just over 60 per cent in such charges.

Further west, the Iberian peninsula entered a period of increasing difficulty in the supply of grain. There had been a foretaste of what was to come as early as 1506 to 1508 in Castile. Whilst it is incorrect to conclude that the favourable treatment of the interests of the migratory sheep flocks of the *Mesta* was the cause of the 'ruin' of Castilian agriculture from the end of the fifteenth century, there were certainly areas where its privileges discouraged the extension of arable farming.[5] The bad harvests of 1506-7 were the result of a temporary combination of climatic conditions. It was relatively easy to obtain additional supplies from Sicily, but the long-term effects of the crisis were the result of the government's attempt to control prices in the interests of the urban poor, which discouraged production, especially as the excessive quantities imported caused a collapse in prices. Gradually as the century proceded, such crises became more frequent, and increasing reliance had to be placed on imports from Sicily and north Africa.

Portugal was even more dependent upon imported grain, especially for the feeding of Lisbon. Expectations from the Atlantic islands proved optimistic, as the supply from the Azores was largely consumed by the Portuguese garrisons in Morocco, and especially as the islands were increasingly concentrating on the production of the vine and the olive. Lisbon had recourse to foreign grain quite early in the century, at first that of Castile and Andalucía, then that of Sicily. The Portuguese commercial interests in the Netherlands led them rapidly to seek grain in Antwerp, of which there is evidence as early as 1509. Small Breton vessels were normally used in large numbers for transport.[6] Brittany itself normally had a surplus of grain and it can be seen from the correspondence of Simón Ruiz of Medina del Campo that Spanish and Portuguese finance was heavily committed to the trade.[7] Annual and seasonal fluctuations in the price made it a risky enterprise, and Ruiz lost more than he made by his ventures, a profit of nearly a million *maravedís* in 1572 contrasting with a loss of over 1½ million in 1582. The loss was the consequence of the arrival in Lisbon of no less than 250 vessels in February 1582, causing a fall in the price of grain from 170 to 120 *reis* in a few days, followed by a new rise to 290 *reis*. Ruiz's losses would seem to have been turned to great profit by the Lisbon speculators. That grain could flow in almost any direction is shown by occasional exports from northern Spain to France though the normal direction was the reverse, even the Cantabrian ports finding it cheaper to import French grain than to transport it from Castile overland. A grain shortage in Seville, growing more serious as the city expanded in size, was matched by surpluses in other parts of Andalucía. Those responsible for victualling the fleet of galleys based on Málaga usually found little difficulty in obtaining supplies at a price a little above the current market level, usually lower than in Catalonia, and only slightly above Sicilian levels. As late as the 1550s the Fugger were granted licences to export grain from Andalucía and from the lands of the Order of Calatrava, up to 36,000 *fanegas* or over 1,500 tons, about half of which was for Barcelona.[8] The 1560s saw a change, however, and the Crown of Castile was forced to buy 100,000 *fanegas* a year from the north, largely for the provisioning of the fleets. Later in the century, despite war with the Dutch and the English, embargoes on the trade of enemy vessels with Lisbon and Seville were frequently lifted for the import of grain from the Baltic.

As early as the 1560s Dutch ships were carrying at least two-thirds of the 60,000 lasts (approximately 120,000 tons) of corn which annually left the Baltic through the Sound. Though the quantities fell to a minimum of 20,000 lasts in 1580, they recovered again in the 1590s to an average of 60,000 lasts a year, and after somewhat lower levels in the early years of the seventeenth century, rose to a peak of over 100,000 lasts in 1608, of which the Dutch share was as high as 80,000 lasts. The overall peak of the trade came in 1618, with the Dutch carrying 100,000 lasts out of about 130,000. The opening of the Thirty Years War, followed by the renewal of direct war between Spain and the Dutch in 1621, and the later activities of Gustavus Adolphus of Sweden caused a violent disturbance both in Baltic sources of supply and in the western and southern European markets. This was most clearly reflected in a catastrophic fall in the trade in grain through the Sound to the almost negligible figure of 12,500 lasts in 1630, of which the Dutch carried some 9,000.[9] Of the Baltic ports, Danzig was undoubtedly the most important centre, controlling between a half and two-thirds of the total before 1590, remaining at around a half until 1620, then dropping to a third, and to almost nothing in 1627-9 when it was besieged by Swedish forces. It was followed in importance by Koenigsberg, with around 25 per cent of the trade between the end of the sixteenth century and the 1620s, when its share of the declining trade rose towards 50 per cent. Riga, furthest to the east, provided a steady 10 per cent of the trade. Together the three ports gave the Dutch merchants access not only to Polish but also Lithuanian and Russian grain.

It is much more difficult to measure the quantities of Baltic grain which reached southern Europe. The Netherlands themselves consumed considerable quantities. The Sound Toll Registers do not give the ultimate destinations of ships before 1618, nor is it possible to deduce from the quantities of salt passing into the Baltic any definite quantity of grain coming out of it for Spain and Portugal or the Mediterranean. The accounts of the Van Adrichem describe in detail 65 voyages between 1569 and 1597. On approximately two-thirds of these the vessel left Danzig carrying corn in far greater quantity than other goods, and almost exactly the same proportion sailed south, though mostly not on through voyages. Of those which sailed to the south, the majority went to Spain or Portugal, nearly half of them to Lisbon or Setúbal, the most important Portuguese centre of the salt trade.[10] It is also clear from the Van Adrichem records that many ships left the Netherlands in ballast, not only for the Baltic, but also for the south. We can only conclude in general terms therefore that a high proportion of the grain brought from the Baltic went to the Iberian peninsula and the Mediterranean. The war of independence did not cut off Dutch trade with Spain and Portugal, but it provided an opportunity for neutrals, especially from Hamburg, to penetrate the Iberian market.

Geneva provides an example of an inland city whose corn supply was increasingly dependent on long-distance transport. Its political history intensified its food problem. Struggling at the end of the fifteenth century for independence from its Bishop and the Duchy of Savoy and increasingly isolated from the Swiss Federation, its later position as the focal point of Calvinism surrounded it with enemies.[11] The inadequacy of the territory under its control put it in a similar position to the city states of north Italy, and its problems were further aggravated by the influx of merchants during the period of its fairs. During the fifteenth and early sixteenth centuries the city government allowed the grain trade to operate freely, only regulating its sale in the town. After the establishment of the Reformation, the new government intervened much more directly to prevent a recurrence of the crisis in supplies accompanying the political troubles of the 1530s, which had provoked a blockade of the city by Savoy. The government was now a producer of grain from the secularised lands of the Church, though of course production was inadequate for needs. The shortage forced Geneva to a political *rapprochement* with the Swiss Cantons, whose own production was adequate for their needs, and provides an example of an exceptionally well-organised and stable market. Geneva was forced to look even further afield, to Germany and France, using a few of its most important merchants who emerged as a new generation of capitalist entrepreneurs virtually monopolising the corn trade.[12]

Salt

Salt was as important indirectly to the food supply as was grain directly. It was essential not only for the flavouring but also the preservation of food, especially fish and meat, and in the more favoured areas and classes of society the heavy salting of butter. In the sixteenth century it was also increasingly used as a basic chemical in industrial processes. Its importance to every family provided a temptation to royal treasuries to impose taxes upon it which in the extreme example of the French *gabelle* became in some regions a heavy burden and a grievance for the poor.

As an object of international trade, salt for the curing of fish was paramount, since the quantity of fish consumed was very high in relation to that of meat, both for economic and religious reasons. In northern Europe the fishing industry was dominated by the herring, but during the course of the period cod was to become of increasing importance, as the English, Portuguese, French and Dutch developed deep-sea fishing in the Atlantic, especially off the Newfoundland coast. Herring demanded large seasonal supplies of salt, because the seasonal nature of the fishing, following the migrating shoals, made its rapid salting essential to its preservation in good quality.

The major centres of salt production were concentrated therefore as close as possible to the largest fishing ports. Around Lüneberg in north Germany, salt was produced from local brine-springs, and in the fourteenth century had been exported as far afield as Stockholm and Riga, its manufacture coming to be dominated by the merchants of Lübeck, who exported it to Scandinavia.[13] The expansion of the Dutch herring fisheries was supported by the production of salt from the impregnated peat of the sea marshes, which enjoyed as high a reputation for quality as the salt of Lüneberg. It was expensive to produce, however, and only its reputation for purity saved it until the sixteenth century from the competition of the salt produced by natural evaporation in the warmer climates of southern Europe.[14] In England salt was produced by both methods—from brine-springs in Worcestershire and Cheshire, and by boiling sea water or peat-ash near the Lincolnshire and East Anglian coasts, where Yarmouth was already a great centre of the herring fisheries.

Long before the beginning of the sixteenth century, the sources of salt around the Baltic and the North Seas were proving inadequate to the demands of the expanding fishing industry. In the Netherlands the supply of peat was inadequate, and in England the drift of East-Anglian labour into more lucrative employment in cloth-weaving made the production of salt more expensive and eventually reduced its volume. A combination of falling production and increasing demand forced northern Europe to turn to more distant sources and to forge a further link between its economy and that of the south-west.

The nearest major area of salt production in a climatic zone which permitted large-scale cheap production was the Atlantic coast of France, from south Brittany to the Basque coast. The most important areas were the Bay of Bourgneuf, south of the Loire estuary, the area round La Rochelle, on the Dordogne and near Bayonne. The export of salt from the more southerly areas probably began as an ancillary to the important wine trade with England, the Netherlands and north Germany. There is evidence that some salt was reaching England from as far south as Lisbon and Setúbal in the mid-fourteenth century, and during the Hundred Years War Spanish and Portuguese sources benefited from the

disruption of the French economy. The region around the Bay of Bourgneuf suffered least, however, and had the advantage of being nearest to
the main centres of consumption and of political immunities deriving
from its position as a 'marchland' between the lands of the crown of
France and Brittany.[15] In the fifteenth century as many as 100 or more
vessels sailed annually to Bourgneuf in the spring, returning to the
north in time for the main herring season beginning in Skania in late
July and continuing in the Netherlands and England until the autumn.
At first the trade was dominated by Hanseatic ships, but the Dutch
began to join increasingly in it, together with the English and the Bretons. The salt trade attracted other goods: English cloth and Breton
canvas were exported, and wines from the Loire and further south were
shipped in the returning fleets. The major part of the salt cargo found
its way to the markets of Bruges, Dordrecht, Middelburg, Antwerp and
Brill, and the re-exportable surplus was sent on by river to the interior
of Germany. By the late fifteenth century the east Baltic ports such as
Danzig and Riga were becoming major markets from which Bay salt
was distributed even further afield to Finland and Russia. In 1478 Danzig received over 70 ships laden with salt.[16]

The steady expansion of demand for salt in the sixteenth century
was a consequence of the rise in population. The ending of the Hundred
Years War opened up more French sources of supply, and those of the
Iberian peninsula increasingly came into play. By the middle of the century Middelburg was receiving salt from Brouage, south of La Rochelle,
from Lisbon, Setúbal and San Lúcar at the mouth of the Quadalquivir.[17]
Later in the century about 15 per cent of the Dutch ships entering the
Baltic carried a cargo of salt, nearly all of it from France or the Iberian
peninsula, though most of it was trans-shipped in the Netherlands where
it was refined to bring it up to the standards of the Dutch peat-salt or
'white salt'.

The north European salt trade bore the marks of a traditional commerce which expanded during the sixteenth century without undergoing much change of structure or direction. It was the natural complement of the Dutch trade in corn, using the same ships, and the same
routes. The growing dependence of the Dutch on Iberian salt both for
their home consumption and the carrying trade led to serious difficulties
when their ships were forbidden the use of Spanish and Portuguese ports.
Only the greater dependence of the southerners on Baltic grain saved
the Dutch from economic disaster, and in the 1590s, during a period
of embargo, they successfully carried out a daring attempt to set up
salt-pans on the shores of the Caribbean.

The ease with which salt could be produced on the coasts of southern Europe meant that it was normally available from local sources throughout the Mediterranean, but some specialisation developed. The islands, especially Ibiza, Sicily, Cyprus and Chios exported their surplus production.[18] Venice attempted to gain control of the salt trade of the Adriatic by channelling it through herself, and subjected Balkan pastoral farmers to her economic control by paying them in salt for their produce. Braudel considers that such control had been an important element in the origins of the economic ascendancy of Venice. By the late sixteenth century, despite the productive capacity of her own lagoon, Venice was drawing salt from Trapani in Sicily, and from Corfu and Cyprus, notwithstanding the capture of the latter by the Turks in 1570. Salt provided a convenient return cargo for Venetian ships on their way home from Syria. Venice's control over the salt trade, largely in the hands of contractors to whom it was farmed by the state, enabled it to enjoy the benefits of prices much lower than those prevailing in the *terraferma*. The profits of the contractors were enormous, the cost of the raw material accounting for a mere 12 per cent, and transport and handling charges only 7 per cent, of the market price, whilst the state's revenue benefited in a similar way.[19]

The demand for salt was further stimulated by the growth of the cod fisheries. Soon after the discovery of Newfoundland at the end of the fifteenth century, the off-shore banks became the hunting-ground of Portuguese, English and French fishermen. The English were slower off the mark than their rivals, perhaps because the proximity of Iceland offered a satisfactory alternative. The French were well-placed, and had access to native supplies of salt. As early as 1504, certainly by 1508-9, Norman and Breton boats headed for the new fishing grounds, and were rapidly joined by those from La Rochelle, Bayonne and St Jean de Luz, with the Spanish Basques joining in by the middle of the century. The Spanish and Portuguese benefited greatly from the fisheries, but rapidly lost ground to the English after the failure of the Armada in 1588 led to a reduction in manpower. Before 1604 brought the restoration of peace with Spain, the English cod fleet, based mainly on the western ports, numbered over 100 vessels in most years, with 50 sailing from Plymouth alone in 1595. Fish landed in England were exported to France, and thence to Spain. After the peace of 1604 the direct trade with Spain and Portugal was opened up. Many ships carried on a triangular trade, crossing the Atlantic to the Newfoundland fishing grounds, returning via Portugal or Spain with their catch, then taking on cargoes of salt, oil, fruit, sugar, raisins and wine for import into England. The deficiency of salt in England thus hindered the growth of the market very little. Much of the cod was carried 'green' to Portugal where it was dried, and some of it was salted and lightly dried on the shores of Newfoundland itself. The Iberian and Mediterranean market for dried cod was an important element in the growing multilateral character of both French and English overseas trade. As with the Dutch, the English balance of trade was improved by a trade which was increasingly carried on without touching the home ports.[20]

Pepper and Spices

The trade in pepper and spices during the sixteenth century was a case of revolution, counter-revolution and a second revolution, deeply affecting the major directions of their distribution in Europe, though deriving from ultimate sources of supply which changed but little. Until the very beginning of the century the trade had suffered little fundamental change since Roman times. The Crusaders, accompanied and followed by merchants, had revived the spice trade through the eastern Mediterranean, and Venice had become the supreme distributor of spices in Europe. Her grip on the market was shaken by the Portuguese discovery and exploitation of the Cape route to India and the spice islands of the Far East, and by the use of Antwerp as a major centre of distribution. From the middle of the century there was a considerable recovery in the pepper trade of the traditional Mediterranean route, until almost a hundred years after Vasco da Gama reached India, first the Dutch and then the English established bases in the spice islands which not only swung the trade back in favour of northern Europe at the expense of Venice, but also spelt the final ruin of the Portuguese trade. Within a few years the Dutch and the English were successfully re-exporting oriental goods to the Mediterranean, almost to the doorstep of the Venetian trade in the Levant.

It must be emphasised at the outset that the Portuguese initiative was not a reaction to any serious crisis in the Levant spice trade caused by the occupation by the Ottoman Turks of the spice markets of Syria and Egypt.[21] Neither Beirut nor Alexandria fell under Turkish control until more than a decade after the dramatic opening of the Portuguese trade, and after the occupation, the Venetians, Genoese and even the Catalans were still able to carry on trade. From the 1480s, the Portuguese exploration of the west coast of Africa had as its objective the rounding of Africa and the establishment of a sea link with India, and it is possible that a desire to rival the Levant spice trade played a part in it, although no direct evidence has been discovered to prove it,

the sources mentioning only access to gold and slaves as the motives.[22]
As early as 1454 efforts were made to persuade some Venetian galleys
which took shelter near Cape St Vincent to join in an expedition to
new lands in search of spices, but it is probable that the proposed des-
tination was no further than Africa, as the Portuguese had already found
'malagueta' pepper near the Gambia river, where it had long been used
as a condiment and a medicine. By 1470 malagueta pepper was being
imported into Lisbon by Fernão Gomes, who secured a monopoly from
the Crown. In the 1480s there followed the strong pepper of Guinea,
some of which found its way from Lisbon to Flanders, England and
Lyons before the end of the fifteenth century. The quantities involved were already significant on a European scale, and exceeded those
of any oriental spice other than pepper itself being imported by the Portuguese after 1500.[23]

The Portuguese initiative, which saw the first arrivals of pepper and
spices from India in Lisbon in 1499, intensified a crisis which already
existed in the trade of the Levant. It was a crisis originating not in Turkish agression, but in the internal politics of Egypt which were to create
the circumstances in which Turkish occupation became possible. It followed the death of the Egyptian Sultan in 1496, inaugurating a period
of political troubles which shook Egypt until it was incapable of resistance to the Turkish invasion of 1516, but which also shook Venetian
commerce. Bankruptcies in Italy became more frequent from about the
same date. A Venetian war with Turkey intensified the crisis, leading
to a great increase in the public debt in Venice, which was attracting
the banks as an alternative investment to the support of commerce.
Venetian commerce was suffering doubly because of a shortage of gold
and silver essential to the Levant as the German merchants of the *Fondaco dei Tedeschi* reduced their purchases of spices. This in turn was
due to a steep rise in their price during the war conditions. The quantity
of spices shipped from Beirut and Alexandria began to decline in 1497
and was reduced to nothing in 1499 and 1500. The price of pepper on
the Venetian market rose from an average of 42-49 ducats the quintal
in 1496 and 1497 to 70-80 in 1499 and 90-130 in 1500, remaining
at 80 ducats or over until 1503. The news of the arrival of the first Portuguese cargoes at the equivalent of 20 ducats a quintal in Lisbon came
at a moment when Venetian prices were at abnormally high 'famine'
levels. The Portuguese competition thus began with a huge short-term
advantage which the Venetians, without adequate stocks to face a price
war, could do nothing to mitigate. Consequently Venice was faced with
a long-term crisis on top of a short-term one.

It was only in 1499 that the Venetians learned that the Portuguese had reached Calicut, and even then a rumour was spread that their ships were not fit for the return voyage, and they would be forced to use the overland route through the Levant. In fact the first Portuguese vessel had already reached Lisbon, and da Gama himself was back in the Azores. In 1501 news of the return to Lisbon of Pedro Alvares Cabral reached Venice in time for the cargo of the Flanders galleys to be reduced. Even after the signature of peace between Venice and the Turks in 1502, the spice markets of Alexandria and Beirut failed to return to normal. The quantities available remained well below the levels of the early 1490s, and later a war between Turkey and Persia ensured that they stayed low, and prices consequently high. In Cairo (which controlled prices in Alexandria), admittedly more affected than Damascus, which dominated the Beirut market, the price of pepper rose from 66 Venetian ducats the *sporta* in 1496 to between 90 and 102 in 1501, and continued to increase to 192 in 1505, and did not fall again below 90 ducats until 1527, rising again to 100-140 ducats in 1531-3. To isolate pepper from the much more valuable true spices nevertheless gives a distorted picture of the threat to the trade of Venice. In the good years before the end of the fifteenth century, the Venetians imported 4,000-5,000 *colli* of pepper, and only a few hundred of spices such as cloves, musk and cinnamon. The trade in the most valuable spices seems to have been much less severely hit by Portuguese competition, whilst their price rose more slowly in the Levant, but stayed high as that of pepper slowly sank back towards its fifteenth-century level, so that the spice trade of Venice was less severely hit in value than in bulk, and the trade in cotton and silks was hardly affected.[24]

Venice made serious efforts to meet the competition of Portuguese spices, as that of their Genoese, Ragusan and French rivals in the Levant. In 1514 it was agreed by the Venetian 'board of trade' (the *Cinque Savii a la mercanzia*) that the spice trade at Beirut and Alexandria should be opened to all Venetians, breaking the monopoly of the syndicates which had previously bid for the right to trade in the state galleys, and to impose additional duties on other merchants who traded in the 'round' ships. This measure proved of little effect in improving the trade and in 1520 the Venetians were forced to ask permission of the king of Portugal for their galleys to purchase pepper in Lisbon. Furthermore the Turks had been successful in opening an overland route from Constantinople to Adriatic ports and thence to central Italy, by-passing the Venetian market.[25] Burying their pride in the interests of their trade, in 1527 the Venetians offered to market all the pepper arriving in Lisbon, but their proposal was rejected. In 1530 the Flanders galleys stopped at Lisbon and were able to purchase some pepper for sale in northern Europe, a poor substitute to fetching spices to Venice for re-sale. This eventually proved possible, but unprofitable because the voyage from Lisbon was longer than that from the Levant. Venice's position at the head of the Adriatic made it an ideal exchange point between the Levant and southern Germany, but a poor competitor with Lisbon for the markets of Antwerp and northern Europe. The Venetians were committed to the Levant by their need for cotton, wheat and sugar, and were not free to abandon it for the sake of an illusory stake in the trade in Portuguese spices.[26]

Since 1501 Portuguese pepper and spices had been arriving in Antwerp, and the Venetian galleys ceased to ply to Antwerp between 1510 and 1518. Sailings to England were kept up, but the trade was dominated by the sale of wines rather than spices in exchange for tin and wool.

It seems probable that one of the objectives of the Portuguese, once they were established in the Indian Ocean, was to impede the transit of spices to the Levant by sea, and thus to perpetuate the shortage in the markets on which the Venetians depended. At the same time their 'blockade' of the Red Sea was a blow against the 'Moors' as well as against the Venetians. This view was certainly expressed in Venice as early as 1506, and the Egyptians talked of a punitive expedition to drive the 'Franks' from the Indian coast. Egyptian naval operations were a failure, and in 1509 the Portuguese destroyed a combined Egyptian and Gujarati fleet off Diu. The Portuguese blockade of Calicut was successful, but they could not prevent Arab vessels from obtaining pepper along the west coast of India, and the fulfilment of their dream of complete control over the spice trade of the Indian Ocean and the Levant depended on a blockade of the Red Sea itself. They failed to establish a base at Aden, though they enjoyed some success in the capture of Arab spice vessels at sea. After the Turkish occupation of Syria and Egypt, Portuguese efforts to stem the flow of spices to the Levant were less successful, the Turks retaining access to Indian spices through Diu, where the Portuguese established a fort only in 1535. Their policy towards the alternative routes which carried spices to the Levant through the Persian Gulf reveals a contrast which at first sight seems difficult to explain. The enmity between Persia and Egypt was well known to the Portuguese, and Persia was therefore an indirect ally.[27] The hope of Persian support made no allowance for the extension of Turkish power, first over Egypt, and then south-eastwards at the expense of Persia. The Portuguese, once firmly established at Ormuz, were able to offer support

to Persia, but were equally compelled to allow the passage of spices into
the Persian Gulf. Ormuz rapidly became the greatest spice market in the
world, with Gujerati merchants obtaining licences from the Portuguese
to trade there. It was impossible to prevent some of these spices reaching the Levant by the caravan routes from Basra, especially to Damascus
and Beirut. In 1543-5 the Turks occupied Iraq, and in 1546 reached
Basra. This was the more serious for the Portuguese since it coincided
with the second Turkish siege of Diu. Though it was as unsuccessful as
the first, it spelt the end of any real hope that the Portuguese could so
dominate the spice routes of the Indian Ocean that they could starve
the Levant of supplies. Far from extinguishing the Levantine spice trade,
the final expansion of Turkish power throughout the Middle East was
the key to its revival.[28]

From 1538 the Portuguese began to review their attitude towards
the Turks. A truce embracing the whole area from the Cape of Good
Hope to China was envisaged, but negotiations broke down. From this
point onwards, the maintenance of an attempted blockade against the
Levantine spice trade was viewed by the Portuguese in India as a limit-
ation on the size of their own market, whilst the monarchy itself, after
the incorporation of the Ormuz customs duties in the Crown in 1543,
also recognised its interest in the maximum possible extension of the
oriental market. Concessions for trade within the Red Sea area became
more frequent, whilst the Portuguese themselves increasingly evaded the
patrols off the Malabar coast. The commercial world of the Portuguese
settled in the Orient was becoming more self-contained, and the views
of Lisbon were counting for less and less as clashes of interest became
more frequent.[29]

The initial advantage gained by the Portuguese in the west European
spice market was the greater because of the crisis in Venetian supplies.
After the first arrivals of Portuguese pepper in Antwerp in 1501, quantities rose rapidly to 2,000 quintals in 1504, 3,000 by 1508 and after
1510 to as much as 8,000 quintals or 400 tons a year. The effect on
prices must not, however, be exaggerated. The price of pepper on the
Antwerp market had been fairly stable during the 1480s and 1490s, even
showing a tendency to fall, until in 1499 and 1500 it reflected the Venetian crisis, but did not rise as steeply as in Venice, probably because of
the cushioning effect of stocks. It fell slightly from 55½ groats the
pound to 51 between 1500 and 1501, and further to 39 groats in 1502
and 1503. By 1504 it had fallen to the levels of 1496 and 1497, and
continued to do so (with the exception of 1510) until 1512, when the
price of 24 groats a pound was lower than any since 1476. The Portu-

guese had probably exploited their opportunity to make very high profits, so that the full effects of the economies of the Cape route were not
passed on to their European customers. Nevertheless it seems from the
series of pepper prices we have for Antwerp that they stayed below
the general trend of prices during the first half of the sixteenth century.
The decennial averages are shown in Table 1.

Table 1: Decennial Averages of Pepper Prices (Brabant groats per lb,
rounded to nearest groat)

1481-90	37	1521-30	45
1491-1500	31	1531-40	42
1501-10	34	1541-50	43
1511-20	32		

Source: Calculated from H. Van der Wee, *The Growth of the Antwerp Market and
the European Economy, 14th to 16th Centuries,* 3 vols., Louvain, 1963.

The short-term rise in pepper prices at the turn of the century masked a
longer-term trend towards falling nominal prices, and even more steeply
falling relative prices. In Antwerp's situation this was partly due to her
emergence as the major redistribution centre both for northern Europe,
and as far south as Lyons and southern Germany.[30]

The Welser were established in Antwerp from 1503, and the *Grosse
Ravensburger Gesellschaft* began to obtain pepper from Antwerp in
1507. From 1508 Portuguese spices began to arrive in Lyons from Antwerp. Before 1530 the strength of Antwerp was enough to prevent the
French Crown from obtaining spices directly from the Portuguese through
the western ports, but from that time onwards increasing quantities entered France through such places as Bayonne. The 1540s heralded the passing of the best days of Antwerp as a spice market, as the French monarchy prohibited the entry of pepper except by the maritime routes
and the attractions of Lisbon itself became greater because of its proximity to Spanish gold and silver. Nor had Antwerp ever controlled enough
of the market to challenge the Venetian supremacy once and for all. The
increasing importance of Marseilles in the spice trade was still testimony
to the supremacy of the Venetians in the French market.

It is difficult to say precisely when the Venetians began fully to
recover their position in the European spice trade. The worst effects of
the Portuguese competition were mitigated by the superior quality of
the Venetian spices, and even pepper, so that they had always not com-

peted directly for the same markets. Gradually too, the Portuguese were losing their price advantage. Towards the middle of the century their position in the Orient ceased to expand, except for the development of trade with China based on Macão, and important changes took place in the markets they tapped. The political consolidation of India under the Moghul emperors seems to have increased local demand for spices, forcing up prices and compelling the Portuguese to seek new sources of supply. Defence costs were also rising steeply and eroding the profits of the Crown. The risks of the voyage did not diminish, and the relatively small number of large vessels employed increased the incidence of loss, which at times in the later sixteenth century became catastrophic.[31] In Europe the markets penetrated by Portuguese spices, especially in southern Germany, were losing their prosperity, and though even after the closure of the Portuguese factory in Antwerp their ships continued to bring spices to Antwerp, the area of the market they could reach was steadily shrinking. In many places Portuguese and Venetian spices were to be found side by side. At Rouen, La Rochelle and Bordeaux the English bought spices from both sources, as they later did at Leghorn. A Spanish merchant at Florence wrote in 1591 that on receipt of the news that no ships from the Orient were expected in Lisbon that year, the prices of spices immediately rose, but not those of pepper, as large quantities had just arrived from the Levant and Venice.[32]

As early as 1543, Venetian merchants had penetrated to the spice market of Ormuz by travelling with the caravans from Aleppo through Baghdad and were also able to purchase larger quantities in Cairo. Between 1560 and 1564 they bought 12,000 quintals of pepper a year in Cairo, as much as they have done before the crisis of the 1490s, and the total quantity of pepper reaching the Levant was greater than that reaching Lisbon, though of course not all of it was for Europe. In 1561 the Turks seized 20,000 quintals of pepper from the Portuguese in the Indian Ocean and sent it to Alexandria. It is probable that rising demand for pepper and spices in Europe made the higher prices now demanded acceptable. Pepper prices in Castile certainly began to rise from 1560 after some years of stability, though they still rose less rapidly than the general price level. In the face of these difficulties, the Portuguese Crown decided in 1570 to abandon its monopoly of the spice trade in Lisbon and to open it to its subjects. The same year saw the outbreak of war between Venice and the Turks, and this time it was her Mediterranean rivals who stood to profit. Marseilles, Ancona and Ragusa benefited most, but there was apparently some increase in the quantities of Portuguese pepper reaching the Mediterranean, and as late as 1577, four years after the restoration of peace with the Turks, the *Cinque Savij alla Mercanzia* were told that four vessels were lading in Portugal with pepper for Venice. On arrival they were permitted to unload, and were even exempted from the tax on 'western' spices levied ever since 1519.[33]

In 1575 there was a project which revealed the competition between Portuguese and Levantine pepper in the Spanish dominions in Italy. It was hoped to draw the Pope into a scheme to drive out Venetian pepper, and to create at Puerto de Santa María or Cartagena a centre for the distribution of pepper to Italy by the royal galleys of Castile. Between 1576 and 1578 the Grand Duke of Tuscany similarly attempted to make Leghorn such a staple, by exploiting the financial needs and the religious fervour of King Sebastian of Portugal during the planning of his ill-fated expedition to Morocco. The Grand Duke had ambitions which went further than the attraction of Portuguese spices, as he negotiated in similar terms with the Sultan at the same time.[34]

After his acquisition of the throne of Portugal in 1580, Philip II hoped to strike a triple blow at the Dutch, the English and the Turks by diverting Portuguese pepper to the Mediterranean. By 1585 he was able to propose to Venice that she should take 15,000 quintals of Portuguese pepper a year, accompanied by Sicilian wheat. The Venetians refused, on the grounds that the price asked was too high and that the effect on their Levant trade would be serious. A similar offer to Milan, Genoa and Florence was also rejected. Their decision was sound, because in 1585 the Welser and the Fugger had again agreed to take on the Asian contract (the organisation of the spice trade between the Orient and Lisbon) and also in 1587 the German and Baltic contract was accepted by the Welser, to be joined by the Fugger in 1591, with other firms accepting quantities of spices for Italy, Spain and Portugal. The consortium was a failure partly because the sea route from the Iberian peninsula to north Germany and the Baltic was now very insecure, and Philip II had to be content with only a part of his plan, which was an aspect of his wider imperial ambitions in these years of the enterprise of England and direct intervention in the French civil wars.[35]

The Levant remained open to the spice trade for the rest of the century and beyond, whilst the security of even the last stage of the Cape route to Lisbon was increasingly threatened by Dutch, English and Barbary corsairs. In 1603 the value of the Venetian trade in Aleppo alone was still 1½ million ducats, and the position of the Mediterranean spice trade remained good as long as the flow of American silver into the area remained strong.

The death-blow to the Levantine spice trade was to be administered in the seventeenth century by the Dutch and to a lesser extent the English. Though both had begun direct trade with the Levant in the last quarter of the sixteenth century, they had not traded greatly in spices, but from 1595 the Dutch and from 1600 the English established direct contact with the spice islands of the Far East. Almost from the outset, they began to import pepper and spices in quantities which rapidly came to dominate the European market. In 1622 the Directors of the Dutch United East India Company estimated the total European market at 7 million pounds of pepper a year, of which the English imported nearly 1½ million pounds, and the Portuguese slightly less, leaving about four million pounds for the Dutch share, if it is legitimate to assume that by that time the Venetian share of the market was negligible.[36] Similar estimates for the late seventeenth century suggest that the market had not expanded greatly, but the picture looks very different if figures for the overall trade of the Dutch and the English companies around the middle of the century are considered. Pepper remained the most important commodity in the imports of both companies, accounting for over half of the value in the Dutch case in 1648-50, as it had done in 1619-21, but the total value of goods invoiced to the Netherlands from the east rose in the same period from 2,943,000 to 6,257,000 florins, implying a doubling in the value of pepper, in spite of a trend towards falling prices.[37] If these figures are reliable it follows that the European market for pepper was capable of considerable expansion, even if allowance is made for the disappearance of Portuguese pepper as a competitor. It is possible that the fall in price widened demand among the poorer classes, though it is generally presumed that they had not been excluded from it in the sixteenth century. On the other hand, the nature of the market was such that stocks could pile up, and supplies from the east could be stored for long periods, especially if the dubious practice of mixing old stocks with fresh supplies was resorted to. This meant that there need not be a close correlation between deliveries of pepper and sales, though naturally an equilibrium had to be established over the long term.

The problem of balancing supply and demand arose even more with the most valuable spices. In 1619 the Dutch and English companies came to an agreement to share the market in the ratio of two to one, at a time when the Dutch estimated that they had stocks of cloves, nutmeg and mace sufficient to supply the whole of the European market for seven or eight years. Their control over the market, and their reserves of capital enabled them to reduce orders and sales, and the total cessation of sales of cloves from 1623 to 1626 enabled them to force the price well up above the uneconomic levels of the preceding years. The Dutch advantage over the English in the scale of their trade, increased by their expulsion of the English from the Moluccas, put them in a position of being generally able to determine the European market price of both pepper and spices, though as late as 1640 a flurry could still be caused by the news of the loss of a single Portuguese carrack. Despite their strength, however, the Dutch were never able to drive the English from their respectable portion of the market by price manipulation, though they had more success with the expensive spices than with pepper.

The English developed their pepper trade by a vigorous re-export drive. The average English consumption of pepper was probably only some 200,000 to 300,000 pounds a year, and by the 1620s imports were reaching an average of 1½ million pounds, with a maximum of over 3 million in 1626. It was perhaps the arrival of this extraordinarily large quantity which led to the decision taken in 1627 to abandon the system of paying dividends of the East India Company in the form of pepper in favour of sale to a single large contractor. Yet the problem of finding an overseas market still remained in the hands of the individual merchant, and only in 1639 and 1640 did the Company consign a quantity of pepper to the Levant on its own account.[38] The problem was a difficult one, especially as far as striking an appropriate price was concerned, as foreknowledge of the state of supplies on the way from the east was impossible to obtain. The English and Dutch adopted a system already seen at work in the spice market of Antwerp in the sixteenth century, which amounted to dealing on a futures market. The failure of the English compared with the Dutch lay in their neglecting to build up adequate stocks in London, so that the merchants were more easily prey to fluctuations in supply and to the speculative cornering of the market. The risks of the trade therefore remained high, both for the East India Company and for the individual trader.

Pepper formed a part of the cargo of English vessels trading with the Baltic, with Italy, and even with the Levant. Whilst Turkey saw supplies of pepper from England only occasionally, for example in 1626, when stocks in England were high and prices low, Italian ports such as Leghorn were regularly receiving consignments, and sometimes members of the Levant Company succeeded in selling pepper to Venice. Though the re-export of pepper formed a part of the potentially important movement of diversification in English trade which was gaining pace in the first half of the seventeenth century, its quantitative importance must not be overestimated. It is not easy to offer a sure estimate of the value either of the re-export trade as a whole, or of the place of pepper within it. It has been calculated that in 1640 the official customs values of all goods exported from London other than 'shortcloths' were no more than £700,000 and that of this, re-exports by English merchants totalled no more than £76,402.[39] It is well know that the official values were most unrealistic, and it is certainly difficult to reconcile such a figure with the quantities of pepper which were re-exported, even though they were smaller than in the 1620s, when the real value of pepper alone, if the statements of members of the East India Company Court are to be believed, must have been over £200,000 a year.

Notes

1. See, e.g., J. Meuvret, 'Le commerce des grains et des farines à Paris à l'époque de Louis XIV', *Revue d'histoire moderne et contemporaine*, III (1956), pp. 169-203, and his collected *Etudes d'histoire économique*, pp. 199-229.
2. M. Aymard, *Venise, Raguse et le commerce du blé pendant la seconde moitié du xvie siècle.*
3. Braudel and Romano, op.cit., pp. 52-3.
4. Braudel, *La Méditerranée*, I, p. 525.
5. J. Klein, *The Mesta*, and R. Ibarra y Rodríguez, *El problema cerealista en España durante el reinado de los Reyes Católicos.*
6. Braudel, *La Méditerranée*, I, p. 531.
7. Lapeyre, *Les Ruiz*, pp. 531-41.
8. Braudel, *La Méditerranée*, I, p. 532.
9. Christensen, op.cit., pp. 423-4, and Diagram XVI. The value of the Sound Toll Registers is critically discussed by P. Jeannin, 'Les tables du Sund comme source pour la construction d'indices généraux de l'activité économique au xviie siècle', *Revue historique*, CCXXXI (1964), pp. 55-102 and 307-40.
10. Christensen, op.cit., pp. 246-8.
11. Spanish lines of military communication between Italy and the Netherlands ran dangerously near to Geneva, but the commanders were given strict orders not to attack the Republic. Nevertheless, the City authorities lived in continuous fear of such an attack. Several Savoyard attempts to destroy Genevan independence came near to success, e.g. in 1582, 1597 and 1602. See G. Parker, *The Army of Flanders and the Spanish Road, 1567-1659*, pp. 63-4.
12. J.F. Bergier, *Genève et l'économie européene de la Renaissance*, pp. 100-9.
13. A.R. Bridbury, *England and the Salt Trade in the later Middle Ages*, p. 1.
14. Ibid., p. 12. Sea water contains quantities of other salts such as magnesium chloride and magnesium sulphate, the last of which could be ruinous to the flavour of food, but more seriously, slowed the curing process to a dangerous extent.
15. Ibid., pp. 56-7.
16. Ibid., p. 88, quoting A. Agate, *Der Hansische Barinhandel*, p. 95.
17. Ibid., pp. 99-100, quoting W.S. Unger, *Bronnen tot de Geschiedenis van Middelburg*, III, No. 683.
18. Braudel, *La Méditerranée*, I, p. 112.
19. Ibid., I, p. 117 and also 'Achats et ventes du sel à Venise, 1587-1593', *AESC*, XVI (1961), pp. 961-5.

150 *Merchants and Merchandise*

20. H.A. Innis, *The Cod Fisheries—the History of an International Economy.*
21. This now familiar fact was first pointed out by A.H. Lybyer in his article 'The Influence of the Ottoman Turks upon the Routes of Oriental Trade', *English Historical Review,* XXX (1915), pp. 577-88.
22. V. Magalhães Godinho, *L'économie de l'empire portugais,* p. 537.
23. Ibid., pp. 541-4.
24. Ibid., pp. 715-26.
25. Ibid., pp. 722-3.
26. Ibid., pp. 731-2.
27. Ibid., p. 765.
28. Ibid., pp. 769-70.
29. Ibid., p. 783.
30. For Lyons and the spice trade see above, pp. 73-6. Gascon, *Grand commerce,* pp. 81-94 and 'Un siècle du commerce des épices à Lyon', *AESC,* XV (1960), pp. 638-56.
31. C.R. Boxer, *The Portuguese Seaborne Empire, 1415-1825,* pp. 207-11, 215-19.
32. Braudel, *La Méditerranée,* I, p. 497, based on the Ruiz correspondence.
33. Ibid., I, p. 504.
34. Ibid., I, p. 505.
35. Ibid., I, p. 510.
36. K.N. Chaudhuri, *The English East India Company,* pp. 143-4.
37. K. Glamann, *Dutch Asiatic Trade, 1620-1740,* p. 13.
38. Chaudhuri, op.cit., pp. 144-51.
39. F.J. Fisher, 'London's Export Trade in the Seventeenth Century', *EcHR,* 2nd Ser., III (1950), pp. 151-61.

7 TEXTILES

The production of cloth was very widely disseminated in sixteenth-century Europe, and its variety was equally great, both in type and quality. Wool, silk, linen and cotton were all used as raw materials, either alone or in a mixture, and the variety of types and nomenclature can cause the historian some confusion. Most areas produced some woollen cloth, and the poorer classes were usually dependent on locally or at least nationally produced cloth. The production of silk goods was more confined to specialised areas, such as north Italy, though it spread to the region of Lyons and Tours in France, and to Antwerp, and was carried on in Spain, especially in Granada and Murcia. Linen was naturally concentrated in northern Europe, from Brittany to Germany. From the point of view of international trade however, Europe was divided fairly clearly into major exporting and importing zones, with England, the Netherlands and Italy providing the principal exports to the rest.

Woollen Cloth

Until the middle of the century and beyond, the southern Netherlands, especially Antwerp, formed the major centre for the marketing of both locally produced and English cloth. The expansion of English cloth exports had already reached the point at which they exceeded the value of raw wool exported before the end of the fifteenth century, and expansion was almost continuous throughout the first half of the sixteenth century, as parts of western England and East Anglia became increasingly industrialised. The coincidence in time between this movement and the rise of Antwerp was not accidental, and an important aspect of Antwerp's industrial growth was the development of the finishing and dyeing of English 'white' cloths. The Merchant Adventurers who had gathered the national cloth trade into their hands, had been settled in Antwerp since 1442, and their future was assured by the *Intercursus Magnus* of 1496. Exports of English cloth reached 80,000 pieces a year by the last years of the reign of Henry VII[1] and were further assisted during that of Henry VIII first by a slight devaluation of sterling in 1526 and much more by the 'great debasement' of the 1540s, at a time when the government of the Netherlands was pinning its faith on maintaining a strong currency. More and more competitive with Netherlands cloth, the English product sold very well in Germany and the Baltic, with exports rising to a peak of 135,000 cloths in 1553.[2]

Alongside the cheaper and lighter English cloths such as kersies, the 'new draperies' of Netherlands manufacture found a rapidly expanding market in southern Europe, which compensated for the troubles which began to afflict Germany and the Baltic from the 1540s. In 1542-3 two-thirds of Antwerp's overland trade to Italy consisted of fabrics manufactured outside the Netherlands. The importance of the southern market is revealed by the export of a number of kersies almost equal to that of traditional 'broadcloths' by the Merchant Adventurers in 1549-50—approximately 50,000 of each, though of course the smaller size and value of the kersies meant that the trade was still dominated in value by the traditional cloth.[3] The crisis of the 1550s hit English cloth very seriously. Revaluation of the English currency in 1554 and 1560 destroyed its price advantage, whilst the economic difficulties of the Netherlands created generally more unfavourable trading conditions. Tensions between English and local merchants led to an embargo on English cloth in 1563, which provoked counter-measures from the government of Elizabeth I and the withdrawal of the Merchant Adventurers from Antwerp to seek an alternative cloth staple at Emden, so linking themselves to the new prosperity of north-west Germany.

War between England and France in 1563, added to that between Denmark and Sweden, had a further serious effect on Antwerp's trade and on cloth production, which the resumption of normal relations with the Merchant Adventurers at the end of 1564 did little to mitigate. To these difficulties were soon to be added the political and religious tensions which led ultimately to open revolt against Spanish rule in the Netherlands. By the autumn of 1566 fear of Calvinist-inspired iconoclasm was leading merchants to quit Antwerp, and the restoration of order led only to a precarious return of confidence, soon to be broken by the measures of the Duke of Alba. According to a correspondent of Simón Ruiz, in 1567 Antwerp dealt in only a quarter of the normal quantity of goods, partly a result of war operations and partly of the ruin of the flax crop by heavy rains.[4] Though the temporary removal of the English staple to Emden had not proved successful, the Merchant Adventurers opened negotiations with Hamburg, which already enjoyed good contacts with central Germany and with Italy through Frankfurt, and was already developing facilities for the finishing of cloth. An influx of workers from the southern Netherlands as the troubles extended was to permit a rapid expansion of Hamburg's industry, and by 1569 the English were better placed to deal with a new embargo on trade with Antwerp, which broke the connection for good.

In the short run, the search for an alternative English cloth staple was only partly successful. The average number of cloths exported between 1571 and 1573 fell to 73,000, and the government was beginning to see the necessity of a more vigorous search for wider markets. Sir Robert Cecil had argued that

> it is to be confessed of all men that it were better for this realme for many considerations, that the commodities of the same were issued out rather to sundry places, than to one, and especially such as the lord thereof is so great a power as he may therwith annoy this realme by way of embargo.[5]

Cecil clearly foresaw that some decline of cloth exports might be expected, but argued that this would help to concentrate the trade in fewer hands, that the drop in exports would be largely at the expense of undyed and undressed cloth, and that if unemployment resulted 'the sturdyer and stronger sort of men' might be sent to Ireland. It is no coincidence that the new charter of the Merchant Adventurers dates from 1564 and contained clauses which further strengthened their monopoly as the 'Merchant Adventurers of England'.

Hamburg nevertheless developed into a reasonably satisfactory alternative centre for the continental distribution of English cloth, and its customs records show a dramatic increase in the quantity entering and leaving the city. Compared with a mere £320 sterling of receipts in customs on English woollens in 1568-9, the following year brought in £8,695. In 1569 over 25,000 broadcloths and 17,000 kersies left Hamburg for Germany and Italy, and the duty paid on them rose to over £12,000 in 1570. The boom was short-lived however, with a progressive decline after 1571. Comparison with figures from the English customs records shows that during the 1570s exports to Hamburg were not representative of the overall picture, as London exports rose to over 100,000 'shortcloths' a year between 1574 and 1576, and over 97,000 a year between 1577 and 1579. It seems certain that Antwerp was still receiving substantial amounts of English cloth, though its official monopoly was broken, and that other Netherlands ports, such as Middelburg, were of increasing importance. Hamburg was alone among the cities of the Hanseatic League in welcoming English merchants, and later in the century the League attempted to force the English from the German market. In 1582 they persuaded the Imperial Diet to expel the Merchant Adventurers from the Empire, but the Emperor, Rudolf II, suspended the decree on the grounds of the harm it would do to German commerce.

The Merchant Adventurers resorted again to Emden, and then to Stade, under the control of the Archbishop of Bremen, but in 1597 they were expelled following a ban imposed by the Emperor. The further English retaliation by the expulsion of the Hanseatic merchants from their London headquarters in the Steelyard in 1598 was a much more effective measure than the Imperial ban, as trade at Stade continued with the connivance of the local authorities.

The increasingly close relations with the Dutch rebels opened up the possibility of the re-establishment of the English cloth-staple in the Netherlands, and it was hoped that a return to a short sea crossing and greater concentration on a single staple might enable the Merchant Adventurers to restore a control over the trade which had suffered from the increased activity of 'interlopers' during the years of dispersion. Negotiations were begun for a permanent site in the United Provinces, and in 1587 it was decided to fix on Middelburg, close to the English garrison at Flushing and well placed on the Rhine-Maas estuary. The tradition of a single staple was never effectively re-established, however, as it was not until 1598 that the headquarters were finally settled at Middelburg, and even then many of the richer merchants continued to trade with Hamburg. The Merchant Adventurers as a company ceased to enjoy an effective monopoly of the trade in cloth. Figures for 1597-8 suggest that they only exported 62,000 short-cloths out of a total of 105,000. Interlopers carried over 8,000 cloths to the Netherlands and Germany, and foreign merchants 3,000.[6]

The remaining 30 per cent of London's cloth exports were now going directly to other markets. The northern French ports had always taken some English cloth, but since the crisis of the 1550s other developments had led to a gradual widening of the markets elsewhere. The Russia Company's trade with Muscovy was modest enough in scale, and was facing competition from English kersies imported into Russia through the Levant by Armenian merchants. The assurance of Arthur Edwards to the Shah in 1566 that England could supply 200,000 kersies a year remained a wildly optimistic dream.[7] Nevertheless the trade was broadened after the opening of the route through Narva in the Baltic, though more to the benefit of private traders than of the Company, and at the end of the century it was exporting only about two per cent of all cloth exports. The Russia Company was therefore more important by the example it set in principle for the widening of markets for English cloth, than in the quantitative importance of its trade.

That example was followed in 1579 by the creation of the Eastland Company. English merchants' trade with the Baltic had been quite active

in the fourteenth century, but had fallen off in the fifteenth, to revive
in a modest way in the sixteenth century. By the 1560s the number of
English vessels passing through the Sound had risen to levels which were
not greatly exceeded until the later seventeenth century, though they
represented only about three per cent of all ships paying duties there.[8]
The revival of England's Baltic trade therefore preceded the withdrawal
from Antwerp. It was based on the export not of the 'white' cloths, but
of fully finished and dyed cloths, and was not so heavily dominated by
the merchants of London as was the trade of the Merchant Adventurers.
The establishment of the Eastland Company was not therefore a response
to the need for the creation of a new trade, but to the desire to organise
an established one, following a period when the trade had undergone
some difficult years, the quantity of cloths exported falling from a peak
of over 11,000 pieces in 1574 to only 3,800 in 1577. The establishment
of the Company was followed by a renewed expansion, cloth exports
climbing back to almost 11,000 pieces by 1582, and reaching a peak of
nearly 36,000 in 1587, a level which was again surpassed in the 1590s,
with an average of nearly 47,000 cloths a year in 1598 and 1599.[9]
Another feature was the very small share of foreign ships in the trade,
averaging less than 2 per cent of the total between 1579 and 1600. As
in the case of the Dutch there is a clear indication that English exports
of cloth to the Baltic were at their highest when imports of grain were
also large, and when at the same time exports to Spain or the Netherlands were low. This is well illustrated in 1586-7, when Anglo-Netherlands trade was experiencing a slump and there were harvest failures
in England.

The domination of London was less great than in the Netherlands
trade. The surviving London Port Book for 1565 agrees remarkably well
with evidence from the Sound Toll Registers, giving London about
2,500 pieces of cloth, whilst Hull had nearly a 20 per cent share of the
trade, rising to nearly 40 per cent in 1585, and as high as 60 per cent
in 1605. The number of pieces is to some extent misleading, as Hull
exported the cheaper kersies, and there is evidence that London merchants were using Hull vessels for some of their goods.[10] The London
figures for 1606 of over 8,000 shortcloths (or 7½ per cent of the total
cloth exports of London) reveal that the Baltic was of growing relative
importance, but understate it nationally since it is likely that the share
of the provincial ports was nearly as great.[11] Ipswich was probably more
important than either Hull or Newcastle. In 1586 Ipswich consigned
over 3,000 cloths to Elbing, mostly heavy traditional broadcloth. Figures from the Elbing records suggest that the share of kersies, especially

from the north of England, was rising faster than the total trade, with over 19,000 imported in 1605.[12]

The early years of the seventeenth century saw a new boom in English cloth exports, despite adverse factors such as outbreaks of plague. The last years for which the enrolled customs accounts are available suggest some buoyancy in the trade: 104,000 shortcloths exported by London in 1601, 118,000 in 1602, 92,000 in 1603, and 112,000 in 1604. Though statistical information is lacking for later years, the dying away of complaints of the over-expansion of cloth manufacture, together with positive contemporary comments on the prosperity of the trade, make it reasonable to believe that the peak of 127,000 shortcloths exported by English merchants from London in 1614 was not an isolated phenomenon, but the culmination of a decade of expansion. The Merchant Adventurers still dominated the trade, using both Emden and Stade as well as Hamburg as official residences at various times, though the new Netherlands staple at Middelburg seems to have been unable to absorb as much cloth as expected. The increasing activities of interlopers and the granting of a special royal licence to the Earl of Cumberland for the export of undyed cloth put the Company into the position of having to defend its monopoly not only against courtiers and interlopers but against Parliamentary criticism, especially from Members representing provincial ports. Within the Company, the trade seems to have been increasingly concentrated in the hands of the greater merchants, and in 1614 23 firms shipped nearly half of the cloths exported to the area of the Company's monopoly.[13]

These years saw what was to be the last boom in the export of traditional broadcloths. In 1614 over half of the cloth exports of London and a much higher proportion of the Merchant Adventurers' trade was in undyed and undressed cloth. Whilst these cloths, because of their size and quality, were worth up to seven or eight times as much as the average kersey, their value would have been enhanced by 50 or 100 per cent had they been exported after finishing. It was a sign of growing self-confidence that the idea of exporting only finished cloth was beginning to seem attractive, and was fostered by the less satisfactory condition of the finishing industry in the new staple towns being used abroad. It was equally characteristic of the age of James I that such a scheme should have been part of a political intrigue. In July 1614 Alderman Cockayne of London succeeded in persuading the government to issue a proclamation prohibiting the export of unfinished cloth, and in December the Merchant Adventurers' Charter was suspended. A body known as the King's Merchant Adventurers was to replace them, guaranteeing to export finished cloths. The government's motives were relatively simple. It was hoped that receipts from customs duties would increase by £40,000 a year, especially valuable in view of the failure of the Addled Parliament in 1614. Membership of the new Company was dominated by merchants engaged in the Eastland and Levant trades, and it was not much more than a confidence trick designed to win the trade of the Merchant Adventurers, most of whom promptly diverted their capital into new fields, including the East India Company. The King's Merchant Adventurers were granted permission to export 30,000 undressed cloths, as well as the right to use the Earl of Cumberland's licence. Their promises to export finished cloths were rapidly whittled down—to 6,000, 12,000 and 18,000 in each of the three following years. The new company lacked the necessary capital and organisation abroad and overestimated the ability of the English finishing industry to meet its relatively modest demands. Consequently it was unable to absorb cloth production. By May 1615

> the great project of dyeing and dressing cloth [was] at a stand, and they [knew] not well how to go forward nor backward, for the clothiers [did] generally complain that their cloth [lay] on their hands, and the clothworkers and dyers weary the King and Council with petitions wherein they complain that they [are] in a worse case than before.[14]

By 1617 the old Company was forced to take over the trade again.

The Cockayne project had caused a serious crisis in the traditional broadcloth industry, and contemporaries blamed it entirely for its poor fortunes in the succeeding years. Yet it has recently been assessed as 'premature by only a few years',[15] and the long crisis which followed had many other causes. It is likely that 1615 would have been a poor year for cloth exports in any event, as the Merchant Adventurers had large stocks left on their hands in the Netherlands after the exceptionally high shipments of 1614. The Cockayne project had shaken confidence at a critical time however, as by 1618 there were clear signs that the uneasy peace of Europe was coming to an end. After a brief recovery the trade in the old draperies was hit by a severe recession. London exports of cloth fell from 102,000 in 1618 to 85,000 in 1620, with the Baltic market even more severely affected than that of the Merchant Adventurers, its cheaper cloth being more easily hit by the competition of local manufacture.[16] Things grew worse in 1621 and 1622. In the latter year only 76,000 cloths were shipped from London by Englishmen, the share of the Merchant Adventurers falling to 50,000, and that of the Netherlands market dropping from 35,000 in 1620 to 26,000 in 1622. Contemporary opinion saw many reasons for the slump, from poor quality workmanship and restrictive practices to a 'shortage of money', but it has recently been convincingly argued that the fundamental cause was monetary, though in a way not properly understood by contemporaries. The crisis was a sudden one and preceded the interruption of trade by military operations in northern Germany. It is therefore likely that the violent manipulations of currency values in the market areas of Germany and the Baltic, known as the *Kipper-und-Wipper Zeit,* rapidly made English exports uncompetitive. It proved cheaper for English merchants to export coin for the purchase of goods in the Baltic region, thus accounting for complaints of a shortage of coin in England.

The traditional broadcloth market was once more the most severely hit, the exports of the Eastland Company more than those of the Merchant Adventurers. The Eastland merchants complained that they were suffering worse than their Dutch competitors in the Baltic because the latter had greater resources in cash with which at least to maintain their import trade, in which great opportunities existed because of the cheapness of Baltic goods. In 1621 Lionel Cranfield pointed out that some of the English outports were thriving on their import trade, a considerable proportion of which was still carried in Dutch ships.

Recovery was nevertheless quite rapid, but not maintained for long. The Merchant Adventurers shipped 59,000 undressed cloths in 1624, aided by greater stability of the currencies in Europe, but in 1625 plague in London, privateers in the Channel and war with Spain, soon to be followed by war with France, caused a new downturn, and 1628 was another bad year for both the Baltic merchants and the Merchant Adventurers alike. The series of crises following the Cockayne project had become a period of chronic stagnation in the traditional cloth trade. Foreign competition was undoubtedly a powerful factor, as well as the declining capacity of England's traditional markets. Cheap supplies of local wool were making cloth manufacture in Germany more competitive, and more suited to the tighter purses of war-time consumers.

The contemporary argument that the Dutch were able to undercut the English in the Baltic market was only a partial explanation of the stagnation of English exports. The Sound Toll Registers suggest that Dutch cloth was entering the Baltic in increasing quantities. Rising from relatively negligible levels in the 1590s, 10,000-13,000 pieces of Dutch cloth passed through the Sound in 1609 and 1610.

falling off again for a few years until a new expansion raised the Dutch share to 29,000 cloths in 1618, compared with 37,000 English cloths. From then onwards Dutch exports of cloth to the Baltic approached or even exceeded those of the English.

Table 2: English and Dutch Cloth Exports to the Baltic, 1618-31

Year	English	Dutch	Year	English	Dutch
1618	37,000	29,000	1625	47,000	32,000
1619	43,000	35,000	1626	34,000	29,000
1620	26,000	23,000	1627	12,000	21,000
1621	19,000	20,000	1628	19,000	20,000
1622	34,000	30,000	1629	8,000	17,000
1623	60,000	55,000	1630	24,000	34,000
1624	57,000	53,000	1631	17,000	37,000

Source: R.W.K. Hinton, *The Eastland Trade and the Common Weal in the Seventeenth Century*, Cambridge, 1959.

The figures for English broadcloths show an even more serious decline, and did not exceed 10,000 after 1624, except in 1633. Not even in the critical years of the middle and late 1620s, when the Dutch were under severe military pressure and there was an indirect threat to their Baltic trade from Imperial and Spanish policy on the south shore of the Baltic, did the Dutch challenge to the English seriously diminish.

The role of the Dutch in the export of cloth to the Baltic clearly dates only from the seventeenth century, despite the great predominance of Dutch shipping in the Baltic from the middle of the sixteenth century or earlier. As the quantity of cloth shipped by the Dutch increased, so did the proportion of it which was woven as well as finished in the Netherlands. Of 4,200 pieces passing the Sound in Dutch vessels in 1605, only 1,000 or so were of English origin.[17] It was only after 1618 that textiles, of whatever provenance, formed more than an insignificant part of Dutch commerce with the Baltic, and then only a relatively small proportion. That the quantity of Dutch cloth nevertheless rivalled and at times surpassed that of the English is a striking testimony of the huge predominance of the Dutch in general Baltic trade.[18]

The German and Baltic markets for traditional heavy cloth failed at best to do more than maintain previous levels for English and Dutch exporters in the seventeenth century, but there was compensation in the expansion of trade in the 'new draperies'. A wide variety of lighter-weight cloths, often mixtures of wool and linen or cotton, had been produced in increasing quantities during the sixteenth century, and in the Netherlands had stepped into the export market as the boom in English cloth exports reached its peak around 1550. The production of says, bays and fustians increased in the rural areas around Hondschoote, where between 1525 and 1560 the number of pieces manufactured rose from 30,000 to 100,000 a year. In many other towns there was a similar trend, and in Arras, Lille, Tournai, Cambrai, Valenciennes, Mons, Weivik and Dendermonde the revival partially restimulated the economy of Bruges, still the centre for the import of Spanish wool, the most suitable raw material for these cloths.[19] This period also saw the expansion of the Flemish linen industry. Though statistical information on exports is lacking, it is clear that the industrial expansion was based on exports to Italy, Spain and the Levant, and to the Spanish colonies in America through the entrepot of Seville. The purchasing power of Spain and her colonies was rising but was not matched by an expansion of the native cloth industry. The export of new draperies to the south through Antwerp was an opportunity eagerly seized by native Brabant merchants to compete more evenly with the French, Italian, Spanish and Portuguese colonists who had previously played the major part in Antwerp's commercial expansion.

Though the troubled years of the 1550s temporarily interrupted the growth of this trade, the restoration of peace between Spain and France in 1559 allowed it to resume. The value of goods exported from Seville to the Spanish Indies began to recover more rapidly than their volume, an indication that the emphasis of the trade was shifting towards such manufactured goods from northern Europe.[20] In 1559 the Spanish merchants in the Netherlands requested the transfer of their consulate from Bruges to Antwerp. The firm of the della Faille turned its attention to the Sevillian trade instead of the Italian, with highly profitable results.[21] Later in the century the Dutch were to overtake the southern Netherlanders as the main exporters of the lighter cloths, which became a part of their commercial system based essentially on control of the grain trade. After the beginning of the blockade of Antwerp, the cloth-manufacturing industry of the southern Netherlands was only saved from total collapse by the dispersion of goods through Nieuwport, Dunkirk, Calais, and even Rouen, St Malo and Nantes.[22] There was some revival of optimism in Antwerp during the early 1580s, when the della Faille were trading directly with Venice and Naples. Following Parma's victories and the fall of Antwerp, the northern provinces, especially Amsterdam, were the main beneficiaries, attracting an increasing quantity of cloth woven in the southern provinces as these regained their stability. From the 1590s the role of the surviving Antwerp merchants was increasingly confined to providing an economic link with the north across the fighting lines, often through their contacts with families like the van der Meulen, who had left Antwerp for Leyden.

The real future in the markets of southern Europe lay with the English and the Dutch. The English had exported some cloth to Spain and the Mediterranean in the first half of the sixteenth century, but for reasons which remain obscure, their trade with the Iberian peninsula slackened after 1550, and inside the Mediterranean it almost entirely ceased. The surviving trade with Spain and Portugal in the old draperies was severely interrupted by the war conditions from 1585 to 1604, and the restoration of peace failed to produce as rapid a return to good trading conditions as had been hoped. The first English merchants to return to Spain after 1604 found low prices obtaining for manufactured goods, the competition from native Segovia cloths, or Italian cloths made with Spanish wool, being too keen. The possibility remained of an expansion of trade in the new draperies, but penetration of the market was made difficult by the intrusion of foreign merchants during the war. Up to the middle of the seventeenth century, only in periods when Spain's relations with France and the Dutch were bad were the English able to benefit to any great extent, though the revival of the English south-western ports was to some extent ascribable to the Iberian trade.[23] The middle years of the sixteenth century had also seen the beginnings of a small trade with Morocco, which absorbed quantities of cloth perhaps equal to those taken by Portugal; this was made possible by the weakening of Portuguese influence in Morocco. By the 1560s the trade was regularly established in the dyed cloths of Suffolk and Kent, and after 1580 the new situation created by Spanish domination of Portugal made the foothold in Morocco even more attractive. In 1585 steps were taken to regulate the trade by the establishment of the Barbary Company. In 1597-8 nearly 2,400 cloths were exported to Morocco, more than to Russia, but still only half as many as to France.

Trade to the Mediterranean was to offer the greatest hope of expanding the range and scale of direct English cloth exports. English cloth, especially kersies, had long found a ready market in the Mediterranean and the Levant. In the fifteenth century the Florentine and Venetian galleys had carried them, and during most of the sixteenth century as much as a quarter of total English exports of cloth found their way via the Netherlands or Hamburg and the overland routes to Italy, and thence in some quantity to the Levant. With the revival of English navigation in the Mediterranean from the 1570s, and especially after the formation of the Levant Company, the cloth was increasingly being sent by the sea route, avoiding the use of continental middle-men. The export of 'new draperies' formed a very large part of English exports other than the traditional broadcloths: in 1640 these woollens, together with some hosiery, were worth £450,000 from London alone at official customs values, Spanish, African and Mediterranean ports taking a steadily increasing proportion of all English goods other than broadcloth. Between 1609 and 1640 their share of a rapidly rising total went up from 46 to 65 per cent.[24]

The major achievement of the Levant Company was, however, the creation of a new market for the flagging English broadcloth industry.[25] In 1598 we have the first record of the export of broadcloth to the Levant, a mere 750 cloths compared with 18,000 kersies, but it was soon realised that many more could be sold in competition with the Venetians. In 1606 the number of broadcloths sent to Italy and the Levant had risen to 2,776 compared with just over 10,000 kersies. By 1621 the proportions had been reversed, with 7,500 broadcloths against 2,300 kersies, and by the 1630s the kersies had ceased to figure significantly in the Levant Company's exports. In some years very large shipments of broadcloth were recorded, the highest quantity being 17,000 in 1634, but they were apparently intermittent, as the market was easily oversupplied. The value of this trade was greater even than the number of cloths suggests, as they were entirely finished and dyed before export, and were the equivalent of at least half their number again of the undyed cloths previously exported to the Netherlands. They were finished and dyed in the producing areas of the west of England, especially Gloucestershire, where the manufacturing industry was rapidly expanding its finishing capacity after the introduction of dyeing at Stroudwater and Gloucester between 1605 and 1608.

The discovery that the hinterland of the Levantine ports was a very large market for heavy cloth for winter wear was perhaps a surprise to the English, but the Venetians had long been aware of it. The English achievement was therefore the more remarkable, and was only made possible by changing economic circumstances both in England and in Venice. Whilst currency changes and war conditions were making English cloth less saleable in the Baltic, her costs, especially in labour, were low in comparison with those in Venice, where industrial wage levels seem to have kept pace with inflation. Not only was Venetian cloth becoming more uncompetitive because of its price, but the growing dependence of the Republic on foreign shipping was a source of serious concern. Measures taken to restore the position only made matters worse. In

1602 the Senate decreed that no foreign vessel might load goods for export unless there were no Venetian ships available, and that imports should be carried in either Venetian ships or ships of the country of origin. Whatever the long-term intentions of such a measure, its short-term consequences were to discourage foreign vessels from making the long detour through the Adriatic on their way to or from the Levant. Undoubtedly the Venetian policy contributed greatly to the rise of Leghorn as a major entrepôt. Venice not only began to lose her Levantine market for cloth, but also suffered progressively from the weakening of demand in Germany, especially after 1618.

Though we have little quantitative information on Venetian cloth exports, the figures for its production are a helpful substitute. The turn of the sixteenth and seventeenth centuries saw the peak in a long period of growth in the production of cloth in Venice. From a mere 2,000 pieces a year at the beginning of the century, by the mid-1550s averages of around 15,000 a year were reached, and after some poor years during the war with the Turks from 1570 to 1573, the last two decades before 1600 brought a new expansion, with an average approaching 20,000 a year. After two exceptionally good years in 1601 and 1602, in which over 28,000 pieces were produced in each, levels returned to those of the 1590s until around 1610, and the decline was by no means serious until 1620, which saw the production of 23,000 pieces. From then onwards the fall was steeper.

Table 3: Cloth Production in Venice, 1621-40

1621	18,883	1631	8,053
1622	14,778	1632	13,000
1623	12,976	1633	13,551
1624	15,272	1634	13,102
1625	16,998	1635	13,999
1626	15,804	1636	12,723
1627	21,124	1637	12,531
1628	18,862	1638	13,640
1629	15,027	1639	11,359
1630	13,275	1640	11,719

Source: D. Sella, 'The Rise and Fall of the Venetian Woollen Industry', in B. Pullen (ed.), *Crisis and Change in the Venetian Economy*, London, 1968.

The decline in Venice was matched by that of other north Italian clothing centres, such as Como and Milan, whilst in Florence the peak of prosperity had been passed a generation earlier than in Venice, and by 1616 production was down to a bare half of the best years of the 1570s.

Whilst it is not certain, it seems very likely that the competition of the Dutch and English in the Levant, superimposed on the decline of the German market, was the principal cause of the decline of the Venetian industry, rather than these northern states stepping into a gap left by the decline in Venetian production. Clearly, by the 1630s there were years in which English exports of broadcloth to the Levant exceeded the total production of Venice.

Alum

The cloth industry was dependent on a wide range of raw materials besides wool. Amongst these alum was vital in the dyeing process for fixing the colour, especially red, black or yellow.[26] Substitutes such as potash, tartar or ashes produced from burning pine-wood with chalk were all used, but produced much less satisfactory results. Alum was consequently much sought after in the middle ages, especially from Syria, Egypt, Greece, and above all from Anatolia, though the Florentine cloth industry seems to have managed with the poorer quality obtainable from the Isles of Ischia. In the fourteenth and fifteenth centuries the eastern alum trade was dominated by Genoa, the capital involved making it her most important eastern trade. The European consumer was protected from the consequences of what was virtually a Genoese monopoly by the existence of two rival syndicates, so that the price fell by 50 per cent at source in Chios during the fifteenth century.

The Turkish conquest of Constantinople in 1453 profoundly shook the Genoese, not only in their Black Sea colonies, but also in their alum trade. Chios was unsuccessfully attacked by the Turks in 1455, but was forced to pay tribute to the Turks, whilst in the same year Phocea was captured. Alum almost disappeared from western Europe, its price rising by 400 or 500 per cent within fifteen years as the Turks exploited their newly won position. Whilst the Genoese were able to obtain supplies for local use from the re-opening of the mines of Ischia, the Venetians were forced to carry out prospecting in Tyrol. Then, in 1462, alum was discovered near Cartagena in south-east Spain and near Tolfa in the Papal States. From this time the Papacy attempted to maintain a monopoly in the supply of alum throughout Christendom, employing spiritual pressures to supplement its economic strength. Absolution from the sin of harming the papal alum trade was withdrawn from ordinary confes-

sors, and in 1505 Henry VII of England was threatened with excom-
munication by the papal legate for having permitted the import of Turkish alum, some of which had been re-exported to Flanders. The Papacy
was to argue that the profits of the alum trade were to be used for the
crusade against the infidel, but as so often even the Spanish government
remained unimpressed. The major hope of the Papacy therefore lay in
the establishment of a monopoly based on economic pressures. It was
able to secure the closure of rival centres of production in Italy, for
example those of Volterra after its seizure by Lorenzo the Magnificent
of Florence in 1472, and those of Massa Maritima, the property of the
Bishop of Massa, by offering an annual pension in exchange.

In areas such as Flanders, where demand was very high, the papacy
achieved some initial success in dominating the market. In 1468, Charles
the Bold signed an agreement for twelve years in which he promised to
forbid the sale of alum other than that of Tolfa in the Netherlands, and
at the same time to prohibit the use of substitute materials. In the
longer term, however, it was impossible for the Papacy to prevent competition from alum from other sources, especially in the Netherlands.
As the mines of south-east Spain became more productive, alum found
its way from Cartagena to the Netherlands, of which there is an example
as early as 1486. By the time the Spanish production reached its peak
around 1560, its output was approaching three-quarters of that of the
Papal States. In 1551 Charles V concluded an agreement with the Grimaldi, farmers of the Tolfa alum, granting them the monopoly of imports
into the Netherlands, but they contracted to supply over a third of it
from Spain. Though this seems surprising, the explanation lies in all
probability in the fact that the Grimaldi were major creditors of the
Spanish government at the time, and were not permitted to export the
proceeds of their financial operations in bullion. Somewhat later Tolfa
was supplying the whole of the 8,000 *cantare* (approximately 400 tons)
of alum needed for the Netherlands and the other cloth manufacturing
areas of northern Europe. Philip II had hopes in the 1560s of supplying the whole of the needs of the Netherlands from Spain, but was dis-
suaded from putting his plan into effect by the advice of the Regent
Margaret of Parma that the Netherlands preferred Tolfa alum for its
quality and that the royal revenues might suffer if the English and Baltic markets were supplied direct from Italy instead of through the Antwerp staple.

Clearly neither the Papacy nor Spain was able to impose a permanent
monopoly of alum supplies to northern Europe, and towards the end of
the sixteenth century new centres of production came to prevent the

re-establishment of any future domination of the trade by a single sup-
plier. In the Bishopric of Liège, in Germany, Bohemia and Scandinavia,
alum production increased not only to satisfy local demand but to provide a surplus for export, and in the early seventeenth century England
struggled to achieve self-sufficiency with the development of quarries
in north-east Yorkshire.

Nevertheless, during the greater part of the sixteenth century, the
papal quarries of Tolfa exported through the port of Civitavecchia a considerable portion of the total European consumption. Until the late
1560s or the 1570s it was almost entirely handled by syndicates of
Italian and Spanish merchants who obtained it from the farmers of the
papal administration, and was carried in ships of Mediterranean origin.
The control exercised by the farmers over the whole production led
naturally to a high degree of concentration in the trade. Of the total
of nearly 20,000 tons of alum exported during the second tenure of
the farm by the Grimaldi, from 1541 to 1553, four single merchants or
groups of merchants handled over two-thirds of the total, with the
Spaniard Martín de Ayala responsible for over 25 per cent, and the
Grimaldi themselves for 20 per cent. The whole trade was under the control of Spaniards and Italians, both in Italy and the distribution centres
of northern Europe, which took nearly 60 per cent of total exports
directly as well as a proportion of the alum sent to Genoa and other
Mediterranean ports.

The exports leaving Civitavecchia directly for ports outside the Mediterranean reached both their absolute peak and their highest proportion
of the total in the period from 1553 to 1565. From this time onwards
there was both a levelling-off in the production of the mines, and a
relative fall in exports beyond the Mediterranean. In part this was compensated by the expansion of the trade of Mediterranean entrepôts, especially with the growth of Leghorn. The evolution of the alum trade in the
later sixteenth and early seventeenth centuries reflects the general change
overtaking Mediterranean commerce. As English and Dutch ships penetrated the Mediterranean, they began to obtain large cargoes of alum
from Genoa and Leghorn, depriving the Italian and Spanish syndicates
of control of the trade beyond the Mediterranean. The considerable
increase in consignments to Genoa and Leghorn is revealed by Table 4.

Woad

Among dyestuffs for cloth, woad had long been the traditional basis of
blue colours, and gave rise to an important and specialised trade. Though
cultivated in many parts of Europe, the woad plant was grown commer-

Table 4: Consignments of Alum to Genoa and Leghorn, 1531-1650 (in cantare)

	Genoa and Riviera	Florence, Leghorn, Pisa
1531-53	50,943	21,407
1553-65	60,401	6,608
1566-78	131,336	24,318
1578-90	48,868	144,881
1590-1602	97,102	99,875
1602-14	34,903	15,765
...	...	...
1638-50	4,467	83,852

Source: J. Delumeau, *L'alun de Rome, xve-xixe siècle*. Paris, 1962.

cially on an intensive scale in Thuringia and in the region south-east of Toulouse. The latter area has been the subject of detailed research.[27] The cycle of production was a long one, the process of growing the plants, drying them and preparing the final product being spread over a year or more, and it was normal for the merchant to advance money to the grower and the technician. Since the main fleet of vessels which shipped the woad from Bordeaux normally sailed in the late autumn, and the peak season for sales in northern Europe was the summer, a full two years normally elapsed from the gathering of the crop until the moment of sale, and the allowance of credit extended the period in which the merchant's capital was tied up. The amount of capital required was therefore as high as three times annual turnover. Some of the larger-scale Toulouse merchants dealt in up to 12,000 bales a year, which at a value of 2 *livres* each, required a working capital of 36,000 *livres*.

There was a considerable market for the woad of Toulouse in Spain, which offered great attractions because of the relative proximity of Bilbao, S. Sebastian and Pamplona compared with the north of Europe, but it is doubtful if even in this sector the turnover of capital was completed in less than two years.

The risks of the trade were also great. The Toulousain merchant was forced to depend for the management of his sales, especially in northern markets, on local agents who frequently caused problems by selling at too low a price, even when they were not dishonest. The larger-scale merchants covered themselves by dealing simultaneously with several markets. Around the middle of the sixteenth century, Pierre Assézat dealt in London, Antwerp, Rouen, Bilbao, S. Sebastian and Pamplona. Even then, in 1557 his Rouen agency failed as a consequence of the dishonesty of junior employees. To these risks had to be added those resulting from more than normal fluctuations in supply and demand. Both the quality and the quantity of the product of the Lauragais area south-east of Toulouse varied as much as that of any agricultural product. The long production cycle also meant that the merchant could not know at the moment of purchase the size of the year's crop. In August 1561, for example, an argument was still raging over the size of the previous year's crop, for which estimates varied from 120,000 to 250,000 loads.

These factors produced a tendency for the woad trade of Toulouse to become concentrated in fewer hands. The Spanish and Lyonese merchants and bankers naturally tended to favour the well-established Toulousain merchants who offered better security. The tendency towards concentration was not continuous or permanent however. It was in years when the quality was high but the quantity was small that competition amongst merchants was at its greatest, and the tendency for the wealthiest and best-established men to dominate the market was at its height.

The greatest days of the Toulouse woad trade lay between 1520 and 1560. Between the middle of the fifteenth century and 1520 the Toulousain merchants had established their grip on the local supplies, at the expense of those from Cahors and Béarn, and to control their sale in Toulouse. Gradually they began to extend their selling operations further afield, first to Castile, where Jean Boisson established an agency at Burgos, and to a lesser extent to Aragon. During the earlier decades of the sixteenth century woad from Toulouse was increasingly finding its way to northern markets through the port of Bordeaux, but largely at the risk of Bordelais merchants who purchased it in Toulouse. In the face of this development, the Spanish market declined in importance, according to the records of individual firms. Between 1514 and 1520 Pierre Lancefoc sold at least 2,360 bales of woad to Bordeaux merchants, and in 1525 began to send quantities outside Toulouse at his own risk, but had already been preceded by several others since about 1520. From this point the trade took on its fully developed character. Partnerships such as that of Lancefoc, Jean Cheverry and Raimond Serravere engaged in the sale of woad in Spain, England and the Netherlands, and were using Lyons as a payment centre in the 1530s and early 1540s. In the late 1550s Pierre Assézat was exporting 12,000 bales (or about 1,000 tons) a year through Bordeaux, a lot of it for the Spanish market, through his associates in Pamplona, but also using the Schetz of Antwerp who had Spanish representatives. In 1557 he consigned 300 tons to the Netherlands, and through his agent Nicolas Duvale, an Aragonese, he sold 200 tons in England in 1558. Assezat had at least twelve factors working for him in various centres, and the magnificence of his house at Toulouse suggests that he was easily the richest of those who concentrated on the woad trade.

Around 1560 the woad trade of Toulouse passed through a period of great expansion, followed by collapse. During a three-year cycle from 1559 to 1562 all the factors involved in the trade, from the climatic chances affecting the crop to the state of the market in northern Europe were exhibited in a combination which was to be fatal. The expectations of an exceptionally good crop in 1559 led merchants to invest heavily, in a wave of buying which became highly speculative, continuing in 1560, with very large quantities being exported in the autumn of 1560. By then it was becoming clear that the crop of 1560 in which such confidence had been placed had turned out after processing to be of the low quality which so often accompanied great quantity, but it had fetched a high price. News began to reach Toulouse of a faltering in the market both in London and Antwerp, causing a collapse in the price of the 1560 crop. Large stocks of the 1559 crop were still unsold, and the hope of disposing of them rested solely on the poor quality of that of 1560. Attempts to open new markets, for example in Florence, were unsuccessful. The consequence was a collapse of the price of the 1561 crop in the Lauragais, which caught many of the less wary who had bought early. Some of the more cautious were caught by a second wave of falling prices as news of the continued stagnation of the markets in the north filtered through. Some of the factors in the crisis were political in origin: the risk of war between England and France over Scotland and the beginnings of religious troubles in France were of importance in further lowering of morale, but were combined with economic conditions in the cloth industry of the Netherlands and England and the intervention of other suppliers.

Recovery from the crisis was incomplete. On top of the worsening political situation, the woad trade was increasingly threatened by the imports of colonial dyestuffs from the Orient and the Spanish Indies. Indigo was more of a psychological threat than a real one in 1560, but increasing quantities began to reach Europe in the second half of the sixteenth century and by the beginning of the seventeenth century it was providing very serious competition for woad.

Notes

1. P. Ramsey, 'Overseas Trade in the Reign of Henry VII—the Evidence of the Customs Accounts', *EcHR,* 2nd Ser., VI (1954), pp. 173-82, at p. 178.

2. F.J. Fisher, 'Commercial Trends and Policy in sixteenth century England', *EcHR,* X (1940), pp. 95-117.

3. Van der Wee, *Growth,* II, p. 186. Also Brulez, 'L'exportation', loc.cit., p. 479.

4. Frias to Simón Ruiz, 27 June 1567, in Vazquez de Prada, *Lettres marchandes d'Anvers,* I, p. 29 n 1.

5. State Papers Domestic, Elizabeth, XXXV, No. 3. Printed in R.H. Tawney and Eileen Power, *Tudor Economic Documents,* II, pp. 45-7.

6. L. Stone, 'State Control in sixteenth century England', *EcHR,* XVII (1947), pp. 103-20.

7. T.S. Willan, *The Early History of the Russia Company,* p. 60.

8. R.W.K. Hinton, *The Eastland Trade and the Common Weal in the Seventeenth Century,* p. 1.

9. H. Zins, *England and the Baltic in the Elizabethan Era,* p. 169.

10. Ibid., pp. 174-6.

11. Ibid., p. 181.

12. Ibid., p. 186.

13. Astrid Friis, *Alderman Cockayne's Project and the Cloth Trade in the Reign of James I,* pp. 92-3.

14. Supple, *Crisis and Change,* pp. 39-40.

15. R. Davis, *English Overseas Trade, 1500-1700,* p. 25.

16. Supple, op.cit., pp. 53-4.

17. Friis, op.cit., p. 231.

18. Christensen, op.cit., p. 361, points out that the cloth and wine together failed to equal other southern European commodities by value in Dutch imports to the Baltic in the seventeenth century.

19. Van der Wee, *Growth,* II, pp. 186-7; III, Graph 24. Goris, op.cit., p. 249.

20. Chaunu, *Séville,* VIII, ii, i, pp. 328-9.

21. Brulez, *della Faille,* p. 24; Van der Wee, *Growth,* II, p. 223.

22. Van der Wee, *Growth,* II, pp. 250-1, referring to Kernkampf, *De Handel op den Vijand,* I, pp. 20, 63.

23. H. Taylor, 'Price Revolution or Price Revision?—The English and Spanish Trade after 1604', *Renaissance and Modern Studies,* XII (1968), pp. 5-32.

24. Fisher, 'London's Export Trade', loc.cit.

25. R. Davis, 'England and the Mediterranean, 1570-1670', *Essays in the Economic and Social History of Tudor and Stuart England in Honour of R.H. Tawney,* pp. 117-37.

26. J. Delumeau, *L'alun de Rome, xve–xixe siècles, passim.*

27. G. Caster, *Le commerce du pastel et de l'épicerie à Toulouse de 1450 environ à 1561, passim.*

TRANSPORT AND INSURANCE

As in other connections, it is important in discussing the organisation of maritime and land transport not to draw too sharp a contrast between the sixteenth century and its predecessor. Nor should we over-emphasise the differences between the types of vessel employed in the Mediterranean and those in use in the Atlantic and the northern seas or the importance of the sea routes compared with those overland.

In the fifteenth century, the merchant galley was still of considerable importance for the long-distance commerce of Venice and Florence. The Venetians used it in their rich Levant trade and for the link with the Netherlands, interrupted only for a decade or so after 1508, but the Florentine galleys ceased to trade with northern Europe in the last quarter of the century. The galley's advantages were its speed and man-oeuvrability and its capacity for self-defence, increased by the large size of its crew. By the fifteenth century, however, it had already absorbed some of the characteristics of the 'round' sailing vessels. It was more often than not powered by sail rather than oars when on the open sea, and frequently a large proportion of the oars were left behind in port. Though it still retained the characteristic of great length in relation to beam compared with the 'round' ships, the fifteenth-century merchant galley had a more highly developed superstructure than that of the smaller galleys designed specifically for naval use. It still normally had only one deck, encumbered by the rowers' benches, and lacked adequate cover for either the passengers or the high proportion of the cargo carried on deck (because of the small capacity of the shallow holds). Nevertheless, the carrying capacity of the Venetian galley approached 250 tons and was comparable with that of 'round' ships of 600 deadweight tons.[1] Its crew was, however, extremely large for its carrying capacity and no longer consisted of slaves, but of free men who were capable of demonstrating on the steps of the Doge's palace for their pay.[2]

The history of Venetian navigation cannot be understood solely in terms of the galley, the numbers of which remained quite small, a fleet of three or four vessels being sufficient in most years for the transport of the valuable cargoes of small bulk between Venice and Flanders. The use of 'round' ships of great capacity was permitted even in the Levant spice trade between 1514 and 1524 and again after 1534,[3] and any hope of measuring Venetian shipping capacity depends on evidence of the fluctuation in their numbers and equally important, of those of the very large number of small sailing vessels. The evidence suggests that around 1560 an average of about 20,000 tons of goods a year was being moved in sailing ships of an individual capacity of more than 240 tons, though it is likely that the total carrying capacity of the fleet was only about 18,000 tons at this time. Later, it seems to have risen by a surprising amount, to about 32,000 tons in 1567, but fell catastrophically to only 8,000 tons in 1574, following the war with the Turks from 1570 to 1573, during which Venice's competitors enjoyed a boom at her expense. Ragusan evidence suggests that trade from this major maritime centre of the eastern Adriatic expanded fourfold during these years.[4]

What was true of Venice was even more applicable to Genoa. By the fifteenth century the galley was hardly used by the Genoese for either their Mediterranean or north European commerce. About the middle of the century the carrying capacity of its fleet of 'round' ships was at least twice that of the Venetian, and was characterised by the enormous average size of the ships. Thirty *navi* had a carrying capacity of 20,000 tons. The adoption of very large vessels was of critical importance in the maritime trade of Genoa. It dictated methods of navigation, sailing techniques and even the routes followed. It is significant that the Genoese ships called much less often at intermediate ports than did those of either the Venetians or the Florentines. The Genoese were accordingly forced to rely on others for the large number of smaller vessels which carried on the short-distance traffic. Whilst the small ports of the Genoese Riviera provided many, the Basques, supplemented by Castilians from Galicia or Seville, were very prominent in the carriage of grain from Sicily and salt from Ibiza.[5]

The evolution of the technique of construction which produced the great 'carracks' of the late fifteenth century had been a long one. The older 'cock' had been developed into a round ship with a greater complexity of sails, and because of the greater ease with which cannon could be mounted, it came into its own with the development of gunnery, with the great advantage of a much smaller crew than a galley of equivalent carrying capacity.[6] The confidence of the designers increased so that ships of 1,000 tons or more were becoming common. A warship of 2,400 tons is said to have been constructed in Venice in 1486, whilst the average official size of their 'round' naval vessels was from 1,200 to 1,500 tons. These innovations spilled over into the building of merchant vessels, and though it was found impracticable to build them much over 1,000 tons, those of 600 tons or more were common. The limiting factor in this period was much more the shallowness of harbours, where they existed, and poor port facilities, rather than the limitations of building techniques.

In sixteenth-century Spain, vessels constructed for the transatlantic trade tended to increase in tonnage. The average tonnage rose from around 100 at the beginning of the century to around 300 at its end and naturally, those vessels which used Cádiz rather than Seville were of the highest average tonnage.[7] The very large vessel was thus an exception, even at the end of the sixteenth century. Most of the ships constructed for the Indies trade and a lot of those used for the links with northern Europe were built in Spain, the majority in the yards of the Biscay coast, originally favoured by good local supplies of suitable timber and iron, and later by its relative proximity to north European sources of raw materials. The proximity of the major Spanish ship-building centres to northern Europe meant also that they were open to northern influences on technique, and influenced the north in turn. The prosperity of Bilbao as a shipbuilding centre lasted until at least 1575. As late as 1583 there were 15,000 tons of shipping under construction in its yards and in the following three years 50 vessels were ordered for the Crown, during the period of build-up for the enterprise of England.[8] Though Spain became more dependent on foreign-built ships, her own construction remained very active until the early years of the seventeenth century, but complaints of design faults became more frequent as losses at sea increased. It seems that the constructors had become mesmerised, as had those of fifteenth-century Italy, by the ideal of building more ships of very high tonnage, whose sailing qualities and safety standards were poor. A drop in the average tonnage of vessels sailing to the Indies in the second and third decades of the seventeenth century may well have reflected technical difficulties as well as economic ones.

It is not easy to calculate the total capacity of the Spanish merchant fleet in the sixteenth century. The most informed estimate is largely guesswork, based on the movement of the port of Bilbao.[9] In one year, 1598-9, a total of 309 vessels entered Bilbao, of which 208 were Spanish. Rough calculations based on the known varieties of vessel give a total tonnage of nearly 68,000, of which nearly 40,000 tons were Spanish-owned. From this limited evidence it is a very large step to estimating the total national tonnage, but an order of magnitude of 250,000 to 300,000 tons for the combined fleets of Spain and Portugal at the end of the century is not unreasonable. It follows from this that the percentage of Spanish shipping engaged in the Indies trade was relatively small, and that the movement of shipping at Bilbao alone exceeded that of the transatlantic trade of Seville. In terms of shipping capacity, the high-volume, low-value cargoes of the European trade were a much more accurate index than those of the Indies.

The large ship of over 400 tons or so was never typical in European trade in either the fifteenth or sixteenth centuries. The exception of fifteenth-century Genoa in fact proves the rule, since she was forced to rely on foreign vessels to service her great ships. There are indeed signs that the proportion of very large vessels in the total European tonnage fell away during the course of the sixteenth century, but that the average tonnage continued to rise. That is to say there was a tendency in the long-distance trades towards a more even distribution of tonnage around the average. Nevertheless, Fernand Braudel goes so far as to say that vessels of small tonnage formed 'a crushing majority'. As early as 1451 a discussion in the Venetian Senate revealed the importance of the smaller vessels even in the Syrian and Catalan trades, whilst in 1478 Andrea Soller wrote from Bruges that the little ships had completely driven out the great. In 1498 four ships loaded 9,000 quintals of goods in Antwerp, whilst 28 caravels took only 1,150 quintals. This contrast is, of course, abnormal and clearly did not represent anything like a full cargo for the caravels. A list of ships in the ports of Asturias in 1538 shows that they averaged only 70 tons, and in the late 1570s a document listing foreign vessels arriving in Andalucian ports shows that they totalled 800 a year, with a total tonnage of 60,000, but an average of only 75 tons. The iron exports of Biscay were almost exclusively carried in small ships because of the number of small ports with shallow water and poor facilities and because the larger vessels were often subject to uneconomic delays whilst they waited for sufficient cargo to be collected.[10] For cargoes of great bulk, such as grain, the smaller vessels were essential because there were insufficient ships of medium size, and undoubtedly many of those entering Andalucian ports were carrying northern grain. The Bretons provided an enormous service around the Atlantic coats of Europe on the basis of very small ships. A third of the cargoes of wine they shipped from Bordeaux in 1482-3 did not exceed 20 tons each, and the values of the cargoes they picked up in the small ports of Cornwall were often only around £10.[11] In the seventeenth century the typical English vessel from the western ports trading with Spain was of only 20-40 tons capacity.

Around the middle of the sixteenth century, if the total capacity of the English merchant fleet was around 50,000 tons, it probably contained no more than 14 ships of over 200 tons. The reign of Elizabeth saw the beginning of a great expansion of English shipping, but it was still largely on the basis of vessels of small tonnage. The encouragement of fisheries and the growth of the coastal trade, especially in coal from Newcastle, were the dominant factors. By 1614, the East Anglian ports employed over 100 vessels in the Iceland fisheries, whilst increasing numbers were sailing from the harbours of Devon and Cornwall for the Newfoundland cod-fishing areas. As Sir William Monson wrote in the 1630s,

> there is no commodity in the world of so great bulk and small value, or that can set so many ships of burden at work. . . A mean merchant may freight his ship of 250 tons with fish that will not cost above £1,600, that forty merchants cannot do of richer and better commodities.

The shipment of coal from Newcastle, mostly for London, rose from 35,000 tons a year in the middle of the sixteenth century to over 400,000 tons by 1633-4.

Whilst these developments stimulated mostly the expansion of shipping of small tonnage, other factors were contributing to the growth of a fleet of larger ships. The gradual diversification of English overseas trade in the late sixteenth century accelerated rapidly after 1580, especially in the Mediterranean, and between 1582 and 1629 the number of English ships of 200 tons and over increased from 18 to more than 145. It has been calculated that the northern European trade was occupying 13,000 tons of shipping, compared with 39,000 for the nearer areas of the Netherlands, France, Scotland and Ireland; 30,000 for the Mediterranean and southern Europe, 36,000 for America and the West Indies and 8,000 for the East Indies.[12]

What was true of England for the late sixteenth and seventeenth centuries was applicable to the northern Netherlands from a much earlier date. There is no doubt that the rise of Dutch shipping was firmly based on the North Sea fisheries. By the middle of the sixteenth century over 1,000 Dutch ships were entering the Baltic each year, and the number continued to grow as the grain trade expanded in the second half of the century. Yet though the size of the Dutch merchant fleet came to surpass that of the combined Spanish and Portuguese, the average tonnage of the vessels employed remained moderate. According to the perhaps not entirely reliable evidence of the Sound Toll Registers, in 1557 only 30 per cent of Dutch ships trading to the Baltic were of over 100 lasts (or 200 tons) capacity, and during the troubled years of the 1560s and 1570s this percentage seems to have fallen to as little as 10. Not until the seventeenth century did it rise again above this figure, but from then onwards the percentage of vessels of over 200 tons rose rapidly—to 50 per cent by the 1620s and as high as 90 per cent by the 1640s. A comparison with the evidence of the records of the port of Koenigsberg suggests a rather different picture however. A total of 127 ships recorded at Koenigsberg in 1549 reached 4,500 lasts, whilst by 1623, 904 ships totalled 65,000 lasts. These averages of nearly 30 and 70 lasts respectively are for all vessels using the port, and since there is evidence that some of the Koenigsberg-based vessels were amongst the largest and the Hanseatics the smallest, the Dutch were probably closest to the average. Though these figures suggest a somewhat lower average size than the Sound Toll Registers, the trend towards vessels of around 100 lasts capacity is evident from both sources.[13]

There is no room for doubt that the Dutch achieved a technical revolution in the design of merchant ships for the European trade which was a major factor in their commercial supremacy in the seventeenth century. The *'fluit'* or flyboat was specifically designed for operation in shallow waters. Speed and manoeuvrability were sacrificed to maximum carrying capacity, and a simplified system of sails reduced the crew required to a minimum. To the same end it carried little or no armament for defence and was thus more suited to northern waters than to the Mediterranean, where the need for heavier armament against the growing activity of corsairs gave the English a decided advantage.

There was no fundamental change during the period in the system of ship-owning. Though owner and master of a small vessel might well be the same person, it was usual for ownership to be shared. The quantity of capital required for the construction and fitting out of an average-sized vessel for long-distance trade was considerable, but the running costs, especially the wages of the crew, could amount to more. Information about the cost of constructing ships is sparse. Even in the fifteenth century, there is an example of a Genoese vessel which was sold without fittings for 10,500 *lire*. For a voyage to Chios, the wages of the crew could amount to 4,500 *lire* in a case where the ship itself was valued at only 4,850.[14] From the point of view of the owner, therefore, each voyage was a serious risk. He was normally paid a fixed sum by the merchants who chartered the vessel for a voyage, the duration of which was extremely variable. The sharing of the capital investment was also a means of sharing the risks of loss from weather or piracy. In Genoa, as elsewhere in the Mediterranean, the system of the *carat* or 24th part was common. The *'armatore'* usually retained some shares himself, other individuals taking a share which could be as small as one quarter of a carat, or only 1 per cent. Investment in shipping was therefore widely spread amongst merchants and financiers, and even amongst the professional classes. The method varied from full participation in a substantial share of a ship to the simple loan to the master. The maritime loan is often regarded as a form of marine insurance, but was sharply distinguished from true insurance by the fact that the lender provided money in advance of the voyage.

Merchants and others increasingly participated in the ownership and fitting out of ships, steadily reducing the independence of the master and although the latter was usually engaged in some small trade on his own account, as were members of the crew, he increasingly lost his freedom of action. It was extremely unusual, both in fifteenth-century Genoa and in sixteenth-century Antwerp, for the master of a ship to enjoy high social or economic status.[15] Joint ownership was the common practice in the Netherlands, at least from the middle of the sixteenth century, as is revealed by the royal ordinances of 1551 and the codification of maritime law of 1563, which repeated earlier regulations concerning the rights of ship-masters and owners. The master retained the rights of command in the interests of the safety of the vessel. He could depart from his instructions, and even dispose of the cargo *en route* if the ship's safety demanded it.[16]

The records of the Delft firm of merchants, the Van Adrichem, give us an insight into the organisation of Dutch shipping in the second half of the sixteenth century. Claes Van Adrichem's connection with shipping dated probably from the 1560s, evolving out of his interests in the fishing industry. He saw in ship-owning a means of bringing his trading activities in corn and herrings more fully under his control and of increasing their profitability. His registers show that he was at various times involved in not less than 26 different shipping companies, involving a somewhat larger number of ships. During the first few years of his investment in shipping, he frequently changed ships and restricted himself to small vessels. Gradually his investment became more stable, and involved larger vessels. In 1579 he owned shares in six ships with a total tonnage of 421 lasts, of which he held 70 lasts, and in 1583 shares in six ships totalling 482 lasts, of which his share was 77. The basic share unit was one-eighth, in multiples or subdivisions. The average number of partners owning a single vessel was nine, so that on average Van Adrichem's shares were somewhat greater than his partners', the ship's master usually participating to about the same extent as the other partners. Van Adrichem's partners were usually drawn from a relatively small and permanent group, amongst whom his relatives were prominent. The owners met from time to time, though often with only half the capital represented.

They were also normally able to equip the vessel from their own resources. Van Adrichem himself was naturally able to supply corn and herrings, whilst other partners provided beer and timber, reliance on the outside market being necessary only for butter and cheese.[17]

Whilst there was no formal legal distinction between the partners, decisions were normally taken by the more active amongst them, usually representing a majority of the capital employed. The relatively subordinate role of the master, even if he owned a share, is clearly brought out by the Van Adrichem records. Those of the formal company meetings shed little light on the conduct of affairs, though these were held regularly once or twice a year for the presentation of accounts, if possible at times when the master could be present. Between these meetings it is clear that the owners met during the voyage to take decisions on such matters as the spending of money received from the sale of the outward cargo, which were communicated to the master as he passed through the Sound, perhaps direct from Lisbon. The function of the company's book-keeper was all-important. The book-keeper in this case was no mere subordinate, but effectively the managing director of the enterprise, though it is not possible to determine the extent of his freedom of action. The master remained subordinate, whether to the instructions of all the owners corporately, or to those of the book-keeper alone. The relative ease of communication between the company in Delft and the master partly accounts for this. Though the master might occasionally take independent decisions, they were usually consequent upon specific permission given on individual voyages, and do not appear to have followed from the wide legal powers of the master. He might, for example, be specifically instructed to engage in trade, and though his authority in such matters, as in the undertaking of charter work, was then great, his use of this freedom was becoming more infrequent as the companies began more and more to employ factors resident in the important centres of their trade. Any complaints from charterers of the vessels were normally made to the owners, not to the master, though he might have been the signatory of the agreement or 'charter party'.

The chartering of a vessel in whole or in part was normal commercial practice. The owners could either charter the whole ship to an individual or to several persons for a specific voyage or for a specific period of time. The written contract (the charter-party), was normally confirmed before a notary. The majority of the Dutch charter-parties surviving from this period were signed by the master of the vessel and give a clear indication of his relationship to the charterers. Though the master remained in full control of the crew and the fitting out of the ship, the charterer laid down the route and the cargo, not necessarily in detail in the original contract, but by orders issued by virtue of his rights under it. There was a tendency for the contracts to become shorter and more stereotyped in form as their use became more widespread, but they never became a standardised *pro forma.* Frequently the charterer granted the master authority equivalent to that of a factor for the disposal of goods abroad and for the purchase of a return cargo with the proceeds. On the other hand, authority to break the terms of the charter-party was strictly limited to the provisions of the law and generally speaking penalty clauses were written into the agreements, reducing the need for resort to law in cases of dispute.

The close relationship in Dutch commerce between trading activity and ship-owning was no sign of primitive organisation, but rather of a tendency to evolve practical solutions to practical problems. Though ship-owning involved an overlapping series of partnerships, it was an essentially simple structure, reflecting the close relationship with the conduct of trade. Though chartering was old, it spread into the Baltic trade during the course of the sixteenth century without leading to a complete separation between ship-owning and commercial activity. It was, however, the beginning of a trend towards the development of the Dutch role in the 'carrying trade' of Europe which was to be a major feature of their seventeenth-century supremacy. The Van Adrichem shipping companies seem to have resorted to the charter of a whole vessel only in a minority of cases, their ships mostly being entirely freighted with the company's own goods, or only partly with those of others, space being usually reserved on the homeward voyage for goods on the common account of the owners. Their attitude towards their ships was far from exclusive, therefore, and they frequently shipped their goods in vessels belonging to other companies. It was in fact normal for six or more individuals or firms to freight a single ship. Evidence from Stockholm at the end of the sixteenth and the beginning of the seventeenth century suggests that the practice of part-freighting developed considerably and that there was a tendency towards increasing subdivision of the cargoes. This tendency was apparently less strong amongst the Dutch who traded with Stockholm than other nationalities and is perhaps a reflection of their greater confidence during a period when the risks of war were great, though its later reversal may well have been due to the evolution of economic attitudes and techniques.[18]

In this latter process the spread of proper marine insurance may well have played an important part.[19] As so often, its techniques were well developed in later medieval Italy, but spread only slowly to the north.

A vessel might be insured by the consignor of the goods when the ship-owner was reluctant to undertake a voyage. Examples of this can be found as early as 1245 and as late as 1526, when in Bordeaux, the factor of the Toulousain merchant, Jean de Bernuys, undertook to insure a ship against capture by Spaniards for a single voyage to Portugalete, at the high cost of 1,240 *livres* for the vessel, its cargo and equipment. It was possible for this risk to be transferred to the purchaser of the goods; there is an example from Rouen in 1528. More normally, the ship-owner could insure the goods he carried. In 1470, 34 *tonneaux* of wine for shipment to Sluys paid three *écus* each for freight, plus a surcharge of eight *écus* if the ship should be attacked by the English. An example from Rouen in 1489 is rather different; the vessel was freighted to a merchant for the transport of 20 *tonneaux* of wine, the merchant paying 9 *écus* per *tonneau.* In case of loss by weather conditions, the freighter promised to pay 12 *écus* per *tonneau,* in case of loss by capture, 16 *écus* payable two months after the event, but in these circumstances the profit on the sale of any wine which was recovered was to remain with the freighter. This practice seems to have survived for a long time, examples being found as late as 1653 in Leghorn and 1655 in Marseilles. Another technique which came close to the modern form of insurance was practised throughout the period: the exchange of risks between merchants themselves.

The essential step in the evolution of modern insurance was the entry of a third party, not directly involved in the ownership or the transport of the goods. A Marseilles contract exists from as early as 1328 which certainly contained a third party. The idea of the wager had of course a very long history, and it was when the two principles of a third disinterested party in taking a risk and the general practice of making bets became fused into one that we can say that the modern concept of insurance was born. City statutes of the late middle ages frequently forbade the making of wagers on the death of individuals, a sure sign that the practice was very current. Whilst it was possible for a third party to help in covering risks by means of a loan, this was very expensive owing to the high prevailing rates of interest. Insurance proper had the great advantage to the insured that, simply because the insurer did not have to lay out any money unless a claim was made, it was possible to offer much lower rates. Insurance did not drive out the loan, because this fulfilled another function, that of providing the merchant with capital. Early Genoese insurance policies took care to disguise the nature of the contract, suspected by the Church of being usurious. Fictitious sales often provided a cover for insurance, but the brevity of the insurance contract enforced by ecclesiastical suspicion carried with it serious legal defects. Since the mention of a premium was often avoided, it was sometimes difficult for the insurer to obtain payment. Pisan and Florentine policies of the late fourteenth century were, on the other hand, much more specific concerning guarantees and risks covered, with open mention of the premium.

Gradually, the 'Florentine' form of policy spread elsewhere, even to Genoa by the mid-fifteenth century. In Venice the practice of insurance was largely carried on by Florentines, even though it was from Venice that the technique spread around the Adriatic and the Levant. From Genoa and Florence it spread to the western Mediterranean, Flanders and England. Lyons was the last centre to be dominated by Florentine insurance as it was in banking, but during the sixteenth century Bilbao, Seville and especially Burgos became important centres of insurance business; Spaniards were prominent in it in the Netherlands, despite Italian competition.

The expansion of insurance business soon gave rise to public regulation. In Florence the statutes of 1525 and 1526 were a model widely imitated. Special officials were established to deal with all insurance disputes, and had the power to approve all contracts, at rates which they fixed. The use of a model or standard form of policy became obligatory. The *Consulado* of Burgos laid down regulations as early as 1500, though their details have not survived. Those of 1538, however, laid down a form of policy, and the authority of the Prior was needed for modifications. In 1556 the officers of the *Casa de Contratación* in Seville laid down regulations giving several alternative forms of policy, one for general trade, and two for the Indies (different forms for the outward and homeward voyages). Those of Burgos stipulated that claims should be settled at once, without the application being in judicial form or even in writing, and the contract had to be deposited with a notary. The insured was not to declare above the true value and there were items which could be excluded from cover. In England jurisdiction over maritime matters lay with the court of the Lord Admiral, but there is evidence that some insurance cases went before the Privy Council in the 1560s and 1570s, when the Lord Mayor of London, Sir Thomas Gresham, was requested to draw up regulations. The Royal Exchange had already opened in 1568, though it was not to receive its title until 1570. Later, an Act of Parliament of 1601 set up a court with a Judge of Admiralty, four lawyers and eight merchants to exercise summary jurisdiction, with appeal to Chancery. The creation of an insurance bureau leading to the standardisation of policy clauses came later, whilst the oldest known English printed policy dates from 1656.

As the use of insurance spread, it was subject to a similar process of standardisation as the bill of exchange, registration before a notary became much less frequent, and even the negotiability of a policy became accepted. The role of the *courtier* or agent was important in its development. As early as 1408 a Genoese ordinance permitted the use of agents to sign insurance contracts. Abuses of the system were, however, frequent, and led to increasingly rigid regulation and penalties. The Duke of Alba hanged a Netherlands insurance agent as well as the master of a vessel which had been insured for a cargo of cloth but which was proved to have been carrying only ballast.

The trend towards specialisation in insurance business was late. Almost invariably during the sixteenth and seventeenth centuries, insurance was effected by merchants for merchants and ship-owners. One of the earliest examples of a specialist was Pierre Tallemont of La Rochelle, who was distinguished by his willingness to engage himself for large sums of up to 3,000 *livres,* but whose experience was clearly unfavourable, as in 1628 he reverted to the more common practice of co-insurance. He was nevertheless a portent of a new trend in which a wider section of society became involved in insurance, especially in Marseilles and Amsterdam, where lawyers, government officials, doctors, peasants and even clergy began to invest in it. Companies specialising in insurance came into existence quite early, however, a Genoese example being known from 1426, whilst in Venice the development of specialists in the calculation of risks was evident from the early part of the sixteenth century.

To the normal risks of the sea very often had to be added those of war and piracy. The rates quoted for the insurance of vessels and cargoes therefore varied enormously in time and place. Whilst transport by sea retained great advantages over that by land or river for bulky cargoes, the cost of insurance could be an important element. A consignment of cloth sent from Genoa to Turkey in the mid-fifteenth century cost 3.5 ducats to transport, whilst the insurance was 3.8 ducats, or about 8 per cent of its value in Genoa.[20] This was apparently quite a normal rate, that to England being somewhat less, whilst the Tyrrhenian sea was costly, presumably because of the risks of piracy. Rates of insurance thus varied more from year to year because of the changing risks of war and piracy than they did from season to season because of weather conditions. When the della Faille began in the 1580s to interest themselves in trade between the Netherlands and the Mediterranean by the sea route, more often than not they did not insure their cargoes because of the high rates which prevailed. In 1591 premiums as high as 18 to 20 per cent were being asked for the voyage to Italy. Clearly, the risks were great. Of thirty recorded voyages of vessels chartered or owned by the della Faille, two ships were wrecked and ten were interrupted *en route* by arrest on suspicion of carrying rebel Dutch goods. Of these, three were released after a few months, two after several years, one was confiscated, and in the remaining cases the voyage was abandoned. As Martin della Faille put it: 'God was the insurer.' It was in fact the custom of the della Faille to give alms on receiving news of the safe arrival of an uninsured vessel. On one occasion when alms were given on the departure of a vessel, it was specifically stated that they replaced insurance, and as the ship was wrecked, their small size gave rise to the suspicion that God was not satisfied.[21]

Piracy was a supreme affliction of the Mediterranean, and it seems to have become worse after the dying out of the official conflict between Spain and the Turks. Venice was forced to spend large sums on the maintenance of galleys to keep the Adriatic clear of pirates, and without permanent success. The most notorious group were the Uskoks, who preyed upon shipping in the northern Adriatic from their impregnable base at Segna, near Fiume. Technically subjects of the Habsburgs, they were regarded by the Papacy as crusaders against the Turks, and an observer noted in 1601 that he had seen them 'going from the harbour to the churches on their knees to give thanks for their uninterrupted robberies'. The local bishop, the friary and the Dominican monastery received their share of the booty as tithes. In 1600 the Austrian Habsburgs decided to intervene against the Uskoks, and their numbers were for a time considerably reduced, but after 1615 they revived, and extended their activities over the whole of the Adriatic, not without Spanish encouragement during the period of the anti-Venetian policy of the Viceroy of Naples, the Duke of Osuna.[22]

The activities of the Barbary corsairs were much more widespread, covering the whole of the eastern and western basins of the Mediterranean, and in the early decades of the seventeenth century extending into the Atlantic, and even as far as the English Channel. Their activities, and the official war between France and Morocco, did much to ruin the trade of Marseilles after 1600, and perhaps helps to account for the wider spread of insurance risks beyond the limits of the purely merchant community.

In the last analysis, the varied risks of the sea were not enough in general terms to outweigh its undoubted advantages in cost compared with the inland routes. Contemporaries had no doubt about this, and some went so far as to say that the overland route, where there was an alternative, was only commercially viable for the more valuable types of cloth. Certainly, the rule holds good that the higher the value of the goods for their weight, the more suitable they were for transport by land. Our concentration on maritime trade is nevertheless usually too great, and our view of the commercial economy of early modern Europe distorted by a relative neglect of inland traffic. Some areas of the greatest economic vitality, such as south Germany, were clearly dependent on overland communications, and others such as Lyons gained their importance from their position on the major land routes linking Italy with the Netherlands.

The relative importance of the land route between Italy and the Netherlands may well have varied during the course of the period, but detailed figures are available only for some years in the 1540s. Then, it seems certain that the land route took the vast majority of the trade. War between France and the Habsburgs may well have affected the traffic during a part of these years, but the rapidity with which land transport could adjust its routes to avoid areas of military action or political difficulty was one of its compensating advantages compared with the sea routes through narrow waters. Goods were often transported from Seville to Alicante by land to avoid both the navigational difficulties of the Straits of Gibraltar and the activities of corsairs in the waters between Morocco and the coast of Granada. As far as the Italian trade of the Netherlands was concerned, it amounted between 1543 and 1545 to about 17 per cent of the total Netherlands exports, and as far as Antwerp was concerned, nearly 40 per cent, almost as great as that to Germany. The predominance of the overland route in Antwerp's trade gave rise to the development of a highly specialised organisation. Firms were established which devoted themselves entirely to the organisation of the complicated routes which linked Antwerp with Germany and Italy, and were able to quote rates for the whole journey, so that the merchant made one payment at the beginning or the end and did not have to concern himself with making arrangements with the local agents who dealt directly with the carriers. By the 1540s half a dozen firms controlled most of this business in Antwerp and as in so much of Antwerp's commercial life, Italians were prominent. The Milanese Giovanni Angelo d'Anoni (or Danon) was the most outstanding, seconded by the German Hans Cleinhaus, but native Flemings seem to have played a greater part in the organisation of overland trade than they did at that time in seaborne traffic, taking perhaps 20 per cent of the total.[23]

The major natural obstacle to trade overland between northern Europe and Italy was the Alps. Here the choice of routes was great. Almost all of the passes were usable by mules and some of them by carts. Political authorities vied with each other to improve the routes under their control, and severe limits were imposed on their liberty to impose excessive tolls by the competition between them to attract the most lucrative traffic. Some villages came to specialise in transport, with almost the whole population dependent upon it for a livelihood. There was considerable collaboration as well as rivalry between them. Those on the same route shared the work of maintaining the roads, the arrangement of stopping-places and the supply of food for men and animals. The winter did not cause the complete stoppage of traffic. For extra payment they would arrange to travel during the night, and in some places sledges were used during the winter months. Road improvements and the spread of inns and hospices began in the late middle ages, but their steady expansion during the sixteenth century is ample testimony of the vitality of the inland routes.[24]

The rise of Lyons was naturally a stimulus to the expansion of new routes through the Alps, especially that of the Mont Cenis, but of equal importance in the growth of Lyons was its position at the confluence of the Rhône and the Saône and its relative closeness to the Loire, which gave it access to western and northern France. Roanne was the southern terminus of the route along the Loire which led via Briare or Orleans to Paris. However, whilst the superiority of the river routes, in the number and length of which France was particularly fortunate, was clear in the downstream direction, the land route was often preferred for the upstream traffic. It was no accident that the route between Paris and Lyons was the first in France to receive a postal system, nor that in 1566 the king ordered the paved road to be extended further south from Paris. Roanne became the centre of a large body of *voituriers par eau,* which became a powerful corporation, able to negotiate with the owners of the many tolls which were levied along the route to Orleans.

The contrast between the river route and that by road was even more marked along the Saône. A natural route for the transport of heavy goods, such as grain, southwards to Lyons, it was much less used in the upstream direction, and the major link between Lyons and the Netherlands was by the revival of the old medieval roads which passed through the fair centres of Champagne to Valenciennes, the southernmost point of navigability on the Scheldt. The land route was thus by no means

uncompetitive even where the river network seemed to provide a preferable alternative. The importance of human transport must not be neglected by an excessive concentration on the large-scale trade of the
greater merchants. Many of them in Lyons had begun life as simple
pedlars and large numbers of peasants brought their goods to Lyons
on foot. In 1578 the taverners of Lyons stated that 'for every merchant
who comes to the fairs on horseback, and who can afford to stay in a
good lodging, there are ten who come on foot who are quite happy to
find some little *cabaret*'. The horse was reserved for the rapid and relatively wealthy traveller, whilst goods went either by cart or mule.
Lyons in fact stood on the border of areas where to the north transport
was predominantly by carts, to the east in the Alps by mule, and to the
west lay a region where the two systems were evenly balanced. The average two-wheeled cart could carry a load of 800 to 1,600 lb, whilst a
mule could manage only about 350 to 400 lb at the most, carried in
two panniers on either side of the animal's back. Where the roads made
the use of the cart practicable its superior efficiency was clear, but
neither could compete with the river-boat in the economy of either
manpower or that of animals. A single river-boat on the Saône, powered by oars or handled upstream by men or horses, could carry as great
a load as 400 mules.

The organisation of transport in the Lyons area seems to have been in
relatively small units, in contrast to that of Antwerp. Most muleteers
seem to have possessed only from five to twelve animals, but they were
grouped together under the charge of a 'driver' on the road. Muleteers
and their animals lived mainly in the suburbs of Lyons, outside the gates
of the city and on the major routes of trade. It is possible to obtain some
idea of the relative cost of the land or river routes to Lyons. In 1543, a
consignment of wheat from Beauce for the *Aumône Général* of Lyons
cost 668 *livres* to transport up-river from Orleans to Roanne and another
686 *livres* for the relatively short distance from Roanne to Lyons by
road, showing an advantage for a comparable distance of almost 75 per
cent in favour of the river, even upstream. Over all, the cost of transport represented three-quarters of the cost price at Orleans, and over
40 per cent of its selling price in Lyons. For goods of higher value for
a given weight, the costs were of course much less significant. Rates for
English 'friezes' coming from Antwerp could be around 14 per cent of
their value, whilst for more expensive varieties of cloth such as Hons-
choote serges they could be as low as 3.5 per cent, and for Bruges satins
as little as 1.4 per cent.[25]

Spain was forced back on land routes for internal transport to a

degree found nowhere else in western Europe. Its rivers were largely un-
suitable for long-distance transport, and though the government introduced grandiose schemes for the development of canals, these came to
little during the course of the period. The number of animals used in
transport was consequently extraordinarily high. Alsonso de Herrera
estimated that as many as 400,000 mules were in use in the 1540s.
Many routes were accessible only to mules, although some routes were
possible for carts, frequently drawn by oxen. Nevertheless from the late
fifteenth century there is evidence that the Crown was systematically
encouraging internal transport, if mostly in the interests of the cam-
paign which led to the fall of the Moorish Kingdom of Granada in
1492. Specific privileges were granted to make transport work for the
Crown more attractive. Freedom was granted for the crossing of local
and provincial boundaries without payment of the usual dues and carters were allowed to cut wood for repairs and cooking fuel. In 1497 a
royal decree established the *Cabaña Real de Carreteros,* but contrary
to customary opinion its existence was limited to the area around the
Kingdom of Granada and it was only at the end of the sixteenth century
that it acquired the full organisation with its own special court, presided
over by a *Juez conservador,* which has led historians to compare its
status and privileges to those of the *Mesta,* or gild of migratory sheep-
owners.

There were many examples of conflict between the interests of the
carters, arable farmers and town authorities. In 1548 the *Cortes* of
Castile complained that the royal judges were failing to suppress the
allegedly illegal practice of the carters in pasturing their animals on
lands used for crops, but despite their protest the privileges of the carters were reiterated by royal order in 1553. By 1590 the carters had been
granted the privilege of a proprietary interest in the lands used for the
winter pasturing of their oxen. The increasing pressure on the food
supply in the late sixteenth and early seventeenth centuries, especially
consequent upon the rapid expansion of Madrid, caused the government
to extend further the privileges of the carters by expanding its cheap
pasture policy, transferring some of the cost of feeding the population
of the capital to the countryside. The carters of Navarredonda were
regularly impressed into service for the transport of grain to Madrid and
in 1643 possessed over 1,000 carts. When the vast number of animals,
especially mules, used in agriculture is taken into account, it is clear that
the feeding of the animal population itself accounted for a considerable
proportion of the production of agricultural land in Spain.[26]

Despite all the advantages of the sea, the land routes of sixteenth-century Europe witnessed an intense activity and on occasions their advantages over sea routes could be exploited. The development of the port of Ancona in the first half of the century is a paradoxical example. It was a port which grew up at the junction of two routes which were essentially terrestrial. During the first quarter of the century Ancona developed from a centre for the exchange of goods within a limited area of the Adriatic into an important entrepôt for foreign merchants. Increasing quantities of English and Flemish cloth, arriving by the over-land route from the Netherlands were sold to Greek and Turkish mer-chants, whilst hides formed the most important commodity brought from the Balkans in exchange. Ancona's development in fact reflected the growing importance of the Ottoman Empire, especially under Suleiman the Magnificent (1520-66), as a market for western European goods and as a source of raw materials. Greater internal security made the overland route from Constantinople through Ragusa much more attractive. It was easier to protect a land caravan on the thirty-day journey from Constantinople to Ragusa with an armed escort than it was to provide a convoy at sea in the Eastern Mediterranean or the Adriatic. The particular insecurity of the eastern Mediterranean meant that it was often possible to carry high-value cloths by land more cheaply than the cost of insurance alone by sea. If the great days of Ancona passed in the second half of the sixteenth century with the revival of Venetian commerce by sea and later the direct entry of the English into the Mediterranean, the middle years of the century saw a conjuncture of circumstances which provide a timely reminder that the land still offered the possibility of safe and rapid transport.[27]

Notes

1. F.C. Lane, *Venetian Ships and Shipbuilders of the Renaissance*, p. 6.
2. Ibid., p. 15.
3. F.C. Lane, 'The Merchant Marine and maritime Trade of Venice through the Centuries', in *Venice and History—the Collected Papers of F.C. Lane*, pp. 143-62.
4. R. Romano, 'La marine marchande vénitienne au xvie siècle', *Les sources de l'histoire maritime, xve—xviiie siècles (Actes du IVe colloque d'histoire maritime)*, pp. 7-32.
5. Heers, *Gênes*, pp. 279-82.
6. Lane, *Venetian Ships*, pp. 40-2.
7. Chaunu, *Séville*, VII, pp. 72-3.
8. A.P. Usher, 'Spanish Ships and Shipbuilding', in *Facts and Factors in Eco-nomic History—Essays in Honor of E.F. Gay*, pp. 189-213.
9. Ibid.
10. Braudel, *La Méditerranée*, I, pp. 275-9.

11. Touchard, *Le commerce breton*, p. 345.

12. R. Davis, *The Rise of the English Shipping Industry*, pp. 1-10, 17.

13. P. Jeannin, 'Le tonnage des navires utilisés dans la Baltique de 1550 à 1640 d'après les sources prussiennes', in *Le navire et l'économie maritime—IIIe colloque d'histoire maritime*, pp. 46-54.

14. Heers, *Gênes*, pp. 285, 292.

15. Ibid., pp. 116-22.

16. Christensen, op.cit., p. 111.

17. Ibid., pp. 116-22.

18. Ibid., pp. 123-51.

19. L.A. Boiteux, *La fortune de mer, passim.*

20. Heers, *Gênes*, p. 319.

21. W. Brulez, 'La navigation flamande vers la Méditerranée à la fin du xvie siècle', *Revue belge de philologie et d'histoire*, XXXVI (1958), pp. 1210-42, at pp. 1235, 1239.

22. U. Tenenti, *Piracy and the Decline of Venice, 1550-1615*, pp. 3-14.

23. Brulez, 'Les exportations', loc.cit., pp. 00-00.

24. Braudel, *La Méditerranée*, I, pp. 188-90.

25. Gascon, *Grand commerce*, I, pp. 141-98.

26. D.R. Ringrose, 'The Government and the Carters in Spain, 1476-1700', *EcHR*, 2nd Ser., XXII (1969-70), pp. 45-57.

27. P. Earle, 'The commercial Development of Ancona, 1479-1551', *EcHR*, 2nd Ser., XXII (1969-70), pp. 28-44.

9 CONCLUSION: RETROSPECT AND PROSPECT

The sixteenth century established trends in the economic life of Europe which have led most historians to characterise it as a period of dynamic change and growth. The level of population was rising and the proportion of it concentrated in towns was also growing. If the purchasing power of the mass of the population failed to grow in real terms (and there is variable evidence that it even tended to diminish), nevertheless the wealth of the classes who provided the capital for commerce and industry grew rapidly, and they themselves tended to increase in numbers. The effect was to stimulate demand for goods which fell into the luxury category, and in the most favourable circumstances to widen the classes of society who could afford to purchase them. The increasing number of the urban masses placed pressure on the available food supply, which, though it expanded, did not do so as fast as the supply of manufactured goods, so that food rose faster in price than the general average of all goods.

The geographical pattern of trade changed in favour of the Atlantic and North Sea regions at the expense of the Mediterranean as a consequence of a number of factors. Heightening tension in the eastern Mediterranean following the Turkish conquest of Constantinople caused the Genoese to swing the balance of their commerce further to the west, and a crisis in Venetian trade with the Levant. The Portuguese were able to exploit the temporary weakness of Venice and force her into a longer-term crisis by the provision of pepper and spices on the markets of north-west Europe at far lower prices. Their arrival in Antwerp provided a new factor in its growth to supplement the prosperity coming from the finishing and sale of English cloth to the Italian and German markets and the arrival of large numbers of south German merchants dominant in the trade in silver and copper. Until the middle of the century German groups, such as the Fugger, played a preponderant role in international finance as a consequence of their control over central European silver mining and established themselves in apparently impregnable positions as the creditors of the Habsburgs.

Gradually the consequences of Spain's development of her empire in America made themselves felt. Increasing quantities of gold flowed through Seville, more than balancing the extra silver from central Europe, so that until about 1550 silver appreciated in value in terms of the more precious metal. From the middle of the century, however, the situation changed in two respects. First, supplies of silver equalled and then exceeded in value the gold coming from the New World, causing a more rapid increase in the stock of silver in Europe, forcing up the value of gold until it largely disappeared as the major circulating medium. Secondly, a higher proportion of Spanish imports of the precious metals was re-exported to the rest of Europe and beyond. Trade with the Iberian peninsula became more attractive as its balance became progressively more unfavourable from the Spanish point of view, and was settled by the largely illegal transfer of silver, mainly to the benefit of the merchants of the Netherlands. At the same time the rising expenditure of the Spanish monarchy in Europe was being financed by official transfers of silver through the agency of mainly Genoese syndicates. The Genoese tightened their grip on the structure of international credit throughout western Europe and registered their success by the transfer of their principal financial fair from Besançon to Piacenza. The profits drawn off by the Genoese undoubtedly played a part in a last temporary revival of the economy of parts of northern Italy, also stimulated by the recovery of an important share in the spice trade by the Venetians in the second half of the century, only temporarily interrupted by the war with the Turks between 1570 and 1573.

From the 1560s onwards, political conditions exerted an even greater influence than before on the economic life of western Europe. In France the Wars of Religion were to kill the only major centre of international commerce and finance. The disturbances in Lyons were to reduce it by the end of the century once more to the position of little more than a regional centre, whilst the growth of Marseilles as its gateway to the Mediterranean was to be put back for almost a century. Internal conflict ensured that the French economy continued to be by-passed by the major currents of commercial and financial expansion. In the Netherlands, the position of Antwerp deteriorated. The Portuguese closed their factory in 1549, the English began their long-drawn-out search for an alternative cloth-staple from the 1560s and from then onwards the progress of the revolt against Spanish rule worked almost continuously against Antwerp. The consequences of the Spanish bankruptcy of 1575 were felt throughout Europe, but in Antwerp they included the sack of the city by mutinous unpaid troops. The siege of Antwerp by Parma in 1584-5 paved the way for some recovery of her position as a centre of key importance for the financing of the Spanish war effort against the Dutch, and for the trade of the slowly recovering southern provinces. But, cut off from her overseas markets by the stranglehold of the Dutch on the estuary of the Scheldt, she depended on the self-interested connivance of the northern provinces for a share of the trade in their industrial products.

The Dutch consequently remained the sole beneficiaries of their conflict with Spain. During the first half of the century they built up a solid foundation of trade in basic essential commodities of little glamour but great economic importance. By the middle of the century their trade in fish, salt and grain already accounted for 50 per cent of the traffic passing to and from the Baltic. From then all the major trends of financial and commercial development worked in their favour. To the growing demand of Spain's colonies in America for northern manufactured goods was added a progressive and ultimately chronic deficit of the Iberian peninsula and of the Mediterranean region in grain, culminating in the great shipments of the 1590s. Much of these cargoes were paid for in silver, and since the differential in price between the cheap corn areas of Poland and the dear markets of southern Europe had hardly narrowed during the course of the century, the potential profit was enormous. It is not surprising that towards the turn of the century large numbers of immigrants came to settle in Amsterdam and other Dutch centres, not only from the nearby southern provinces of the Netherlands, but also Portuguese New Christians from Lisbon.

Before the century came to its end, there were intimations that the shift of the centre of economic gravity was about to accelerate.
Even before the Dutch arrived in the Mediterranean in strength the English had returned there to trade directly with the Levant and to undermine still further the position of Venice in the eastern Mediterranean, not only by cutting her out of most of her share of the market there for English cloth, but also by making use of the rapidly developing entrepôt of Leghorn. During the 1590s the Dutch and the English made the exploratory ventures to the Orient which were to result in the formation of their East India Companies in the very first years of the seventeenth century and the sale of spices in Leghorn as early as 1605. To the west, the establishment of salt-pans on the shores of the Caribbean by the Dutch in the 1590s revealed that they were ready to pursue a policy of breaching the monopoly of Spain by direct seizure of territory in central and south America.

By 1600 the process by which Italian methods of business organisation and technique were disseminated throughout western Europe was virtually complete. The use of letters of exchange had become normal in north-west Europe, and their endorsement, together with that of internal means of payment such as letters obligatory, had become widespread. Without entirely removing the dependence of the credit structure, and therefore that of commercial life, on the supply of the precious metals, the expansion of the credit mechanism had assisted the growth of trade to the point at which discounts for cash settlement of credit instruments was customary. The existence of such a structure, operated by professional specialists, had been among the factors which had permitted men of moderate capital to engage in long-distance commerce almost on equal terms with the great, especially when combined with a system of commission agents. Within this kind of framework, the structure of the individual enterprise had altered little, and in some fields, such as the ownership of vessels, risks were shared by groups which interlocked but were as temporary in late-sixteenth-century Holland as they had been in fifteenth-century Genoa. Though the techniques of insurance were well developed, they were not universally used, nor were there yet many examples of narrow specialisation in risk-bearing business. The early examples of companies based on the joint-stock principle were equally characterised by the impermanence of their capital, and were rather another method of sharing risks in new long-distance ventures than of gathering extraordinarily large quantities of capital together.

As the seventeenth century dawned, it might well have seemed to contemporaries that the expansive trends established in the later sixteenth century were to continue. For more than a decade after 1600 there was room for continuing optimism about the future. If the quantities of American silver reaching Spain had reached their peak in the 1590s, there was as yet little cause for concern at the rate of their decline. It seemed that an era of unusual peace was about to settle on Europe. Peace between Spain and France in 1598 offered the French a much-needed opportunity for reconstruction at home after a generation of civil war culminating in foreign involvement and offered the Spaniards an opportunity to concentrate their energies on the struggle with the Dutch. In 1604 the now desultory conflict between Spain and England was liquidated in an equally inconclusive peace. Finally in 1609 a truce between Spain and the Dutch provided Spain with a breathing space in which she might recuperate from financial and social exhaustion and the Dutch with an opportunity to devote themselves even more vigorously to the exploitation of their newly won dominance in north European trade and the consolidation of their footholds in the Orient and the Caribbean.

It is only with the hindsight permitted to the historian that we can see that there were already signs of a major change of trend, and an almost universal crisis which was to see the irrevocable confirmation of the trends established during the sixteenth century. It was no accident that Spain was the first to feel the effects of the crisis. Though it is not possible to be specific about the date, it is generally agreed that the population of Spain passed its peak sometime before 1590. The census of 1591 in Castile showed that the major towns were still for the most part much more highly populated than they had been sixty years earlier, whilst the majority of smaller towns and villages of New Castile had reported in the mid-1570s that they were larger in size than a generation before. In the rural areas of Old Castile, and even more in the remote north-west coastal areas, some depopulation had almost certainly occurred by 1590. The bad harvests of the 1590s were to culminate in malnutrition and a severe outbreak of plague between 1599 and 1601 which caused serious losses, especially in Old Castile. Further outbreaks were to occur at more frequent intervals during the first half of the seventeenth century, especially between 1627 and 1631, affecting most regions, but particularly the Mediterranean littoral. These demographic disasters hit the harder because Spain was entering a deep and sustained period of economic and financial distress. Whilst reliable figures are not available, and there is strong reason in particular to suspect the abnormally low figures produced by the census of 1646, it seems reasonably certain that by the middle of the seventeenth century Spain had lost almost all of the demographic growth of the sixteenth century. Policy had intensified the work of natural disaster, in the deliberate decision of 1609 to expel the badly integrated Morisco population, particularly numerous in Valencia. The most recent estimate of a minimum of 250,000 persons expelled, perhaps nearly 300,000, was in itself equal to the losses from a major outbreak of plague, and in many areas was not made good by internal migration in the middle of the century.

With a delay which varied by as much as twenty or thirty years, the rest of Europe began to suffer a significant decline of population. War undoubtedly played as large a share as plague, bringing with it not only local catastrophes resulting from military operations such as sieges, but attendant diseases including smallpox. The Thirty Years War hit Germany and Bohemia the hardest and estimates for the loss of population in Germany between 1618 and 1648 go as high as 40 per cent. The north-west escaped most lightly, but areas in south-west Germany, especially the Palatinate, lost over half their population, with most of the rest losing over 40 per cent in a great swathe extending north-eastwards to Brandenburg and the Baltic coast, where Mecklenburg and Pomerania again lost over 50 per cent. Elsewhere in Europe, the

intensification of outbreaks of plague, the universal companion of malnutrition, probably accounted more than war for the reversal of the
population trend. Switzerland suffered greatly in 1610 and 1611, whilst
in the Netherlands the unfavourable factor of the war against Spain was
interrupted only briefly between 1609 and 1621. In the southern provinces, the growth in population up to the 1570s was completely wiped
out by the middle of the seventeenth century. The northern provinces
were more fortunate in their relative freedom from invasion, but suffered
from plague, especially from 1623 to 1625, from 1635 to 1637 and
again from 1663 to 1664. The power of growth in great centres such as
Amsterdam was, however, too strong for these disasters to cause more
than a series of temporary setbacks to an expansion which continued in
the long term, if at a reduced rate.

Urban Italy suffered greatly from the plague which raged throughout
the Mediterranean around 1630, and as in Spain its effects were superimposed on severe social and economic stresses. A further wave of
plague which struck in 1656 was equally severe, and though Rome was
saved from its worst ravages by the energetic action of the Pope in ordering sanitary and quarantine measures, this time rural areas were as badly
affected as the cities.[1] In France the late sixteenth century saw a period
of decline in population as the inevitable consequence of civil war, so
that by contrast the first quarter of the seventeenth century was a period
of recovery. This was ended from about 1628 by a decade of famine,
plague and rural unrest. From then onwards the eastern provinces
especially were harmed by French entry into the Thirty Years War and
the years following the Westphalia settlement were ones of continued
war against Spain and of the internal struggles of the Frondes, coinciding with yet another series of very poor harvests. The demographic consequences were certainly serious, if even more difficult to quantify at
the national level than elsewhere.

In the short term, a combination of war, dearth and plague was to
send the price of grain to famine levels at more frequent intervals and
over a wider area simultaneously than had occurred in the sixteenth century. In the long term, however, the effects seem to have been generally
much as they had been in the late fourteenth century. Dearth had
resulted from the pressure of a rising population, more concentrated in
the towns, upon a European agriculture which had barely been able to
keep pace with demand, despite the important entry into western and
southern markets of Baltic supplies of grain. Increasing poverty, especially
around the Mediterranean, meant that the mass of the population could
not afford to buy the minimum quantities needed for survival. In the

long run 'Malthusian' principles operated so that the population was reduced to a point at which the reserves of the agricultural system were
again adequate to meet demand in all but the most unfavourable years.
The consequence was that the price of grain began to fall. Despite high
peaks in certain years, the overall trend lay downwards throughout the
second half of the seventeenth century, and very gradually the extreme
contrast between the dear grain areas of southern Europe and the cheap
grain areas of the Baltic zone was reduced.[2]

The long-term demographic trends do not tell us with certainty that
trade was declining. They are merely a pointer which suggests that it is
as logical to assume that the market was unfavourably affected by the
stagnation or decline of the population as it was to assume the opposite
from the rising demographic curve of the sixteenth century. Greater
precision is clearly essential. A strong argument was constructed by
Ruggiero Romano that the European economy passed through a sharp
and decisive crisis which coincided with the first years of the Thirty
Years War, specifically between 1619 and 1622.[3] Whilst it is fair to say
that the case was not completely proven by the evidence presented, and
that some of the evidence in fact suggests that the onset of the crisis
was slower and its effects more prolonged, the wide geographical spread
and diverse character of his evidence enables it to transcend most criticism based on doubts concerning the worth of any of the individual sets
of statistics used.

Of the two most important continuous series of statistics available
for the measurement of European trade during the sixteenth and seventeenth centuries, one is really only of indirect relevance. The records of
the *Casa de Contratación* at Seville have not received detailed discussion
here because they provide us with information only concerning the trade
between Spain and America. However, if, as was suggested earlier, an
increasing proportion of the export traffic to the Indies was in goods
of north European origin, it follows that within broad limits we can
deduce from the fluctuations of the American trade those of an important element in that of Europe itself. This conclusion is of course subject to at least one vital *caveat*; it has to be admitted that this becomes
progressively less valuable as an index, as Seville loses its monopoly of
trade with the Spanish Indies. Until about 1630, however, it is likely
that the inroads being made upon it were relatively minor in relation to
the total volumes recorded. It is not surprising that the peak figures of
Seville's Atlantic trade measured by value should have occurred during
the 1590s, when official shipments of silver from the Indies also reached
their peak. But the volume of traffic as measured by the tonnage of the

fleets remains (whatever criticisms may be justly levied against the method of calculation employed by Pierre Chaunu) by far the best index we have of the total tonnage of the cargoes, which were dominated by the exports to America.[4] Judged by this standard, the peak years of Seville's trade lay in the years 1606 to 1610. From the latter date there was a parallel, if not very steep, fall in both the values of the traffic and the tonnage of the fleets employed, with some temporary recovery between 1616 and 1620. In 1621 and 1622 there was a very severe slump, from which recovery was never complete. From what might have seemed to contemporaries to have been no more than an unusually long inter-cyclical slump, Seville's situation became increasingly clearly one of a steady and permanent decline.

> In the heart of the crisis of 1622-23, the *Carera de Indias* found itself face to face with an abnormal situation—the liquidation of its former prosperity was almost completed. After 1622, without the slightest doubt, the great turning-point was passed.[5]

Even so, we must be careful not to overstate the rate of decline. It was only after 1630 that the levels of trade fell below those normal at a relatively late stage of the period of expansion, those between 1630 and 1635 being roughly equal to those of 1571 to 1575, as were also the imports of treasure.

The second point at which it is possible to approach an accurate quantitative assessment of the levels of trade over the whole period is the Sound, controlling access to the Baltic, and thus of a region whose activity was almost entirely concerned with trade within the limits of the European continent. The numbers of ships recorded in the Sound Toll Registers rose to a maximum of 5,623 a year in both directions between 1590 and 1599, falling to 4,525 a year between 1600 and 1609, to 4,779 from 1610 to 1619, to only 3,726 from 1620 to 1629, and again to a minimum of 3,015 between 1650 and 1657. The share of the Dutch in this trade was of course very great, and followed a slightly different course. Though the tonnages of ships recorded are perhaps not entirely reliable, rough orders of magnitude are possible to determine, giving the following results. Between 1591 and 1600 an average of 250,000 tons of Dutch ships passed through the Sound, falling to 240,000 between 1601 and 1610, rising again during the Twelve Years Truce with Spain to the huge total of 360,000 from 1611 to 1620, but falling dramatically to 230,000 from 1621 to 1630, and recovering to 260,000 from 1631 to 1640. These figures bring home the huge relative size of Baltic trade measured by volume, and imply an enormous capital investment in shipping, even allowing for the shortness of most of the voyages. In terms of value, Baltic goods were cheap and bulky, but in terms of grain alone must have closely approached the value of trade through Seville, inclusive of the imports of treasure. It follows that the impact on mercantile incomes of the falling values of Baltic trade must have been relatively as serious as that of Seville.

In other areas too, though our evidence is not so systematic a kind, it points in the same direction, and sometimes helps to confirm that of the Sound Toll Registers. The values recorded by the customs at Danzig held up well until 1623, but from that date collapsed to less than a third of the 1620-3 average by 1627. Figures for the export of both English and Dutch cloth to the Baltic reveal a sharp crisis, beginning in the case of the Dutch in 1619 and in the case of the English in the following year. In both cases there was a recovery which began in 1622, to reach boom proportions in 1623, but again decline during the mid and late 1620s.[6] The English trade in 'traditional shortcloths', partly recovered from the after-effects of the Cockayne project by 1618, fell by over 25 per cent by 1622, and never recovered to the levels of the prosperous years of the middle of the reign of James I.[7]

There is evidence too of a temporary decline in Dutch and English trade with the Levant. If the declining number of Dutch ships which fell prey to pirates in the Mediterranean is a rather indirect indicator of a decline in the trade, there is certainly a lack of any evidence that the pirates were in retreat, and some positive evidence that they were a great menace to the shipping of Marseilles, and had extended the range of their operations to the Atlantic coasts of Europe as far as the English Channel. Certainly the Dutch consul at Constantinople complained in 1623 that he had received no dues for two years.

Though it would be dangerous to stretch the evidence for a general crisis in European trade between 1619 and 1622 or 1623 too far, and especially to explain the drop in the levels of activity in southern Europe by the same causes as those which affected Baltic markets, there is little doubt that the political crisis in Bohemia and Germany, accompanied by war between Poland and Sweden, provided an unfavourable environment over a very wide area. Where there is evidence that a decline in trade was delayed for a few years more it is possible to relate it to the same causes but with a time-lag. Such might be the case of the declining receipts from the Venetian anchorage tax, which held up well to their early seventeenth century levels until 1622, but then declined steeply.

Statistics of industrial production are even harder to come by than those for trade and are more difficult to generalise from because it was much easier for industry to change its centres of production from one town to another (or more often than not, outside the towns altogether) than it was for maritime trade to avoid the major ports. Nevertheless, there is some evidence that similar forces were at work. Though the 1620s were the peak period for the production of cloth in Leiden, there were signs that the rate of expansion was considerably slowed and an absolute decline set in from the 1630s. Figures for the production of soap in Amsterdam reach their peak between 1617 and 1620, and the rates of admission of immigrants to citizenship in the United Provinces falls off after 1620.

There is a fundamental distinction to be drawn about the long-term consequences of such a general crisis. For some areas it was a temporary setback after which expansion was renewed, for others it was a crucial blow which accelerated their permanent decline. For Spain there was to be no recovery until after the end of the seventeenth century, apart from the modest revival of Valencia and Barcelona from about 1650. Spain's domestic market, or such of it as survived, lay increasingly open to the industrial products of the northern states. Similarly, her colonial markets were penetrated directly with the connivance of the colonists who received illegal traders with open arms. An increasing proportion of the silver production of Potosí found its way direct to northern Europe, and that production fell far less rapidly than the official imports of treasure into Spain itself. In Italy the last revival of Venetian commerce was at an end and was rapidly followed by the contraction of its cloth industry, priced out of the markets of the Levant by English and Dutch competition, so that by the end of the century the city and the *terra-ferma* were producing only the same pitifully small quantities they had done at the beginning of the sixteenth century. The financial supremacy of Genoa ended when her bankers withdrew from the great business of the Spanish *asientos* in 1627 and the fairs of 'Bisenzone' began to wither. Sicily, one of the granaries of the Mediterranean in the sixteenth century, failed to escape the famines which swept the region, the earliest in 1607.

The future clearly lay with the English and the Dutch. Though they were both to suffer from internal political crises around the middle of the century, they were less affected than others by the general dearth in the 1630s. The English enjoyed the advantages of neutrality in the Thirty Years War, whilst the Dutch, after some dangerous moments in the 1620s, which included an abortive threat to their Baltic commerce from a grandly conceived but poorly executed Habsburg plan to occupy its shores, managed to exploit the new advantages given to them by their grip on the copper and iron trade of Sweden.

Even in their old markets in the Netherlands, the English managed to create a larger market for their dyed cloths as a partial substitute for the stagnating trade in unfinished broadcloth. In one specialised sector, they succeeded in producing a new version of the traditional broadcloth. Even more successful was the use of imported Spanish wool to produce expensive cloths of a new style. From the Wiltshire-Somerset border and from Devon the export of these 'Spanish' cloths began some time after 1622, and by 1628 the equivalent of over 3,300 standard shortcloths was exported from London to northern Europe, over three-quarters of them to the Netherlands. By 1632 the total had grown to over 6,000 and by 1640 to over 13,000, with nearly 50 per cent going to the north Netherlands, 30 per cent to Germany, and 25 per cent to Flanders. In 1640, these cloths amounted to 20 per cent of London's total exports of cloth to northern Europe, so that the Privy Council was justly able to claim that the Spanish cloths had 'become one of the best and most requested manufactures of this Kingdom'.[8]

On the other hand, it was the lighter and cheaper 'new draperies' which most expanded their production, their export growing by 500 per cent between 1600 and 1640, mostly to the markets in Spain and the Mediterranean which by 1640 were taking nearly two thirds of London's exports of goods other than the traditional broadcloths. Three-quarters of these goods, worth over £450,000 at official customs values, were still in the form of woollens and hosiery.[9] Produced in areas which were free of rigid gild restrictions the new draperies represented an industrial potential which was the essential basis of an expanding export trade. Though the Civil War to some extent interrupted the process of renewal and expansion, the Commonwealth and Protectorate period was to see the full recognition by the government of the importance of colonial development. The last war against Spain at the end of the 1650s was characteristic of a new approach. Superficially, it was an apparent anachronism in its concern for the re-establishment of a base on the south side of the English Channel, but the hopes of the capture of Dunkirk gave promise of an end to the depredations of her privateers on English commerce.

If the concept of a Protestant alliance against the leader of the Counter Reformation looked backwards, the operations of Admiral Blake in the Mediterranean and in the Caribbean were a statement of England's future intentions which was not misunderstood by contemporaries. The cession of Tangier by Portugal at the time of the marriage of Charles II to

Catherine of Braganza provided a base from which the security of English Mediterranean commerce could be guarded until Gibralter was finally acquired at the beginning of the eighteenth century. As rivalry with France came to succeed that with the Dutch the presence of English naval forces in the Mediterranean became more frequent until their superiority was clearly established after 1713. Blake's seizure of Jamaica was the only success of an expedition of which the original objective had been Santo Domingo. It secured a valuable addition to England's existing Caribbean colony of Barbados and contributed greatly to the enormous increase in the cultivation of sugar and tobacco, which together with that from Virginia was to place England in a dominant position in both the sugar and tobacco markets of Europe by 1700.

By the end of the seventeenth century England had built on the foundations laid before the Civil War a commercial structure which saw both the maintenance of her traditional exports at their earlier levels and a vast expansion in the new. In 1700, of a total export trade worth nearly £6,500,000 a year, woollens accounted for less than half, other native manufactures, foodstuffs and raw materials for another 20 per cent and the re-export of non-European goods the rest. Among her markets, Europe north of the Alps and the Pyrenees still accounted for over 60 per cent, with southern Europe and Turkey taking over 26 per cent, and America and Asia 15 per cent. Among her imports of £5,800,000 textiles (mostly linen goods) accounted for over 26 per cent, foodstuffs and raw materials, especially wool and cotton, for no less than £4,000,000 or nearly 70 per cent. England's overseas trade was therefore worth over £12,000,000 at the official valuation, and she was already the exporter of manufactured goods worth twice those which she imported.[10] The mercantilist ideal of an economy which imported raw materials, largely from a closely controlled colonial source, and exported its own manufactures with an overall favourable balance, had been fully realised.

In the meantime, England had overcome the competition of the Dutch both in European and overseas markets.[11] The Dutch resumed their progress after the setbacks of the 1620s and 1630s, and their prosperity perhaps reached its peak about the middle of the century. From that time, the fundamentals of their wealth were slowly undermined. The great trade in Baltic grain began to slacken, as a combination of reduced population in many parts of Europe and a series of good harvests in the west took effect.[12] Though the East India Company continued to expand both the scale of its business and its profitability, it is doubtful if in the long run this was sufficient to counterbalance the decline in the Baltic.

The process was a slow one, however, and it was only from the 1670s that it could be said that the Dutch position was being undermined. The series of wars with England during the third quarter of the century were clearly dominated by commercial considerations, although they were certainly harmful to the commerce of both sides whilst they were being fought. The English Navigation Act of 1651, re-enacted at the Restoration, was a sign that at last English shipping was strong enough to make enforcement possible, and by the end of the wars the Dutch had been driven from their North American foothold of New Amsterdam. The Dutch reputation for competitive shipping rates was somewhat reduced, but they retained the important advantage of a cheap money market. Indeed, a plentiful supply of capital kept interest rates lower than in England, and eventually the Dutch were to swing the balance of their investment away from commerce towards international finance. This ultimate development invites comparison with the experience of the Genoese a century earlier.

The late seventeenth century was a period during which the traditional rivalry of England and the Dutch gradually gave way to a sense of identity of interest against the threat of the French. The French economy had recovered slowly, and as late as the period of the ascendancy of Colbert economic and commercial expansion was a half-reluctant response to state initiative. The effort to imitate the English and Dutch in the development of powerful trading companies for the Atlantic and Oriental trades was slow to produce results. Initially, response from the maritime and commercial communities was lukewarm, with the greatest share of investment being taken by courtiers, officials and the Crown itself. Nevertheless, the protectionist programme of Colbert was designed to lessen the grip of the Dutch on the trade of the northern and western ports of France. At the same time a policy of colonial expansion was beginning, which was to lead to an important element in the struggle with England in the eighteenth century. Nevertheless, France, for all its huge resources of population (perhaps nineteen or twenty million people in the middle of the reign of Louis XIV), played a relatively minor role in world trade at the end of the seventeenth century. The size and relative self-sufficiency of the internal market was probably a more important factor than is often realised, a point stressed by the contemporary who stated that more goods changed hands in a few days at the fair of Beaucaire than passed through the port of Marseilles in a year.

Only by the end of the seventeenth century is it fair to speak of world trade rather than European. Despite the emphasis placed on the spice trade, and the undeniable importance of American treasure, the sixteenth and early seventeenth centuries were a period in which European commerce was essentially inward-looking when judged by the standard of the volume and value of goods exchanged, and of the quantity of capital and shipping employed.

Notes

1. Helleiner, 'The Population of Europe', loc.cit., pp. 50-1.
2. F. Braudel and F. Spooner, 'Prices in Europe from 1450 to 1750', *Cambridge Economic History of Europe,* IV, Ch. VII, Graphs, pp. 470-1.
3. R. Romano, 'Tra xvi e xvii secolo—una crisi economica, 1619-1622', *Rivista storica Italiana,* 74 (1962), pp. 480-531.
4. Imports were of course dominated in value by the small volume of treasure.
5. Chaunu, *Séville,* VIII, ii, 2, p. 1529.
6. Hinton, *The Eastland Trade,* Appendix D.
7. Fisher, 'London's Export Trade', loc.cit., See W.E. Minchinton, *The Growth of English Overseas Trade in the 17th and 18th Centuries,* pp. 64-77.
8. Supple, *Commercial Crisis and Change,* pp. 149-52.
9. Fisher, loc.cit., p. 68.
10. R. Davis, 'English Overseas Trade, 1660-1700', Minchinton, op.cit., pp. 78-98.
11. On Anglo-Dutch rivalry, see C.H. Wilson, *Profit and Power, a Study of England and the Dutch Wars.*
12. J.A. Faber, 'The Decline of the Baltic Grain Trade in the second half of the seventeenth Century', *Acta Historiae Neerlandica,* I (1966), pp. 108-31.

General

alcabala   Castilian sales tax, existing from the Middle Ages. Nominally at the rate of 10 per cent, it was in practice often much less. From 1537 in many areas it was compounded by a local assessment or *encabezamiento*.

arbitrista   Writer on Spanish economic and social questions, especially in the seventeenth century, who propounded plans for recovery.

asiento   A contract, normally between the Castilian monarchy and financiers who arranged the transfer abroad of financial resources for current expenditure on short-term credit. Also a slave-trade concession.

aubaine, droit d'   French tax levied on property of deceased persons.

caravel   A ship, normally of modest tonnage, used in exploration and early transatlantic trade. Its main characteristic was a mixture of lateen- and square-rigged sails.

fluit (flyboat)   Dutch merchant ship, evolved in the late sixteenth century. Slow in speed but of cheap, sometimes semi-standardised construction, with a small crew in relation to carrying capacity.

Fondaco dei Tedeschi   Headquarters of German merchants in Venice.

gabelle   Salt tax levied in most parts of France.

hidalgo   Spanish gentleman (lit. *hijo de algo*). Cf. *hidalguía,* the status of gentleman.

juros   Castilian government bonds; long-term or funded debt, yielding interest at rates varying from 5 per cent upwards.

meseta   Central Castilian plateau.

Mesta   Castilian gild of owners of migratory sheep-flocks, from the thirteenth century onwards.

Relaciones Topográficas   Name usually given to the surviving replies from numerous villages of Castile to questionnaires sent out by the government of Philip II in 1575 and 1578. They contain valuable information concerning population trends, agricultural production and local commerce. See N. Salomon, *La campagne de la Nouvelle Castille à la fin du xvie siècle.*

Says   English name of a variety of cloth (usually woollen), finely woven similar to serge.

Sound Toll Registers   Records of the tolls levied by the Crown of Denmark on ships passing to and from the Baltic.

Taula Municipal banks, especially of Barcelona and Valencia.

Weights and Measures

aune French unit of length, used especially for cloth, which varied
    between 2/3 and 1¼ yards.
cántara Italian unit of weight, approximately 1 cwt.
collo (pl. *colli*) Italian (especially Venetian) unit of volume, varying
    between 250 and 300 lb, lit. a bale.
fanega Spanish unit of volume; approximately 55 litres.
quintal Spanish and Italian unit of weight, approximately 100 lb.

Money

cruzado Portuguese gold coin, from 1457, 64 being coined from a
    mark of gold. Equivalent to 253 *reis* (q.v.).
ducat Initially a Venetian gold coin, imitated by Castile from 1497;
    officially the *excelente de Granada*. 65 were coined from a mark of
    gold. Equivalent to 375 *maravedís* (q.v.).
écu French gold coin of varying weight. In 1488 it was valued at 1
    livre 10 sols (sous) 3 deniers, rising to 2 *livres* by 1540. In 1567, the
    écu au soleil d'or was valued at 3 *livres,* and was itself made a money
    of account, until its intrinsic value rose even higher.
escudo Castilian gold coin, replacing the ducat in 1537. Equivalent to
    350 *maravedís.*
groat silver coin, here the Brabant groat is alone mentioned.
grosz (pl. *groschen*) Polish money of account.
lira (pl. *lire*) Italian money of account (cf. French *livre*). Equivalent to
    20 *soldi* or shillings, or 240 *denari* or pence.
livre French money of account, strictly the *livre tournois.*
maravedí Castilian money of account. Originally a gold coin of Arabic
    origins, much devalued.
peso here used for a quantity of gold or silver worth 450 *maravedís.*
    There were other meanings with substantially different values.
real (pl. *reales*) Castilian silver coin valued at 34 *maravedís.* Frequently
    coined in multiple form, e.g. *reales de a ocho* or 'pieces of eight'.
real (pl. *reis*) Portuguese silver coin.
Rhenish florin German money of account.
scudo (pl. *scudi*) Italian (Venetian) gold coin.
vellón (cf. French *billon*) Coinage consisting of a mixture of copper
    with a small quantity of silver. In Castile, after 1598 it was minted entire-
    ly of copper, the practice spreading to France and elsewhere during the
    early seventeenth century.

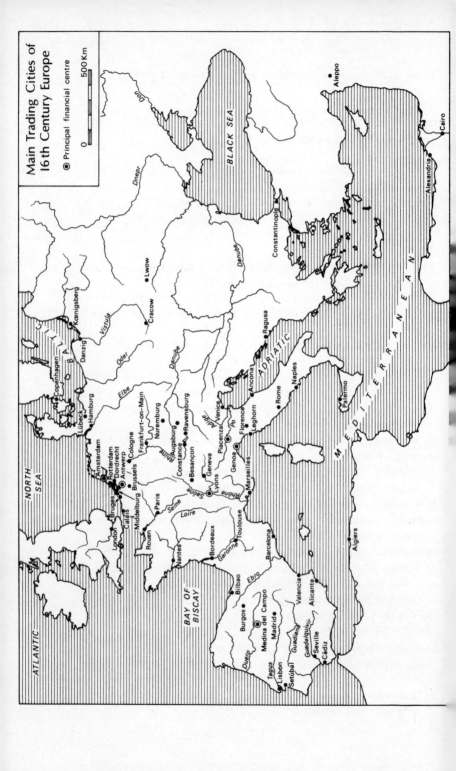

Main Trading Cities of
16th Century Europe

⊙ Principal financial centre

0   500 Km

NORTH
SEA

ATLANTIC

BAY OF
BISCAY

MEDITERRANEAN

BLACK SEA

ADRIATIC

Aleppo
Cairo
Alexandria
Constantinople
Ragusa
Ancona
Rome
Naples
Palermo
Algiers
Venice
Florence
Leghorn
Po
Adige
Genoa
Marseilles
Piacenza
Lyons
Geneva
Besançon
Ravensburg
Constance
Augsburg
Nuremburg
Frankfurt-on-Main
Cologne
Dordrecht
Rotterdam
Amsterdam
Bruges
Brussels
Middelburg
Antwerp
London
Calais
Rouen
Paris
Nantes
Bordeaux
Toulouse
Barcelona
Bilbao
Burgos
Medina del Campo
Madrid
Valencia
Alicante
Seville
Cádiz
Setúbal
Lisbon
Lübeck
Hamburg
Copenhagen
Kœnigsberg
Danzig
Cracow
Lwow

Rhine
Elbe
Oder
Vistula
Dnepr
Don
Danube
Saône
Rhône
Seine
Loire
Garonne
Ebro
Duero
Tagus
Guadiana
Guadalquivir

SELECT BIBLIOGRAPHY

Annales–Economies, Sociétés, Civilisations – AESC;
Economic History Review – EcHR.

Attman, A. *The Russian and Polish Markets in International Trade, 1500-1650.* Goteborg, 1973.

Aymard, M. *Venise, Raguse et le commerce du blé pendant la seconde moitié du xvie siècle.* Paris, 1966.

Baehrel, R. 'Prix, superficies, statistique, croissances.' *AESC,* XVI (1961), pp. 699-722 and 922-38.

Baehrel, R. *Une croissance–la Basse Provence rurale (fin du xvie siècle – 1789).* Paris, 1961.

Bailyn, B. 'Communication and Trade – the Atlantic in the 17th Century.' *Journal of Economic History,* XIII (1953), pp. 378-87.

Barbour, V. *Capitalism in Amsterdam in the Seventeenth Century.* Baltimore, 1950.

Basas Fernández, M. *El Consulado de Burgos en el siglo xvi.* Madrid, 1963.

Baulant, M. *Lettres de négociants marseillais – les frères Hermite, 1570-1612.* Paris, 1953.

Bec, C. 'Mentalité et vocabulaire des marchands florentins au début du xve siècle.' *AESC,* XXII (1967), pp. 1207-26.

Bennassar, B. 'Facteurs sévillans au xvie siècle.' *AESC,* XII (1957), pp. 60-70.

Bennassar, B. *Valladolid au siecle d'or – une ville de Castille et sa campagne au xvie siècle.* Paris, 1967.

Bergier, J.-F. *Genève et l'économie internationale de la Renaissance,* Vol. I, Paris, 1963.

Bernard, J. *Navires et gens de mer à Bordeaux (vers 1400-vers 1550).* 3 vols. Paris, 1968.

Billioud, J. and Collier, J.-R. *Histoire du Commerce de Marseille.* Vol. III, Paris, 1951.

Boiteux, L.A. *La fortune de mer.* Paris, 1968.

Bonnassié, P. 'Contrats d'affrêtement et commerce maritime à Barcélone au xviie siècle.' *Revue d'histoire économique et sociale,* XXXV (1957), pp. 255-65.

Bourgouin, E. 'Nantes port du sel au xvie siècle – de la légende à l'enquête.' *Annales d'histoire économique et sociale,* VIII (1936), pp. 140-50.

Boutruche, R. (ed.) *Bordeaux de 1453 à 1715. (Histoire de Bordeaux sous la direction de Ch. Higounet,* Vol. IV.) Bordeaux, 1966.

Bowden, P.J. 'The Wool Supply and the Woollen Industry.' *EcHR,* 2nd Ser., IX (1956-7), pp. 44-58.

Boxer, C.R. *The Portuguese Seaborne Empire, 1415-1825.* London, 1969.

Braudel, F. 'Monnaies et civilisations – de l'or du Soudan à l'argent d'Amérique. Un drame méditerranéen.' *AESC,* I (1946), pp. 9-22.

Braudel, F. 'La vita economica di Venezia nel secolo xvi.' In *La Civiltà veneziana del Rinascimento.* Sansoni, 1958.

Braudel, F. 'Achats et ventes de sel à Venise, 1587-1593.' *AESC,* XVI (1961), pp. 961-5.

Braudel, F. *La méditerranée et le monde méditerranéen à l'époque de Philippe II.* 2nd revised edition, 2 vols. Paris, 1966. (English translation, 2 vols. London, 1972.)

Braudel, F. and Romano, R. *Navires et marchandises à l'entrée du port de Livourne, 1547-1611.* Paris, 1951.

Braudel, F., Jeannin, P., Meuvret, J., and Romano, R. 'Le declin de Venise au XVIIᵉ siècle', in *Aspetti e cause della decadenza economica Veneziana nel secolo XVII.* (Fondazione Giorgio Cini: Centro di Cultura e Civiltà, Istituto di Storia della Società e dello Stato Veneziana, Studi, 9). Venice, 1961, pp. 23-86.

Braudel, F. and Spooner, F.C. 'Prices in Europe from 1450 to 1750.' *Cambridge Economic History of Europe,* Cambridge, 1967, Vol. IV, Ch. VII, pp. 374-486.

Braunstein, P. 'Livres de compte et les routes commerciales dans les Alpes Orientales et les Balkans au xviᵉ siècle.' *AESC,* XXVII (1972), pp. 247-55.

Bresard, M. *Les foires de Lyon au xvᵉ et xviᵉ siècles.* Paris, 1914.

Bridbury, A.R. *England and the Salt Trade in the later Middle Ages.* Oxford, 1955.

Brown, R. *A History of Accounting and Accountants.* Edinburgh, 1905.

Brulez, W. 'La navigation flamande vers la Méditerranée à la fin du xviᵉ siècle.' *Revue belge de philologie et d'histoire,* XXXVI (1958), pp. 1210-42.

Brulez, W. 'L'exportation des Pays Bas vers l'Italie par voie de terre au milieu du xviᵉ siècle.' *AESC,* XIV (1959), pp. 461-91.

Brulez, W. *De Firma della Faille en de internationale handel van vlaamse firma's in de 16ᵉ eeuw.* Brussels, 1959.

Brulez, W. 'Les routes commerciales de l'Angleterre en Italie au xvie siècle.' *Studi in Onore di Amintore Fanfani*, Milan, 1962, IV, pp. 181-4.

Brulez, W. 'Anvers de 1585 à 1650.' *Vierteljahrschrift für Sozial- und Wirtschaftsgeschichte*, LIV (1967), pp. 75-99.

Brulez, W. 'Le commerce international des Pays Bas au xvie siècle – essai d'appréciation quantitative.' *Revue belge de philologie et d'histoire*, XLVI (1968), pp. 1205-21.

Brulez, W. 'The Balance of Trade of the Netherlands in the Middle of the xvith Century.' *Acta Historiae Neerlandica*, IV (1970), pp. 20-48.

Burwash, D. *English Merchant Shipping, 1460-1540.* Toronto, 1947.

Carande, R. *Carlos V y sus Banqueros.* 3 vols. Madrid, 1943-67.

Carter, F.W. 'The Commerce of the Dubrovnik Republic.' *EcHR*, 2nd Ser., XXIV (1971), pp. 370-94.

Caster, G. *Le commerce du pastel et de l'épicerie à Toulouse, 1450-1561.* Toulouse, 1962.

Castillo, A. 'Les banquiers portugais et le circuit d'Amsterdam.' *AESC*, XIX (1964), pp. 311-16.

Castillo, A. *Tráfico maritimo y comercio de importación en Valencia a comienzos del siglo xvii.* Madrid, 1967.

Chaudhuri, K.N. *The English East India Company – the Study of an Early Joint-Stock Company, 1600-1640.* London, 1965.

Chaunu, P. 'Autour de 1640.' *AESC*, IX (1954), pp. 44-54.

Chaunu, P. *Séville et l'Atlantique.* 8 vols. in 12. Paris, 1955-60.

Chaunu, P. *Conquête et exploitation des nouveaux mondes.* Paris, 1969.

Christensen, A. *Dutch Traffic to the Baltic about 1600.* Copenhagen/The Hague, 1941.

Cipolla, C.M. *Mouvements monétaires dans l'état de Milan, 1580-1700.* Paris, 1952.

Cipolla, C.M. 'The decline of Italy: the Case of a fully matured Economy.' *EcHR*, 2nd Ser., V (1952), pp. 178-87.

Coleman, D.C. (ed.), *Revisions in Mercantilism.* London, 1969.

Coornaert, E. *La draperie-sayetterie d'Hondschoote.* Rennes, 1930.

Coornaert, E. 'Grand capitalisme et économie traditionelle à Anvers au xvie siècle.' *Annales d'histoire économique et sociale*, VIII (1936), pp. 127-39.

Coornaert, E. *Les Français et le commerce internationale à Anvers, xve –xvie siècles.* 2 vols. Paris, 1961.

Craeybeckx, J. *Un grand commerce d'importation – les vins de France aux anciens Pays-Bas (xiiie – xvie siècle).* Paris, 1958.

Darnsholt, T. 'Some Observations on four Series of Tuscan Corn Prices, 1520-1630'. *Scandinavian Economic History Review,* XII (1964), pp. 145-64.

Davis, R. 'English Overseas Trade, 1660-1700'. *EcHR,* 2nd Ser., VII (1954-5), pp. 150-66.

Davis, R. 'England and the Mediterranean, 1570-1670.' *Essays in the Economic and Social History of Tudor and Stuart England in Honour of R. H. Tawney,* Cambridge, 1961, pp. 117-37.

Davis, R. 'Influences de l'Angleterre sur le déclin de Venise au XVIIe siècle.' *Aspetti e cause della decadenza economica veneziana nel secolo XVII.* (Fondazione Giorgio Cini: Centro di Cultura e Civiltà, Instituto di Storia della Società e dello Stato Veneziano, Civiltà Veneziana, Studi, 9). Venice, 1961, pp. 185-235.

Davis, R. *The Rise of the English Shipping Industry.* London, 1962.

Davis, R. *English Overseas Trade, 1500-1700.* London, 1973.

Delumeau, J. *Vie économique et sociale de Rome pendant la seconde moitié du xvie siècle.* 2 vols. Paris, 1957.

Delumeau, J. *L'alun de Rome, xve-xixe siècle.* Paris, 1962.

Denuce, J. *La Hanse et les compagnies de commerce anversois aux pays baltiques.* Antwerp, 1938.

Deyon, P. 'La concurrence internationale des manufactures lainières au xvie et xviie siècles.' *AESC,* XXVII (1972), pp. 20-32.

Doehard, R. 'Commerce et morale à Anvers au xvie siècle. A propos d'un manuscrit de la bibliothèque de Leyde.' *Revue historique,* CCIV (1950), pp. 226-33.

Doehard, R. *Etudes Anversoises.* 3 vols. Paris, 1962-3.

Dollinger, P. *The German Hansa.* London, 1970.

Domínguez Ortiz, A. 'Guerra económica y comercio en el reinado de Felipe IV.' *Hispania,* XXIII (1963), pp. 94-120.

Dow, J. 'A Comparative Note on the Sound Toll Registers, Stockholm Customs Accounts and Dundee Shipping Lists, 1589, 1613-22.' *Scandinavian Economic History Review,* XII (1964), pp. 79-85.

Earle, P. 'The Commercial Development of Ancona, 1479-1551.' *EcHR,* 2nd Ser., XXII (1969-70), pp. 28-44.

Ebersholt, J. and Chomel, V. *Cinq siècles de circulation internationale vue de Jougne.* Paris, 1951.

Ehrenberg, R. *Capital and Finance in the Age of the Renaissance.* London, 1928.

Eldridge, H.J. *The Evolution of the Science of Book-keeping.* London, 1931.

Faber, J.A. 'The Decline of the Baltic Grain Trade in the second half of the seventeenth Century.' *Acta Historiae Neerlandica,* I (1966), pp. 108-31.

Fasano-Guarini, E. 'Au xvie siècle — comment naviguent les galères.' *AESC,* XVI (1961), pp. 279-96.

Fisher, F.J. 'Commercial Trends and Policy in sixteenth Century England.' *EcHR,* X (1939-40), pp. 95-117.

Fisher, F.J. 'London's Export Trade in the early seventeenth Century.' *EcHR,* 2nd ser., III (1950-51), pp. 151-61.

Fisher, R.H. *The Russian Fur Trade, 1500-1800.* Berkeley, 1943.

Friis, A. *Alderman Cockayne's Project and the Cloth Trade — the Commercial Policy of England in its main Aspects, 1603-1625.* London, 1927.

Gascon, R. 'Un siècle du commerce des épices à Lyon, fin xve — fin xvie siècle.' *AESC,* XV (1960), pp. 638-66.

Gascon, R. *Grand commerce et vie urbaine au xvie siècle — Lyon et ses marchands (environs de 1520 — environs de 1580).* 2 vols. Paris, 1971.

Gioffré, D. *Gênes et les foires de change — de Lyon à Besançon.* Paris, 1960.

Girard, A. *Le commerce français à Séville au temps des Habsbourg.* Paris, 1922.

Glamann, K. *Dutch Asiatic Trade, 1620-1740.* The Hague, 1958.

Goris, J.A. *Les colonies marchandes méridionales à Anvers de 1488 à 1567.* Louvain, 1925.

Goubert, P. 'Une fortune bourgeoise au xvie siècle — Jehan Pocquelin, bisaïeul probable de Molière.' *Revue d'histoire moderne et contemporaine,* I (1954), pp. 8-24.

Goubert, P. *Familles marchandes sous l'ancien régime — les Danse et les Motte de Beauvais.* Paris, 1959.

Goubert, P. *Beauvais et le Beauvaisis.* 2 vols. Paris, 1960.

Grassby, R. 'The Rate of Profit in Seventeenth Century England.' *English Historical Review,* LXXXIV (1969), pp. 721-51.

Grice-Hutchinson, M. *The School of Salamanca, Readings in Spanish Monetary Theory, 1544-1605.* Oxford, 1952.

Hamilton, E.J. *American Treasure and the Price Revolution in Spain, 1501-1650.* Cambridge, Mass., 1934.

Hammerstöm, I. 'The "Price Revolution" of the Sixteenth Century— Some Swedish Evidence.' *Scandinavian Economic History Review,* V (1957), pp. 118-54.

Harsin, P. 'Bodin et la théorie monétaire du xvie siècle.' *Revue belge de philologie et d'histoire,* VII (1928), pp. 1301-23.

Hauser, H. 'Réflexions sur l'histoire des banques à l'époque moderne, xvᵉ–xviiiᵉ siècles.' *Annales d'histoire économique et sociale*, I (1929), pp. 335-51.

Hauser, H. *Les débuts du capitalisme*. Paris, 1931.

Hoszkowski, S. 'L'Europe centrale devant la révolution des prix.' *AESC*, XVI (1961), pp. 441-56.

Hecksher, E.F. *Mercantilism*. 2 vols. London, 1935.

Heers, J. *Gênes au xvᵉ siècle. Activité économique et problèmes sociaux*. Paris, 1961.

Heers, J. *L'Occident au xivᵉ et xvᵉ siècles – aspects économiques et sociaux*. Paris, 1966.

Helleiner, K.F. 'The Population of Europe from the Black Death to the Eve of the Vital Revolution.' *Cambridge Economic History of Europe*, Cambridge, 1967, Vol. IV, pp. 1-95.

Hinton, R.W.K. *The Eastland Trade and the Common Weal in the Seventeenth Century*. Cambridge, 1959.

Ibarra y Rodríguez, E. *El problema cerealista en la España durante el reinado de los Reyes Católicos, 1475-1516*. Madrid, 1944.

Innis, H.A. *The Cod Fisheries – the History of an International Economy*. Toronto, 1954.

Jeannin, P. 'L'économie française au milieu du xviᵉ siècle et le marché russe.' *AESC*, IX (1954), pp. 25-43.

Jeannin, P. 'Les relations économiques des villes de la Baltique avec Anvers au xviᵉ siècle.' *Vierteljahrschrift für Sozial- und Wirtschaftsgeschichte*, XLIII (1956), pp. 193-217.

Jeannin, P. *Les marchands au xviᵉ siècle*. Paris, 1957.

Jeannin, P. 'Le tonnage des navires utilisés dans la Baltique de 1550 à 1640 d'après les sources prussiennes.' *Le navire et l'économie maritime du Nord de l'Europe du moyen âge au xviiiᵉ siècle. IIIᵉ Colloque d'histoire maritime*. Paris, 1960.

Jeannin, P. 'Le commerce de Lübeck aux environs de 1580.' *AESC*, XVI (1961), pp. 36-65.

Jeannin, P. 'Les comptes du Sund comme source pour la construction d'indices généraux de l'activité économique en Europe, xviᵉ–xviiᵉ siècles.' *Revue historique*, CCXXXI (1964), pp. 55-122, 307-40.

Jeannin, P. 'En Europe du Nord: sources et travaux d'histoire commerciale.' *AESC*, XXIII (1968), pp. 844-68.

Jørgensen, J. 'Denmark's Relations with Hamburg and Lübeck in the 17th Century.' *Scandinavian Economic History Review*, XI (1963), pp. 73-108.

Kellenbenz, H. *Unternehmekräfte im Hamburger Portugal- und Spanien-*

handel, 1590-1625. Hamburg, 1954.

Kellenbenz, H. 'Le commerce du poivre des Fugger et le marché international du poivre.' *AESC*, XI (1956), pp. 1-28.

Kellenbenz, H. 'Le déclin de Venise et les relations économiques de Venise avec les marchés au nord des Alpes.' In *Aspetti e cause della decadenza economica Veneziana nel secolo XVII.* (Fondazione Giorgio Cini, Centro di Cultura e Civiltà: Istituto di storia della Società e dello Stato Veneziano, Studi, 9). Venice, 1961, pp. 107-83.

Kellenbenz, H. 'Industries rurales en Occident de la fin du moyen âge au xviiie siècle.' *AESC*, XVIII (1963), pp. 823-82.

Kepler, J.S. 'Fiscal Aspects of the English carrying Trade during the Thirty Years War.' *EcHR*, 2nd Ser., XXV (1972), pp. 261-83.

Kernkamp, J.H. *De Handel op den Vijand, 1572-1609.* 2 vols. Utrecht, 1931-4.

Klein, J. *The Mesta: a Study in Spanish Economic History, 1273-1836.* Cambridge, Mass., 1920.

Klein, P.W. *De Trippen in de xviie eeuw.* Assen, 1965.

Lane, F.C. *Venetian Ships and Shipbuilders of the Renaissance.* Baltimore, 1945.

Lane, F.C. 'La marine marchande et le trafic maritime de Venise à travers les siècles.' *Les sources de l'histoire maritime en Europe du moyen âge au xviiie siècle. IVe Colloque d'histoire maritime*, pp. 7-32. Paris, 1962.

Lapeyre, H. *Simón Ruiz et les asientos de Philippe II.* Paris, 1953.

Lapeyre, H. *Une famille de marchands – les Ruiz. Contribution à l'étude du commerce entre la France et l'Espagne au temps de Philippe II.* Paris, 1955.

Lapeyre, H. 'Banque, change et crédit au xvie siècle.' *Revue d'histoire moderne et contemporaine*, III (1956), pp. 284-97.

Lapeyre, H. 'Banque et crédit en Italie du xvie au xviiie siècle.' *Revue d'histoire moderne et contemporaine*, VIII (1961), pp. 211-26.

Larraz, J. *La época del mercantilismo en Castilla.* Madrid, 1963.

Lee, R.L. 'American cochineal in European Commerce, 1526-1625.' *Journal of Modern History*, XXIII (1951), pp. 205-24.

Lipson, E. *Economic History of England.* 3 vols. London, 1947 (4th ed.).

Lohmann Villena, G. *Les Espinosa: une famille d'hommes d'affaires en Espagne et aux Indes à l'époque de la colonisation.* Paris, 1968.

Luzzato, G. 'Les banques publiques de Venise (siècles xvi-xvii)', in J.G. van Dillen, *History of the Principal Public Banks.* The Hague, 1934.

Luzzato, G. *Storia economica di Venezia dell secolo XI al XVI*. Venice, 1961.

Lybyer, A.H. 'The Influence of the Rise of the Ottoman Turks upon the Routes of Oriental Trade.' *English Historical Review*, XXX (1915), pp. 577-88.

Maddalena, A. de. 'Les archives Saminiati.' *AESC*, XIV (1959), pp. 738-44.

Maddalena, A. de. 'Affaires et gens d'affaires lombards sur les foires de Bisenzone – l'example des Lucini.' *AESC*, XXII (1967), pp. 939-90.

Magalhães Godinho, V. 'Création et dynamisme du monde atlantique.' *AESC*, IV (1950), pp. 32-6.

Magalhães Godinho, V. *L'économie de l'empire portugais au xve et xvie siècles*. Paris, 1969.

Mahn-Lot, M. 'Colomb, Bristol et l'Atlàntique Nord.' *AESC*, XIX (1964), pp. 522-30.

Di Majo, S. 'Rinascimento e declino economico dell Italia secondo A. Sapori e R. Lopez.' *Economia e Storia*, XIV (1967), pp. 349-58.

Di Majo, S. 'La posizione dell Italia nell' economia mediterreanea secoli xvi e xvii secondo Fernandino Braudel.' *Economia e Storia*, XIV (1967), pp. 149-66.

Di Majo, S. 'La decadenza economica d'Italia a l'inizio dell'età moderna secondo G. Luzzato.' *Economia e Storia*, XIV (1967), pp. 17-27.

Mallet, M.E. *The Florentine Galleys in the fifteenth Century*. Oxford, 1967.

Malowist, M. 'L'évolution industrielle en Pologne du xive au xviie siècle.' *Studi in Onore di Armando Sapori*. Milan, 1957, pp. 571-604.

Malowist, M. 'Les produits des pays de la Baltique dans le commerce international au xvie siècle.' *Revue du Nord*, XLII (1960).

Malowist, M. 'Un essai d'histoire comparée—les mouvements d'expansion en Europe aux xve et xvie siècles.' *AESC*, XVII (1962), pp. 923-9.

Manca, C. *Il commercio internazionale del sale*. Milan, 1966.

Manca, C. 'Aspetti dell'espansione economica catalano-aragonese nel Mediterraneo occidentale – il commercio internazionale del sale.' *Biblioteca della Rivista Economia e Storia*, XVI. Milan, 1966.

Mandich, G. *Le pacte de Ricorsa et le marché italien des changes au xviie siècle*. Paris, 1953.

Mandrou, R. 'Les Français hors de France aux xvie et xviie siècles.' *AESC*, XIV (1959), pp. 662-75.

Mankov, A.G. *Le mouvement des prix dans l'état russe du xvie siècle*. Paris, 1957.

Marciani, C. *Lettres de change aux foires de Lanciano au xvie siècle.* Paris, 1962.

Masson, P. *Histoire du commerce français dans le Levant au xviie siècle.* Paris, 1896.

Mauro, F. *Le Portugal et l'Atlantique, 1570-1670.* Paris, 1960.

Mauro, F. *Le xvie siècle européen – les aspects économiques.* Paris, 1966.

Meuvret, J. 'Circulation monetaire et utilisation économique de la monnaie dans la France du xvie et du xviie siècle.' *Etudes d'histoire moderne et contemporaine,* I (1947), pp. 15-28.

Meuvret, J. 'Le commerce des grains et des farines à Paris à l'époque de Louis XIV.' *Revue d'histoire moderne et contemporaine,* III (1956), pp. 169-203.

Meuvret, J. *Etudes d'histoire économique – recueil d'articles.* Paris, 1971.

Minchinton, W. (ed.). *The Growth of English Overseas Trade in the 17th and 18th Centuries.* London, 1969.

Mollat, M. 'Anglo-Norman Trade in the XVth Century.' *EcHR,* XVII (1947), pp. 143-50.

Mollat, M. *Le commerce maritime normand à la fin du moyen-âge.* Paris, 1952.

Moret, M. *Aspects de la société marchande de Séville au début du xviie siècle.* Paris, 1967.

Morineau, M. 'D'Amsterdam à Séville – de quelle realité l'histoire des prix est-elle le miroir?' *AESC,* XXIII (1968), pp. 178-205.

Nef, J.U. *The Rise of the British Coal Industry.* 2 vols. London, 1932.

Nef, J.U. 'Silver Production in Central Europe, 1450-1618.' *Journal of Political Economy,* XLIX (1941), pp. 575-91.

Nübel, O. *Pompejus Occo, 1485 bis 1537 – Fuggerfaktor in Amsterdam.* Tübingen, 1972.

Pach, Zs. P. 'En Hongrie au xvie siècle – l'activité commerciale des seigneurs et leur production marchande.' *AESC,* XXI (1966), pp. 1212-31.

Parker, G. 'Spain, her Enemies and the Revolt of the Netherlands.' *Past and Present,* 49 (1970), pp. 72-95.

Parker, G. *The Army of Flanders and the Spanish Road, 1567-1659 – the Logistics of Spanish Victory and Defeat in the Low Countries' Wars.* Cambridge, 1972.

Parker, G. 'The Emergence of modern Finance in Europe, 1500-1730.' In *Fontana Economic History of Europe,* London, 1974, Vol. 2, Ch. 7, pp. 527-94.

Pélékidis, M.N. 'Venise et la Mer Noire du xie au xve siècle.' In *Venezia e il Levante fino al secolo XV*, A. Pertusi (ed.). Florence, 1973, Vol. I, pp. 541-82.

Pérez, J. *La révolution des Comunidades de Castille.* Bordeaux, 1970.

Pike, R. *Aristocrats and Traders – Sevillian Society in the Sixteenth Century.* Ithaca, New York, 1972.

Plaisse, A. 'Le commerce du port de Brest à la fin du xvie siècle.' *Revue d'histoire économique et sociale*, 42 (1964), pp. 499-545.

von Polnitz, G.F. *Anton Fugger.* Tubingen, 1958.

Posthumus, N.W. *De Uitvoer van Amsterdam. 1543-45.* Leiden, 1971.

Rabb, T.K. 'The Effects of the Thirty Years War on the German Economy.' *Journal of Modern History*, XXXIV (1962), pp. 40-51.

Ramsey, P. 'Overseas Trade in the Reign of Henry VII – the Evidence of the Customs Accounts.' *EcHR*, 2nd Ser., VI (1954), pp. 175-82.

Rau, V. *A Exploração e o comercio do sal de Setúbal.* Lisbon, 1951.

Rau, V. 'Affari e mercanti in Portogallo dal xiv al xvi secolo.' *Economia e Storia*, 14 (1967), pp. 447-56.

Richards, G. *Florentine Merchants in the Age of the Medici.* Cambridge, Mass., 1932.

Raveau, P. *Essai sur la situation économique et l'état social en Poitou au xvie siècle.* Paris, 1931.

Renouard, Y. *Les hommes d'affaires italiens du moyen âge.* Paris, 1949.

Ringrose, D.R. 'The Government and the Carters in Spain, 1476-1700.' *EcHR*, 2nd Ser., XXII (1969), pp. 45-57.

Ringrose, D.R. *Transportation and economic Stagnation in Spain, 1750-1850.* Durham, North Carolina, 1970.

Romano, R. 'La marine marchande vénitienne au xvie siècle.' *Les sources de l'histoire maritime, xve – xviiie siècles. Actes du IVe colloque d'histoire maritime.* Paris, 1962.

Romano, R. 'Tra xvi e xvii secolo – Una crisi economica: 1619-1622.' *Rivista storica italiana*, 74 (1962), pp. 480-531.

Romano, R. 'Encore la crise de 1619-22.' *AESC*, XIX (1964), pp. 31-7.

Romano, R. and da Silva, J.G. 'L'histoire des changes – les foires de "Bisenzone" de 1600 à 1650.' *AESC*, XVII (1962), pp. 715-21.

de Roover, F. Edler. 'The Effects of the Financial Measures of Charles V on the Commerce of Antwerp, 1539-42.' *Revue belge de philologie et d'histoire*, XVI (1937), pp. 663-77.

de Roover, F. Edler. 'The van der Molen – Commission Merchants of Antwerp – Trade with Italy, 1538-44.' In *Mediaeval and Historiographical Essays in Honor of J.W. Thompson.*

de Roover, R. 'Les origines du comptabilité à partie double.' *Annales d'histoire économique et sociale*, IX (1937), pp. 171-93 and 270-98.

de Roover, R. 'Le contrat de change.' *Revue belge de philologie et d'histoire*, XXV (1946), pp. 111-28.

de Roover, R. *The Medici Bank – its Organisation, Management and Decline.* New York and London, 1948.

de Roover, R. *Money, Banking and Credit in mediaeval Bruges.* Cambridge, Mass., 1948.

de Roover, R. *L'évolution de la lettre de change.* Paris, 1953.

Rörig, F. 'La Hanse – les raisons intellectuelles d'une suprématie commerciale.' *Annales d'histoire économique et sociale*, II (1930), pp. 481-98.

Ruiz Martín, F. *Lettres marchandes échangées entre Florence et Medina del Campo.* Paris, 1965.

Salomon, N. *La campagne de la Nouvelle Castille à la fin du xvie siècle.* Paris, 1964.

Sardella, P. 'L'épanouissement de Venise au xvie siècle.' *AESC*, II (1949), p. 19.

Savary des Bruslons, J. *Dictionnaire du commerce.* 2 vols. Paris, 1735.

Sayous, A.E. 'Le rôle des Génois dans les premiers mouvements réguliers d'affaires entre l'Espagne et l'Amérique.' *Compte rendu de l'académie des inscriptions et belles lettres,* 1932.

Sayous, A.E. 'Une caisse de dépôts – la "Table des Changes" de Valence, 1407 et 1418.' *Annales d'histoire économique et sociale*, VI (1934), pp. 135-7.

Sayous, A.E. 'La déchéance d'une capitalisme de forme ancienne – Augsbourg au temps des grands faillites.' *Annales d'histoire économique et sociale*, X (1938), pp. 208-34.

Sayous, A.E. 'Le rôle d'Amsterdam dans l'histoire du capitalisme commercial et financier.' *Revue historique,* CLXXXIII (1938), pp. 242-80.

Schick, L. *Un grand homme d'affaires au début du xvie siècle – Jacob Fugger.* Paris, 1957.

Sée, H. 'Quelques aperçus sur le capitalisme commercial en France au xvie siècle.' *Revue d'histoire économique et sociale*, XII (1924), pp. 165-80.

Sée, H. 'Le commerce en France au xvie siècle.' *Annales d'histoire économique et sociale*, I (1929), pp. 551-61.

Sella, D. *Commerci e industrie a Venezia nel secolo xvii.* Venice and Rome, 1961.

Sella, D. 'Crisis and Change in Venetian Trade.' In *Crisis and Change in the Venetian Economy in the 16th and 17th Centuries.* B. Pullan (ed.),

London, 1968.

Silva, J.G. da. *Stratégie des affaires à Lisbonne entre 1595 et 1607. Lettres marchandes des Rodrigues d'Evora et Veiga.* Paris, 1956.

Silva, J.G. da. 'Philippe II et les problèmes de l'argent.' *AESC*, XIV (1959), pp. 736-7.

Silva, J.G. da. 'Trafics du Nord, marchés du "Mezzogiorno", finances génoises – recherches et documents sur la conjoncture à la fin du xvie siècle.' *Revue du Nord*, 41 (1959), pp. 129-52.

Silva, J.G. da. 'Echanges et troc – l'example des Canaries au début du xvie siècle.' *AESC*, XVI (1961), pp. 1004-11.

Silva, J.G. da. 'Richesse et enrichissement dans une économie pré-capitaliste.' *AESC*, XVII (1962), pp. 967-87.

Silva, J.G. da. 'Au xviie siècle – la stratégie du capital florentin.' *AESC*, XIX (1964).

Sjøberg, A.G. 'Swedish Foreign Trade in the mid sixteenth Century.' *Scandinavian Economic History Review*, VIII (1960), pp. 175-9.

Sluiter, E. 'Dutch-Spanish Rivalry in the Caribbean Area.' *American Historical Review*, XXVIII (1922-3), pp. 165-96.

Spooner, F.C. *The International Economy and Monetary Movements in France, 1495-1725.* Cambridge, Mass., 1972.

Steensgaard, N. 'European Shipping to Asia, 1497-1700.' *Scandinavian Economic History Review*, XVIII (1970), pp. 1-11.

Steensgaard, N. *Carracks, Caravans and Companies.* Copenhagen, 1972.

Stephens, W.B. 'The Trade of the Port of Barnstaple at the End of the Civil War'. *Devon and Cornwall Notes and Queries*, XXXI (1970), pp. 6-15.

Stone, L. 'State Control in sixteenth-century England.' *EcHR*, XVII (1947), pp. 103-20.

Supple, B.E. *Commercial Crisis and Change in England, 1600-1642 – a Study in the Instability of a Mercantile Economy.* Cambridge, 1959.

Tadić, G. 'Les archives économiques de Raguse.' *AESC*, XVI (1961), pp. 1168-77.

Tanguy, J. *Le commerce de Nantes au milieu du xvie siècle.* Paris, 1956.

Tawney, R.H. and Power, E. (eds.). *Tudor Economic Documents.* 3 vols. London, 1924.

Taylor, H. 'Price Revolution or Price Revision? – The English and Spanish Trade after 1604.' *Renaissance and Modern Studies* (University of Nottingham), XII (1968), pp. 5-32.

Tenenti, A. *Naufrages, corsaires et assurances maritimes à Venise, 1592-1609.* Paris, 1959.

Tenenti, A. 'A Venise au début du xviie siècle – autour d'un livre de

Gaetano Cozzi.' *AESC*, XVI (1961), pp. 780-90.

Tenenti, A. and Vivanti, C. 'Le film d'un grand système de navigation – les galères vénitiennes xive–xvie siècles.' *AESC*, XVI (1961), pp. 83-6.

Tenenti, A. *Piracy and the Decline of Venice, 1550-1615.* London, 1967.

Trasselli, C. 'Richerche sulla seta siciliana—secoli xv—xvii.' *Economia e Storia,* 12 (1965), pp. 213-58.

Trocmé, E. and Delafosse, M. *Le commerce rochelais de la fin du xve siècle au début du xviie.* Paris, 1952.

Usher, A.P. 'Spanish Ships and Shipbuilding.' In *Facts and Factors in Economic History – Essays in Honor of E. F. Gay.* Cambridge, Mass., 1932.

Usher, A.P. *The Early History of Deposit Banking in Mediterranean Europe.* Cambridge, Mass., 1943.

Van der Wee, H. *The Growth of the Antwerp Market and the European Economy, 14th to 16th Centuries.* 3 vols., Louvain, 1963.

Van der Wee, H. 'Typologie des crises et changements de structures aux Pays-Bas – xve-xvie siècles.' *AESC*, XVIII (1963), pp. 209-51.

Van der Wee, H. 'Anvers et les innovations de la technique financière au xvie et xviie siècles.' *AESC*, XXII (1967), pp. 1067-89.

Van Dillen, J.G. (ed.). *History of the Principal Public Banks.* The Hague, 1934.

Van Houtte, J.A. 'La genèse du grand marché international d'Anvers à la fin du moyen-âge.' *Revue belge de philologie et d'histoire*, XIX (1940), pp. 87-126.

Van Houtte, J.A. 'Bruges et Anvers, marchés nationaux ou internationaux au xvie siècle?' *Revue du Nord*, 34 (1952), pp. 89-108.

Van Houtte, J.A. 'Anvers au xve et xvie siècles – expansion et apogée.' *AESC*, XVI (1961), pp. 248-78.

Van Werveke, H. Review of J. Kernkamp, *De Handel op den Vijand, 1572-1609* (2 vols., Utrecht, n.d.), *Annales d'histoire économique et sociale*, V (1933), pp. 413-14.

Van Werveke, H. 'Monnaie de compte et monnaie réelle.' *Revue belge de philologie et d'histoire*, XIII (1934), pp. 123-34.

Vazquez de Prada, V. *Lettres marchandes d'Anvers.* 4 vols. Paris, 1960.

Vidalenc, J. Review of H. and P. Chaunu, *Séville et l'Atlantique, Revue d'histoire économique et sociale*, 40 (1962), pp. 110-30.

Vilar, P. 'Histoire des prix, histoire générale.' Review article on E.J. Hamilton, *War and Prices, 1650-1800*, *AESC*, IV (1949), pp. 29-45.

Vilar, P. 'Remarques sur l'histoire des prix.' *AESC*, XVI (1961), pp. 110-15.

Vilar, P. *La Catalogne dans l'Espagne moderne.* 3 vols. Paris, 1962.

Wagner, D.O. 'Coke and the Rise of Economic Liberalism.' *EcHR*, VI (1935-6), pp. 30-44.

Wallerstein, I. *The Modern World-System – Capitalist Agriculture and the Origins of the European World-economy in the sixteenth Century.* New York, 1974.

Westermann, J.C. 'Statistiche Gegevens over den Handel van Amsterdam in de zeventiende eeuw.' *Tijdschrift voor Geschiedenis,* 61 (1948), pp. 3-15.

Willan, T.S. *The early History of the Russia Company, 1553-1603.* Manchester, 1956.

Wilson, C.H. *Profit and Power – a Study of England and the Dutch Wars.* London, 1957.

Wood, A.C. *A History of the Levant Company.* Oxford, 1935.

Yamey, B.S. 'Accounting and the Rise of Capitalism.' *Studi in onore di A. Fanfani*, VI, pp. 835-57.

Yamey, B.S. *Accounting in England and Scotland, 1543-1800.* London, 1963.

Yamey, B.S. and Littleton, A.C. *Studies in the History of Accounting.* London, 1956.

Zanetti, D. 'Contribution à l'étude des structures économiques – l'approvisionement de Pavie au xvie siècle.' *AESC*, XVIII (1963), pp. 44-62.

Zeller, G. 'Deux capitalistes strasbourgeoises du xvie siècle.' *Etudes d'histoire moderne et contemporaine*, I (1947), pp. 3-14.

Zins, H. *England and the Baltic in the Elizabethan Era.* Manchester, 1972.

INDEX

221